The Microstates of Europe

D1521180

The Microstates of Europe

Designer Nations in a Post-Modern World

P. Christiaan Klieger

LEXINGTON BOOKS
Lanham • Boulder • New York • Toronto • Plymouth, UK

Published by Lexington Books
A wholly owned subsidiary of The Rowman & Littlefield Publishing Group, Inc.
4501 Forbes Boulevard, Suite 200, Lanham, Maryland 20706
www.rowman.com

10 Thornbury Road, Plymouth PL6 7PP, United Kingdom

Copyright © 2013 by Lexington Books
First paperback edition 2014

All rights reserved. No part of this book may be reproduced in any form or by any
electronic or mechanical means, including information storage and retrieval systems,
without written permission from the publisher, except by a reviewer who may quote
passages in a review.

British Library Cataloguing in Publication Information Available

Library of Congress Cataloging-in-Publication Data

The hardback edition of this book was previously cataloged by the Library of Congress as
follows:

Klieger, P. Christiaan, author.
  The microstates of Europe : designer nations in a post-modern world / P. Christiaan
Klieger.
     pages cm
  Includes bibliographical references and index.
   1. States, Small. 2. Europe, Western—Politics and government. I. Title.
  JC365.K5554 2012
  320.1—dc23
                          2012041641

ISBN : 978-0-7391-7426-5 (cloth : alk. paper)
ISBN : 978-0-7391-9796-7 (pbk : alk. paper)
ISBN : 978-0-7391-7427-2 (electronic)

♾™ The paper used in this publication meets the minimum requirements of American
National Standard for Information Sciences—Permanence of Paper for Printed Library
Materials, ANSI/NISO Z39.48-1992.

Printed in the United States of America

To H.E. Richard Dunn, Bailiff Grand Cross of Honor and Devotion in Obedience, Sovereign Military Hospitaller Order of St. John of Jerusalem, of Rhodes, and of Malta.

Contents

Figures

Foreword
Anomalies that Reaffirm

Dibyesh Anand
University of Westminster, UK

We live in a clichéd world—an interconnected world where boundaries are said to be becoming less relevant, where flows of ideas, goods, services, peoples, problems, opportunities, challenges, loyalties and desires are not confined to the bounded community of the nation-state. Cautionists who argue that states remain powerful entities mostly recognize that the nation-states are being transformed in a way that makes the conventional concept of sovereignty of the state and the boundedness of the nation problematic. It is usually the big and/or powerful states that are seen as having the capacity to retain their autonomy and sovereignty in the face of relentless tides of globalization and fragmentation, homogenization, and pluralization.

Sovereignty as an idea had a wide purchase until the end of the Cold War but since then has often been recognized for what it actually is—a fiction, a fiction that emerged in Europe a few centuries ago and got universalized through imperialism and decolonization. But a fiction that in the post-Cold War era of humanitarian interventions, wars against non-states and ideologies, emerging norm of responsibility to protect, human security, and so on is seen as increasingly archaic and unhelpful. It is rare for powerful Western states to invoke sovereignty. And yet, nationalism remains the main form of political community that collectives imagine; the state remains the primary form of institution through which people are governed. Bounded political communities therefore remain a vital subject of inquiry. This work is in the tradition of a study of several bounded political communities. And yet it is innovative and interesting both in terms of the subject matter and its approach.

Microstates is about political entities that have been rarely studied seriously. They have invoked merriment, curious amusement, ridicule, or exoticization, but not considered important enough to be studied rigorously. Studies of individual entities exist, e.g. the Vatican, but there are no studies that investigate them all without reducing them to a dull comparativism. This book is an exception.

Studying these "curious" entities spread in various parts of Europe allows us to raise new questions about the meanings of statehood and nation. Why did these entities not only survive but also flourish? Was it merely an accident of history? What role did the ruling elite play and to what extent was their autonomy a product of strategic calculations made by powerful bigger neighbors? What do these states tell us about the interesting trajectory of sovereign nationhood in microstates in the home continent of modern concepts of state sovereignty and nationalism?

This book is also about the persistence of an idea despite all odds stacked against it. This is self-determination being invested in the people, while the legitimacy is shared between the people and the ruling elite. Self-determination is often understood in secularist terms—the struggle of the people against the rule by the outsiders. However, this study allows us to perceive self-determination in a new and fresh light. Religious vocabulary, medieval codes of conduct, and traditional valorization of honor also play a role in determining how these entities have expressed themselves. It is commonplace to argue that nation-states are products of tradition and modernity. The tiniest of political entities here are no exception. In fact, they show a remarkable amalgam of traditional and the modern. The experiences of different entities are different. Some like the Vatican are all mostly about traditional religiosity even though the Roman Catholic Church has often intervened in problems of modern life. Others make little appeal to any traditional religious culture and more to the self-interest of their super-rich citizens. Is a generalization of the experience of tradition and modernity of these microstates possible?

Microstates re-emphasizes the crucial importance of recognition in sovereignty and self-determination. It is international recognition by neighbors and other actors that assure distinct political identity to these entities that otherwise may be deemed too weak, small, or irrelevant. Should Liechtenstein's commitment to fostering new thinking about self-determination be understood in this light? Is the commitment as much about helping other entities in the world that are usually ridden roughshod by brutish *realpolitk* of great power as the self-interest of preservation? One hopes this book will rekindle the debate over self-determination in International Relations.

The book's innovation also lies in terms of its hybrid approach. The narrative is a mix of historical and contemporary, politics and culture, personal and objective. It is an anthropology in that does not shy away from making generalizations across different cases. It is a political analysis that shows an appreciation of cultural specificity and yet at the same time identifies the myriad ways in which sovereignty and nationhood are articulated.

Klieger provides a pen picture and analysis of what could be seen as "anomalies" in the larger stories of national self-determination, state sovereignty, and

Europeanization and argues that the anomalies in fact reaffirm the stories. What are better illustrations of continued relevance and attraction of sovereignty and nationhood than the super-tiny entities that survive and flourish? This narrative of European microstates thus contributes to an understanding of macropolitics of identity in international relations.

Preface

I entered graduate studies years ago with an all-consuming interest in learning about the peoples of Tibet, representatives of a culture that seemed to be the last archaic civilization in the modern world. I was immediately presented with the existence of tens of thousands of Tibetan refugees from Chinese occupied-Tibet. These displaced people, it seemed, wasted no time in reproducing vital cultural institutions in exile. Their monasteries, language centers, arts organizations, government-in-exile offices, and other agencies have provided amazing cultural resources, helping to allow Tibetans to remain Tibetans. This quickly became my thesis question throughout: the Tibetan people as a group have shown remarkable resistance towards the agents of assimilation between the dominant cultures of India to the south and China to the east, that are especially pronounced during this period of occupation and diaspora. Throughout its long history, Tibet has as shown times of great independence, and times of subordination, yet throughout the people remain Tibetan. Despite the Marxist-based minorities policies of the Peoples Republic of China, the people of Tibet were not, and are not accepting the new political reality. Similarly in exile, Tibetan refugees were not assimilating into their host countries. Why was this? Work on this question has led me to an interest in the tiny countries of Europe. Why are they still here, when larger states have disappeared?

In trying to answer these sorts of questions, I stumbled upon the structural historiography of the French Annales School, the works of great scholars like Le Roy Ladurie, Marc Bloch, Fernand Braudel, and Jacques Le Goff. I discovered by examining deep social structures existing over the long term (*longue durée*) rather than conventionally focusing on event, it may be possible to explain how some so-called marginal groups in the world persist despite constant pressures to be absorbed. Where anthropologists such as Fredrik Barth and Edward Spicer recognized the tenacity of ethnic boundaries, it seemed that structural history was able to explain the process by which these boundaries were created and maintained in the first place. The scholars of the Annales School, by concentrating on regional records, journals, and *ethnohistories*, were able to see through the miasma of centralist official historiography and its emphasis on transitory event and provide a deep, longitudinal tool for explaining change over the long term. This perspective provided me with a solid method and interpretive viewpoint for nearly all my subsequent interpretations of Tibetan history and culture.

The litany of scholars that have been influenced by the Annales has itself grown deep, and I could be characterized as standing, rather wobbly, on the shoulders of great scholars, who in turn stand on the broader shoulders of anthropologists like Marshall Sahlins, who stand on the anterior parts of French intellectuals of the Annales School, themselves walking Wallenda-like between history and anthropology.

This book has come about in a similar fashion, noting that some of the tiny states of Europe seem particularly tenacious, and illogical under the determinism of Marxism and modernist social theory. Places like Andorra and San Marino should have disappeared ages ago. Why haven't they? And what does that say about the power of nationalism? By examining the process of ethnogenesis over the long term, one may be able to finally break away from the banality of the synchronic "ethnographic present" that has characterized much of anthropology for far too long, a method that has often presented inter-ethnic difference in too great of a contrast. And we are most fortunate that the narratives available about the microstates of Europe are very long indeed, these little places possessing among the oldest institutions and continuous communities in Europe. Presenting a rich, descriptive narrative of present cultural expressions is one thing, but to be able to explain how a people develop and preserve their ethnic and national groups over time is perhaps a higher goal.

Finally I must say a word on sources. Unfortunately, historical sources are not homogenous by any means, making comparison between data problematic. Even within the Annales, journals of everyday people living mundane lives are encumbered with bias and prejudice. It is the same on the other end of the spectrum, with "official histories" and popular narratives such as those that are used in tourist propaganda. I cannot suggest an easy historiographic solution, except to express the observation that even widely disparate sources often share glimpses of the shared memories and "national disposition" that persists over time. Wikipedia entries, first-person accounts, tourist literature, palace histories, and scholarly accounts all share to some extent knowledge of these national configurations. It is these memories that are called to play in the construction of the collective consciousness. As the basis of emotive, "national sentiment," these shared ideas are the primary elements for ethnogenesis and the development of the nation. It is our task to find these widely held, persistent ideals, and examine how they traverse the course of time.

Acknowledgements

Research began on the book in 2000, an appropriate millennial milestone to herald the victory of post-modernism in the interpretation of the state. Field research has included a dozen or so field trips to Europe, some of which included audiences with larger-than-life heads of microstates. Very little has been seriously written about this subject, and I hope not to break that trend.

So many people offered me substantial information and encouragement to construct this work, that I am apprehensive to crawl down the path of acknowledgement lest I forget anyone. But first and foremost I must give my thanks to H.E. Richard Dunn, Bailiff of Honor and Devotion in the Order of St. John of Jerusalem, of Rhodes, and of Malta. The challenge I felt in 2000 was that no book on the microstates of Europe would be complete without adequate understanding of the Sovereign Military and Hospitaller Order of Malta, which as a subject of international law, might be the smallest microstate of all. Believing it was relative impossible to "visit" the Order, I discerned that if I could not mount a first-hand study of the Order, it would be useless to continue research on the subject of the microstates. Fortunately, Bailiff Dunn stepped in and made the whole project possible. First, as President of the Western Association-USA, he introduced me to the operations of the Order at the local level, as is practiced throughout the world. Then, as member of the Sovereign Council, he invited me to Rome, and arranged for an audience with H.M.E.H. Frà Andrew Bertie, Prince and Grand Master of the Order at the Magistral Palace.

I thank the late Grand Master for his enthusiasm for the project and his friendship throughout the years, as we both were students of the people and religion of Tibet. I was also graciously welcomed by the Order's archivist and curator of the time, Frà John Critien. Since then, other Sovereign Council members such as H.E. Antonio Sanchez-Corea and Frà John MacPherson have been instrumental in my journey to make sense of this ancient political, military, and religious force of Europe. With a deep sense of gratitude I must thank Erik Cimini, KM, and H.S.H. Prince Andreas von Liechtenstein of Sweden for inviting me to participate in the 2011 pilgrimage to Lourdes by the Scandinavian Association. This provided me with a strong European perspective to the works of the Order, essential for an understanding of both the past and how the Order operates in the world today. I also must thank David Fencl, Monsignor Steven Otellini, and Frà Carl Nolke for continual prodding to finish the book, as it trailed on for ten years or so. John Porter, administrator at the Western Association-USA of SMOM, provided great support and knowledge in navigating the nine hundred-year history of the Order.

I am also appreciative of the encouragement of the late Lieutenant of the Equestrian Order of the Holy Sepulchre of Jerusalem, Sir John McGuiken, and the current Lieutenant of the Northwest Lieutenancy (USA), Lady Mary O'Brien.

In Liechtenstein, a mutual interest in Tibet precipitated in an audience with another microstate sovereign, H.S.H. Prince Hans-Adam II. I am very grateful to the Prince for his time and perspectives on ruling a tiny principality.

This book has benefitted greatly from discussions on self-determination I have had with former Tibetan government-in-exile prime minister Kazur Tenzin Tethong, current prime minister Kazur Lobsang Sangay, and international law experts Fred Shepardson and Michael van Walt van Praag.

I am thankful that old friends were willing to help me augment, read, or criticize the manuscript. This includes Dibyesh Anand of Westminster College, Anthony Ordona, and Jan Magnusson of Lund University. Professor Anand, a noted expert in international studies, has generously provided a foreword to this research. Of course, Amy King and Emily Natsios, editors at Lexington Books of Rowman & Littlefield, are praised for their thoroughness, patience, and perseverance in insuring that the production of this book was always on track.

P. Christiaan Klieger
San Francisco

Chapter One
Introduction—Toward the Post-Modern State

Along the endless corridors in the Louvre Museum of Paris is a rather monumental painting from the late eighteenth century that visually summarizes the hypothesis of this essay. Jacques-Louis David's "Oath of the Horatii" depicts three brothers of the ancient Roman army, arms outstretched to the father who is holding their swords. Off to the right side, the women of the family quietly shed tears as their men folk go off to war. This famous allegory about loyalty to the state over family was painted in 1784, just before the revolution in France that forevermore changed the relationship between the individual and the state. The famous painting is metaphorical for the basic irrationality of modern nationalism: nations are artificial social constructs formed by a transformation of family loyalties to the symbols of a greater collective. And like family affections, they are not necessarily based in logic and rationality. Nationality seems essentialistic—always there and immutable precisely because they are an extension of familial affect. But national consciousness is nevertheless an artificial construct. In an age of developing modernism, emotions were considered an impediment to rationality. That the modern state nevertheless has these qualities of irrationality is best seen in the tiniest of states, whose continued existence in the modern world seems to be irrational given the widely held sentiment that globalism will ultimately triumph. There is nothing seemingly logical about the continued existence of San Marino in the Apennine Mountains of modern Eurozone Italy, yet it has been continuing as a functional sovereign nation for over seventeen hundred years. And there are six other examples in Europe. Why are they still here? Is there a common thread in the historical narratives of the microstates that can explain the persistence of peoples, ethnic groups, tiny states, and other high-level collectives despite seemingly insurmountable pressures towards world community?

The current microstates of Europe are arbitrarily:[1] Andorra, Liechtenstein, Monaco, San Marino, Sovereign Military Order of Malta, Vatican City, and the Republic of Malta (Figure 1.1). They are all unlikely survivors of the great social upheavals that have characterized Western Europe since the fall of Rome.

1

These states are pre-modern in the sense that they are not like contemporary, multicultural states like France. Many retain institutions that seem more appropriate to the feudal age than to ours. Most are snippets of borderland regions between great empires that have managed to surf the crest of history and survived. They are post-modern in the sense of being wholly imagined and artificially contrived polities, what Benedict Anderson[2] would call imagined communities. Tourists flocking to them from the superpowers are sure to ejaculate a snicker or two as they pose themselves in front of quaint guard stands with stoically suffering security forces in antiquated military costumes. These pocket countries are reminders of an imagined, mythological past, with damsels in towers, knights on horseback, and grumpy little kings who chastise the palace cook for spoiling their *hasenpfeffer*. Are the anachronisms simply theatre?

Like your parents, the church, a hallowed university, and apple pie, we tend to think of states and their borders as essential, ever-existent. While we know there will always be an England, we are not so sure about a Monaco or Liechtenstein. That ambiguity adds to the sense of indistinct anachronism we experience when visiting these microstates. Odder yet is that many of the microstates themselves were of differing shapes and forms through the passage of time. Andorra, a little island of land now surrounded by large states (France and Spain) was for a long time just another principality among an archipelago of tiny lands running the extent of the Pyrenees. Monaco, now a gilded fly-speck of a country, was for most of its existence a polity whose territory was more the size of Luxembourg. And Vatican City, which is now pretty much a big church and a palace, was once the chewy center of the Italian peninsula, if not the whole Christian world. These countries have persevered, for a thousand, for seventeen hundred years—what can this persistence tell us about the nature of sovereignty, ethnic group formation, and other boundary regulating mechanisms?

This book is not a grand history of petite places—rather, it is an "ethnographic anthology" of a few places in Europe that should not logically exist. It is a post-modern critique of normative globalism, which examines the countertrend of increasing nationalism, particularism, and cultural relativism. It is also a study in ethnogenesis—the care and feeding of ethnic and national identities. I have attempted to be totalizing, in the sense that the individual historical narratives presented here, together, may show deep structures that may be useful in sociological comparison and the study of cultural change and continuity in Europe through time. Rather than being eclectic exceptions, the microstates may demonstrate the survival of extremely long enduring mechanisms of collective boundary maintenance that may be present in many communities throughout the world. Most social scientists, as Llobera has argued,[3] have been caught unaware of the continuing power of nationalism to account for political change. Many Marxists and other modernists assumed that nationalism would simply fade away in the process of social evolution.

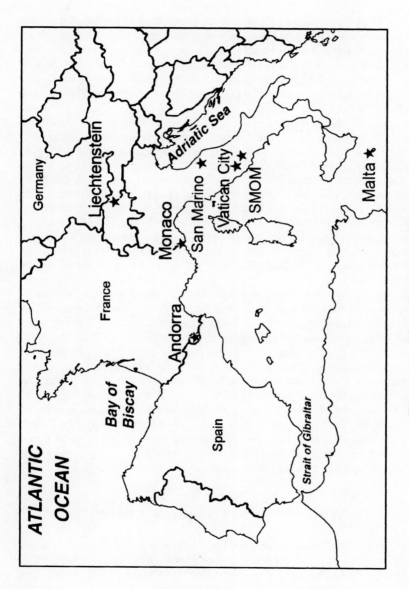

Figure 1.1 The Microstates of Europe

The power of emotion to motivate a national collective has been largely ignored in the bright lights of the modern age. The rupture of the Soviet Union,
the break-up of Yugoslavia in 1991, and the persistence of the microstates are
clear examples of the fact it has not. The microstates seem illogical because they
do not neatly fit in the Modernist scheme of how states are supposed to evolve.
This leads to a general hypothesis: Are the microstates of Europe eclectic outliers of general sociopolitical development or do they possess ethnic and national structures of the *longue durée* that could inform how states and nations form
everywhere?

In many of the microstates we also see the development of something
beyond the nation-state, in fact, which I will refer to in several examples as post-
modern polities. We also see two examples of ancient transnational organizations that are now represented as internationally recognized states. At the risk
of forcing comparison, the seven microstates presented in this book can show
that political viability is not necessarily unilineal or must robotically track positivist agenda. Nor is ethnic and state viability based on size. The microstates,
because they are tiny, may be able to serve as prototype for understanding
broader trends in nation-building occurring throughout the world. The microstate case studies may serve, like the architect's maquette, as objects from which
far larger and more complex state formation and maintenance processes may be
examined.

Although many of the European microstates were established as borderlands between developing empires, they are currently far from being economically marginal. Andorra receives nine million tourists a year; the Vatican is the
religious focus of at least twenty percent of the world's population; the demi-
monde of Monaco are familiar faces to the millions of readers of supermarket
check-out glamour magazines. In fact, the total combined visitor count for the
seven microstates described here is well over twenty million each year and
growing. In places like Liechtenstein and San Marino, the perceived evidence of
quaint anachronisms is a strong motivation for the herds of visitors to swerve off
the *autostrada* in their giant buses to descend upon these tiny places. Economic
survival remains an important factor for maintenance of the state, but it is not
necessarily the lead factor as most modernists would argue. The tourist popularity of the microstates is a phenomenon worthy of examining.

What Are You Laughing About?

Many of the previous works on the subject of microstates are slim and couched
in the genre of humor rather than political anthropology, nationalism, or international studies. This is because of their marginalization and seeming triviality, as
evident in both the social sciences and popular works. A few examples include
John Sack's humorous 1955 *Report from Practically Nowhere*[4] and Lonely Pla-

net's inane *Micronations*.[5] Although examining real places, both works treat their subject matter with one-sided humor, as if these little countries are but mere parodies of the larger states. As such they share the giggles of tourists who actually visit these places. Only perhaps writers in the United States or China could get away with this sort of paternalism—witness the humor generated around the naïve Fourth World character in the popular film *Borat*.[6] Nationalist "big-brotherisms" occult social phenomena that underlie the formation and maintenance of smaller states, not to mention microstates and would-be countries. That is really the issue that this book addresses, and it is not a broadly shared perspective. The closest academic work to my subject area is Jorri Duursma very exhaustive look at five microstates in 1996.[7] Thomas Eccardt, a high school teacher, wrote a hastily descriptive travel book on seven microstates in 2005.[8] This observation leads us to our first inquiry: Why does the persistence of these microstates strike many as ludicrous or trivial?

In the same year Sack's book on microstates appeared, a series of novels, written by Leonard Wibberley was launched that satirized the Cold War competition of the superpowers. Wibberley presented a plucky European microstate that accidentally defeats the United States. *The Mouse that Roared*[9] series chronicled the fictitious Duchy of Grand Fenwick, located between Switzerland and France, as an archaic (still using bows and arrows) maternal monarchy, humorously frozen in time. The parody closely follows a hybrid of the Grand Duchy of Luxembourg, then ruled by the beloved World War II resistance leader, Grand Duchess Charlotte, and the minute Principality of Liechtenstein lying on the east side of Switzerland. The premise of the series was made into a popular movie in 1959 starring Peter Sellers as the Duchess Glorianna XII, as well as playing other characters. The work was cast as an improbable farce, pitting modernity against antiquity and antiquity winning. What is the genesis of this humor?

In a more sinister expression of the improbity of the smaller European states existing, or just having the right to exist in the modern world was the famous speech of Adolf Hitler given at the Berlin Sports Palace, 30 January 1941. The address, given in defense of German aggression, was a specific response to F.D. Roosevelt's ultimatum to the chancellor not to invade a list of countries in Europe and the Middle East. As Hitler read off the litany, "Finland, Lithuania, Latvia...," the audience, detecting the sarcasm in the führer's voice, began to giggle. When Hitler reached Liechtenstein, the house roared with laughter.[10] It was absurd to think that the little states in Europe, in particular the microstates, had any chance or right to remain independent under the modern logic of liberation and the scientific "progress" of National Socialism. Why did the Nazis find the tiny states' struggles for freedom humorous?

As an attempted explanation of why the microstates were considered ludicrous, especially during the first half of the twentieth century, I suggest that there are several mechanisms operating. First, the modernist standpoint from which the unlikely team of Sack, Lonely Planet, Hitler, and Wibberley

pan the microstates, is a scientific and rationalistic perspective ultimately
deriving from the Age of Reason and the Enlightenment and expressed in
Mid-Century sensibilities. The individual's loyalty, no longer bound to church
and crown, but to the secular state, stands as the foundation of the modern state.
The modern state, itself striving for a pure, homogenous, and ideal nation-state,
flattens cultural difference in a dictatorship of the majority. Anachronism is just
a chronological or developmental wart in the streamlined formation of the modern nationalist state.

Anachronism, because it juxtaposes symbols apparently from the archaic past into modern constructs, often catching the viewer by surprise, is
also a fertile territory for the creation of humor: carrying the President of
the United States to the Senate in a sedan chair by liveried coolies would
probably strike many people as funny. The extant microstates seem anachronistic—under the logic of the modern state they should have merged with
their larger neighbors after feudalism broke up—but they did not. Why?

Another observation is that since anachronisms are a discordance of time,
microstates also appear to exhibit a discontinuity of space. The microstates
that exist in borderlands between powerful states, i.e. Andorra, Liechtenstein, Monaco, and the Republic of Malta, are in a political no-man's land
of ambiguity. Andorra, for example, is neither French nor Spanish nor a blend
of the two. As such it does not share the ideals of Liberty, Equality, and
Fraternity hatched during the creation of the French Republic, nor subscribe to
the shared patriotic memory of the unification of Spain under Ferdinand
and Isabella and the subsequent development of a Castilian world empire.
Andorra is a Catalán state of the larger ethnic region, or nation, of Catalonia. Its
ethnogenesis is facilitated by the use of the language and its invocation
of the Frankish emperor Charlemagne as its founder. These states, are in
effect, liminal from the standard boundaries of modern Europe; they are
"betwixt and between" and belong to no one but to themselves.

I suggest that part of the popular appeal of visiting the microstates is based
on their ability to suspend belief and provide transcendence from routine life, to
enter into a state of liminality. Liminality is a concept useful in anthropological interpretation since it was first discussed by Arnold van Gennap
in his *Rites of Passage* of 1909.[11] The anthropologist Victor Turner used
it extensively in describing the ritual process and especially rites of initia-
tion. Here actors transform from a previous social category to a higher
one through a period of liminality. The rites of passage from childhood
to adult status is common throughout the world, for example. During a
state of liminality, categories of belonging are ambiguous and rites associated with this process are rich in surprise, humor, and anachronism, in
addition to danger and chaos. Among structure-as-process social scientists such
as Sahlins, the structure of the previous social construct is utilized in the process
of its own attempted social reproduction. This often happens in a period of li-

minality, when all categories of meaning and their references are destroyed in the chaos. These facilities are, in effect, transformational. There is also a strong connection between ritual and play, as was so carefully discussed by Johan Huizinga[12] and brought more firmly into anthropological thought through the work of Edward Norbeck.[13] Christian Church ritual, for example, is largely re-enactments, with priests playing the part of Jesus at the Last Supper. The sacred spaces, e.g. the church sanctuary, are functionally equivalent to the playground, ball court, or stage according to Huizinga. They are places set apart; they are liminal, on the threshold between normative and transcendental states of perception.

The microstates are liminal in the modernist sense that they are set apart, geographically and seemingly chronologically. Andorra and Liechtenstein are still rather isolated mountainous polities off the main highways, lacking railroads and airports. San Marino has no railroad. Malta is a rather isolated island group in the mid-Mediterranean. The Vatican and SMOM are isolated by social class and position—most of their territories cannot be visited without special permission, only obtainable through highly placed officials within. Monaco, although no longer geographically isolated, is generally not available to outsiders without the expenditure of substantial wealth. Andorra, Liechtenstein, and Monaco are often referred to as playgrounds for the rich and famous. San Marino and Malta try to parrot that image in their tourist literature. While not necessarily playgrounds, the Vatican and SMOM are certainly sacred spaces, functionally equivalent as arenas for ritual games and activities set apart from the mundane world, in the sense of Huizinga.

Since the microstates are liminal, they are seen to be set apart from the modernist march of history. But are they really the clowns of Europe? These days no one would think of laughing at Prince Hans-Adam II of Liechtenstein, owner of a major European bank and the largest private art collections in the world. And most people take the pope seriously. But even at the Vatican, anachronisms must be occasionally pruned to avoid creeping incredulity. The grand papal coronation, with its bejeweled triple tiara, skyscraping sedan chairs (*sedia gestatoria*), and pharonic ostrich feather *flabella* was already looking rather silly when Paul VI was crowned in St. Peter's in 1964. The ceremony was suspended subsequently, the crown given to the poor in a stunning rite of reversal (a liminal act). But many of the microstates do seem to be lands of make-believe, "what-if" countries that encourage the visitor to suspend belief that they are even of this earth. It is within this symbolic field of juxtaposed categories, unknown traditions, and seemingly illogical customs that these outliers of historical development at once strike the outsider as comical exceptions to the rule.

In deference to the more sensitive of cultural relativists, if the microstates are not funny at least they tend to be intriguing, even exotic. The tens of millions of yearly visitors to these marginal places attest to this. The idea of play comes again into resolution. Humans, especially children, have an inordinate interest in possessing and playing with miniatures. From Barbie dolls to Easy-Bake Ovens to Märklin trains, children (and many adults) know the pleasures of lording over a world in miniature. Working with models is metaphorical for interacting in the real world, with many more controls and much less risk. I am not suggesting that the citizens of Andorra and San Marino feel they are "playing country,"[14] but their national founders may have been. The strongest evidence for this possibility is Liechtenstein, where an Austrian noble family purchased two ancient Alemannic feudatories to elevate their standing at the Imperial Court. Same is true of the Crusader knights, who spent much of their history shopping around from territory to territory to establish a state that could help vouchsafe their "natural" independence.

Tribe and the Nation-State

From the anthropological and political science perspectives, the microstates are not trivial at all—rather they can possibly demonstrate the mechanism of nation-building, self-determination, survival, and ethnogenesis, ever-present and compelling public preoccupations of that "tribal" collective known as the nation. No discussion of microstates would be complete without acknowledgement of the term "tribe."

The tribe is an ancient phenomenon, not yet forgotten by anthropologists but also not talked about much in polite professional circles. It is useful here. The tribe lies quick to the marrow; it is a deep, unquestioning emotional essence negotiated between self and the familial collective. The Romans had a clear idea about the equivalency of tribe and nation as ethnic units, sharing similar language, culture, and origins. In the original Roman sense tribe specifically refers to the three ethnic groups, the Latins, Sabines, and Etruscans that formed the early Roman state. "Race" in this sense refers to people of common descent, thus related by bonds of kinship, in particular corporate descent groups.

Some anthropologists have highjacked the term "tribe" and applied it to a particular phase of political development in pre-state societies, as in tribes, bands, chiefdoms, and states. This has unfortunately generally confused the original sense. In the Roman sense however, a nation-state is the largest unit of social organization in which a tribal, kin-based, or corporate descent group identification is the primary organizing principle. Tribe itself connotes emotive, human relationships of affinity, heredity, and passion born of the family. Many of the smaller states of Europe have been at least mythologically based on kin-based affiliations observed during Roman days: Belgium is named after the Belgae tribe, Denmark from the Dani, Sweden from the Suiones, and France from the Franks. Their rulers originated from among peoples who shared a common language, culture, and descent. To what extent has this original concept of tribe served in the nation-building efforts of the European microstates? And to what extent are these microstates "nations" in the original sense?

Most of the European microstates are indeed survivals of the great feudal period within the Holy Roman Empire when princelings and their manifold estates were suzerain to a universalist emperor. Being immediate vassals, they ruled their tiny lands with nearly absolute authority and sovereignty, deferring to their imperial lord or ecclesiastical authority only in the most important of issues. With the Reformation and the break-up of the notion of Universal Christendom, Protestant princes became the sole sources of civil and churchly authority in their own realms. The kings of England, Sweden, Prussia, and many other northern Protestant monarchies were absolute—they took their share of the Holy Chrism that effected rule by Divine Right. The smaller princelings were removed from the emperor and enfeofed to kings, much to the princes' annoyance. They were forcibly "mediatized" as the larger nation-states grew. Formerly "immediate" principalities that owed allegiance only to the emperor, new kings wedged themselves into the mix by the late eighteenth and nineteenth centuries.

One by one, the hundreds of tiny kingdoms ruled by patriarchal princes, heads of their own tribal, ethnic-based microstates, were amalgamated into the voracious maws of accreting kingdoms like Prussia and Italy. One thinks of fairy tale castles ruled by an avuncular prince, with a roaring fireplace and a roast beef on the spit turned slowly by a barefoot scullery boy. The lord of the manor is clad in padded slippers and a maroon velvet topcoat and writes his cousin in Florence while the valet selects the proper insignia and orders for tonight's gala. These images were gathered up by the brothers Grimm in the nineteenth century, based on the mediated princelings of Germany and Italy who now had little to do except hunt, grow roses, and otherwise cultivate their parochial realms. By and large, the surviving microstates are non-mediatized realms that escaped the nation-building enterprises of its larger neighbors.

The nation-state is the largest unit of social organization by which tribal identification is still the primary unifying principle of identification. According to Anthony Smith, a nation-state consists of people cognizant of an ancient bond of affiliation based in descent or other agency, encompassed by a recognized territory, in one-to-one correspondence that is acknowledged by neighbors on an equal footing.[15] This is similar to the stand of Smith's professor Ernest Gellner who stated that "nationalism is primarily a political principle that holds that the political and the national unit should be congruent."[16] Here "nation" is used in the old Roman sense of tribe. The nation-state stands in opposition to an empire or other multicultural polity, which are usually defined as organizations of many nations and peoples, usually possessing autonomous units or colonial dependencies. Contemporary Europe is largely defined by the weakening of multinational polities and nation-states and the transference of solidarity downward to substate ethnonations or to post-modern collectives such as the Eurozone.

The modern, secular state, especially those in the West, is largely defined by Enlightenment-inspired republics and philosophical ideals and ideas that are traceable to Kant and his notion of self-determination. This ideal has, in fact, now spread throughout post-colonial Africa, much of the Middle East, and to Asia. This is a position well articulated by Benedict Anderson, who takes a Marxist view that the modern nation-state arose developmentally as America and France overthrew absolutism and the Divine Right of Kings of universal monarchy.[17] Of particular importance to the dynamics of this fundamental change was the development of moveable type and the rise of vernacular literature. These acts alone tended to break various dialect chains in European cultural continua into discrete language-specific parcels, many of which went on to become nation-states. One can clearly see this framing of linguistic specialty in most of the microstates: Catalán is the primary language of Andorra; Monégasque (Genovese Ligurian) is the official tongue of Monaco; Latin of Vatican City (where it is extinct as a living language everywhere else); the Semitic Maltese of the Republic of Malta; Liechtenstein uses Alemannic German. San Marino Italian is a distinct accent. It is in the utilization of these once marginalized languages that the performance of national uniqueness is clearly seen within the microstates (the universalistic Sovereign Order of Malta uses standard English, French, Spanish, and Italian, as its official languages).

The larger "modern" states, now mostly multinational and multicultural, are a far cry from the parochial little fiefdoms and principalities of the Middle Ages that were headed by tribal *patres familias* who had absolute power over their subordinates. Its subjects, slaves and citizens alike, were bound to the ruler in bonds of consanguinity, fictive or otherwise, marital affinity, and feudal alliances all the way up to the Emperor, the universal monarch. Engels, in his developmental history, felt that these archaic principalities, as "ethnographic monuments," would eventually be overwhelmed and absorbed by the larger nation-states as a process of social evolution. This positivist determinism is primarily where we get the notion that smaller states are not as viable as the larger ones, and that assimilation is inevitable. Writing in 1849 about the Slavs, having witnessed the great uprisings of 1848, Engels posited "we repeat: Except for the Poles, the Russians and at best the Slavs in Turkey, no Slavic people has a future, for the simple reason that all other Slavs lack the most basic historic, geographic, political and industrial prerequisites for independence and vitality."[18]

According to Marx and Engels, nationalism is a post-feudal bourgeois construct that artificially melds classes within nations to defend their ruling classes. These constructs tend to pit nations after each other, when the true unity of people is within the classes themselves regardless of national bountries.[19] Nationalism was considered the ultimate detriment to the development of the international class struggle movement. Within this coming struggle, certain nations will be assimilated into "fitter," more viable polities as a part of the evolutionary process, according to the historical materialism discourse of Marxism. There is little room for emotion and national sentiment in such clinical approaches.

Anthropologists Morton H. Fried[20] and Elman Service[21] were also pioneers in the discussion of the evolution of the state, positing that states and "civilizations" gradually developed from stratified tribal societies. Social Darwinism (sociobiology) and Marxism are the most deterministic of the various schools of social evolution, with societies lineally evolving from band to tribe to chiefdom to state. Polities that do not fit the perfect trajectory are somehow considered in stasis or "degenerate." The study of deterministic state formation and social evolution in general, has fallen out of fashion in recent years, particularly among ethnologists. The essentialist concept of nation as a group of people who have remained unchanged for thousands of years is also now relegated to the dustbin of paradigms past, as much as the scientific concept of human races has. To what extent, if any, are Andorra, Liechtenstein, Monaco, Malta, and San Marino nation-states?

The nation, as defined as an extension of the tribe with codified relationships between individuals being the primary institution of social interaction, is referred to by Smith as an ethnic community, or *ethnie*.[22] Smith has fused some of the modernist concepts of nation with more traditional ones such as the mythological origin of the ethnic community. On a nation-state level, this is quite evident in a few, large and complex countries like Thailand and Japan, where the monarch is the mythical father of the nation. It was also true of the core of the Roman Empire, where the ruling Julians, as descendents of Aeneas, were the Latin family descended from the founders of Rome and the gods themselves. The ethnic community underlying the origin of the nation is perhaps now most clearly demonstrated within some of the smaller monarchies of Europe such as Denmark, and includes several microstates.

The modernist school of nationalism scholars, including Anderson, Gellner, and Smith, generally posit that all nations are artificial, that they are created by peoples who have recognized bonds of affinity, whether genuine or spurious, and have acted successfully to create polities that are sovereign, i.e. entirely free from similar polities. Throughout the world, this sort of nationalism is on the rise—the process of nation-creation being essentially the same as ethnogenesis as a primary type of identity formation and maintenance. The count of independent countries around the globe has been steadily increasing since the break-up of the old European empires that began in the first half of the twentieth century. Well over 200 sovereign states color the modern international landscape. While the tribe appears ascendant, Gellner has pointed out that there are six thousand ethnonations and only two hundred states. There is some way to go before national self-determination is achieved universally, if such a thing were possible. Clearly the well-crafted logic of social evolution, including the Marxist variety, has not fared well in the retro-reality of post-colonialism. The microstate is counterintuitive, but nevertheless valid.

Like vicious ant colonies to the sociobiologists, nation-states are collectives that maintain their solidarity of perceived "race, language, and culture" for the inclusive fitness of the genome. Anachronisms of political form may be maintained, however illogically, if they are seen to contribute affectively to the continuation of the polity. E.O. Wilson argues that our Neolithic emotions are currently at war with our high-tech sophistication.[23] Is this why the generous Facebooker will share pix of colorful, feather-helmeted honor guards in San Marino, pointing out the unusual anachronism to global audiences?

Many of us were witness to the dissolution of the Soviet Union in the late 1980s and the fracturing of Yugoslavia in 1991, a process that seems to continue to spawn new countries to this day. We might think of the People's Republic of China as a *sinica irredentia*, but it too may one day fission into a myriad of sovereign national entities. In their 1911-12 republican revolution, the various national components of Qing Empire of the ruling Manchu coalition were recast into a Han-based nation-state, with non-Han peoples officially labeled as "ethnic" minorities. Historians are only beginning to learn how artificial the Manchu ethnic group behind the Qing Dynasty was (comprised of Han, Tungus, Mongolian, and other peoples as a military force designed to conquer and rule China proper), and how the nationalism of modern China has transformed them into an essentialistic minority group. The breakup of the Soviet Union, unthinkable during the height of the Cold War, says something powerfully deep about peoples' volition and affiliation for the collective, *as they themselves define it*. This is the motivational essence of ethnogenesis and self-determination.

Gellner suggests, in a functional and somewhat Marxist manner, that nation-states had to come into being as the increasing specialization of labor in the shift away from agrarian life in the West demanded specialization in education and political affiliation. Each country, then, serves a specific niche in the European and global schemes that is fully subject to sociological type formation and vulnerable to selection of the fittest. And following the Marxist imperative, either a country has something valuable to offer the world, or it disappears. The phenomenon of nation-states by this definition is clearly comprehended in the seemingly improbable microstates of Europe, which not surprisingly tend to be culturally homogeneous, wealthy, and of very long duration. Each of the current microstates of Europe seems to provide services that their larger brother nations do not. In a sense, most microstates serve specific niches in the global world; they are boutique nations who have most self-consciously removed themselves from any taint of political evolution or the seemingly inevitable process of historical determinism. They have, in effect, set Engels' beard on fire.

History of the *Longue Durée*

In searching for analytic tools for understanding the continued existence of European microstates, a clue lies in the bare fact that most of these polities have existed in some form for many, many centuries. This indicates that, at the very least, they have been successful in reproducing core institutions and collective memories to which national identities are built. Second, the histories of the microstates should not be those written in Madrid or Paris, but ideally should use memories gathered, stored, and passed on by the actors themselves. In one context, this method may be called ethnohistory; in another, it is structural history, most often associated with the French intellectual school of social scientists known as the *Annales*, after the periodical they established. Writers such as Braudel, Comaroff, Ellias, La Durie, Le Goff, and Wallace have turned the classic, official historiographic world on its head by utilizing sources close to the people being memorialized. Considering the difficulties of Marxist as well as many synchronic paradigms in utilizing the dimension of time, structural history seems a Holy Grail for many.

Most modern ethnography deals with the present, or "ethnographic present." While synchronicity seems suited for making comparisons with other cultures, it generally does not excel at making such comparisons through time or showing the processes involved with cultural change or persistence. The social sciences were also burdened for eons by the structural/semiotic paradigm (e.g. Levi-Strauss), which does not possess great aptitude to smoothly handle the dimension of time. The structure itself often has to disappear in order to allow for change. Structure is seen here as a completely different conceptual order than time or process. As such, structure has the capability only of reproducing itself endlessly through time or to disappear, throwing cultures and its actors into chaos. This is one reason cultures are often seen as delicate phenomena, at great risk to external forces of assimilation and modernization.

Structural history generally assumes that many cultural characteristics and institutions that have existed for long periods of time have done so through a continual, rather than punctuated or event-based process of cultural reproduction. Cultural knowledge, borne by actors participating in a community of shared descent, collective memory, or affiliation, is always being utilized to interact with the vicissitudes of everyday life and to inform the decision-making process. The "structure" is the "process." The collective will continually utilize the knowledge of the past to interpret present circumstances.

In the structural/semiotic view of history, however, the collective, in attempting to reproduce the pre-existing social construct, often encounters unintended consequences of their actions. Things change in these conjunctures, which are themselves liminal. With further passage of time, the pre-existing constructs will often have been rearranged in order to better adapt to the changing circumstances. Thus "event" seems the dominant force in driving history.

The work of the Annales School, on the other hand, has sought to find conservative structures and patterns of the *longue durée* that have provided a relative consistency of meaning throughout long periods of time. Such work characteristically looks at the values and behavior of everyday life and common actors as opposed to histories of important individuals.

One interesting facet of cultural change, whether driven by dramatic event or everyday process, is that cultural labels tend to be conservative, yet the relationships between actors may have been radically changed. I believe this is what Fredrik Barth is referring to by stating that ethnic boundaries tend to be conservative, but the personnel within may come and go. In this process, culture changes, yet is called the same thing by the people living it. This is why, perhaps, that the Papacy is still around, and after seventeen hundred years the Principality of San Marino still governs itself. The pope is no longer a high official of the Roman Empire, nor is he Universal Sovereign, but he still is the pope. The *apparent* continuity with the past is the most important feature of this process. Neither the event nor the substance of the transformational outcome is as important as the name people give it.

So by placing process over event, one can see how an institution like the Knights Hospitallers can continue for nine hundred-plus years, sequentially becoming knights of St. John of Jerusalem, then of Rhodes, then of Malta, and finally settling in Rome, while still doing their twin jobs of defending their faith and seeing to the needs of the poor and sick.

The Post-Modern State

> Causality according to the laws of nature, is not the only causality operating to originate the phenomena of the world. A causality of freedom is also necessary to account fully for these phenomena—Kant[24]

In mainstream international studies, very small countries may seem illogical or even trivial in the modern age because when viewed under the arc lamp of many positivist sociopolitical theories, cultural differences are supposed to eventually evaporate under the forces of assimilation inherent in these modern global superpowers. Modernists have difficulty accepting that microstates still exist in Europe, that indeed they have been viable as states for centuries and are likely to continue as such. Are they something other than archaic survivals? Imperialism and globalism are mere waves of political modernity that seem to leave the bedrock identity of these small places intact. What are some of the underlying processes that construct, shape, and maintain these seemingly illogical polities into the twenty-first century? What does it say about the power of self-determination?

I suggest, in this critique of the apparent inevitability of global uniformity, that many of the European microstates presented here can be thought of as post-modern states rather than archaic relics. Post-modernism in general is a reaction to the assumed absolute of science and the philosophy of reason. A post-modern state is one has transformed from a modern nation-state, often through agencies of immigration and multicultural development, into a polity that promotes ideals other than ones based in ethnic or origin-based nationalisms. Wealth, freedom from entangling political alliances and warfare, excellent educational and social services, environmentally sound business practices, and similar values are emphasized in these newer expressions of statehood.

The microrepublic of the Sammarinese fascinated Napoleon and Cavour for being a true "primitive" democracy in the Roman or Greek city-state sense. If one had a problem, one could simply attend the council and be heard. In the monarchial microstates, one could, and still can, visit the sovereign and present your problem directly. So the relative size of the microstate may be an expedient for direct democracy and ease in relations between the individual and the state. I conjecture that many visitors and citizens prefer their microstates because there is a humanity, a "face" in the smallness that is absent or abstract in the larger realms in the modern age. With this human touch, the microstates could be envisioned as simultaneously pre- and post-modern.

The post-modern state term has been introduced to political studies by Robert Cooper. It refers most specifically to a relatively new entry on the world political stage, the European Union.[25] Cooper defines the post-modern state as one that emphasizes the deconstruction of borders, rejects force for resolving disputes, is characterized by institutional transparency, and maintains no distinction between domestic and foreign affairs. I suggest that Andorra, Monaco, San Marino, and Liechtenstein are good examples of the post-modern state. They embrace free trade, secure banking, provide no distinction between foreign and domestic activity, have renounced their standing armies, impose almost no restrictions on customs, and are generally neutral. In the larger world, Hong Kong and Singapore would also qualify as post-modern states, although reunited Hong Kong is now only a "special administrative region" within an essentialized, highly nationalistic People's Republic of China. Singapore, also long a British colony, separated from Malaysia in 1965. These "boutique" or designer states have quickly developed unique world market economic and service niches, which through the wealth and power they generate, undoubtedly help maintain their viability and their political status. Malta and SMOM may be considered as post-modern on this basis.

Andorra, Monaco, San Marino, and Liechtenstein were transformed from pre-modern feudatories to post-modern states, with only the briefest of time spent as modern nation-states, if ever. They quickly learned that the sale of postage stamps could not support their continued national ambitions.

The Vatican City State is unique in that it is the territorial expression of the Holy See, the remnant of the Universal Church and the ideals of unified Christendom. This concept is traceable to Constantine, who first established Christianity as an organ of the Roman Empire. The Crusader knights, of which SMOM is a modern expression, was the army of the Church. While the Papal States were certainly feudal, the Vatican and the Holy See per se were never that. The universalism of the Church was continued as an ideal throughout the Holy Roman Empire, and brought into the succeeding Austro-Hungarian Empire by the Habsburgs. It is no coincidence that the last crown prince, Otto von Habsburg, was one of the founders of the European Community, now the European Union. This is Cooper's prototype of the post-modern state. There are aspects of post-modernity with both religio-political organizations: Both SMOM and the Vatican are now strictly neutral in international affairs; both have renounced the use of force to defend their territories and missions.   What the Knights Hospitallers and the Papal States never developed was an ethnically based nation-state. In general, the subjects of the Papal States did not develop a social *communitas* in the manner that the Italian unificationists of the nineteenth century were able to ignite throughout Italy.   Similarly, the elite, knightly occupiers of Jerusalem, Rhodes, and Malta were never able to assimilate, but rather contributed indirectly to native ethnogeneses that excluded them.

Despite the European Union, the United Nations, Star Alliance, and Starbucks, individualism does count in the post-modern world—in fact it helps define post-modern. One laughs at the Orwellian visage of Colonial Sanders looming over the sense-addled diners at a KFC in Kuala Lumpur. In fact, transnational angst and the grey conundrum of state conformity may be causing the resurgence of nationalism that is clearly evident in the explosion of new countries in the last thirty years. From the end of European colonialism in the early twentieth century, and accelerated by the shattering of the USSR, there has been a steady increase in new countries—polities and names that perhaps the world had only glimpsed at in the grinding and slippage of great empires. Lithuania and the other Baltic states, Montenegro, Croatia and the nascent Balkan republics, the ancient states of Central Asia rekindling over the edge of the horizon—the tribes are ascendant in this post-modern age. Who had even heard of South Ossetia or Abkhazia until Russia recognized the break-away Georgian regions? They are clear examines of the artificiality of the "national" concept and a bane to essentialism where the warm and fuzzy of affect is the primary collectivizing agent. In the age where idiosyncrasy can triumph over uniformity, the custom-tailored state shines in opposition to the generic, off-the-rack world of modernity.

Sovereignty and the State in International Law

There of course is a great difference between nation and state. The nation, whose definition became clearer with the Enlightenment, is much more of an ethnically defined social aggregate in the old Roman sense, which may or may not have statehood. The *Deutscher Nation* qualifier of the *Heiliges Römisches Reich Deutscher Nation* is a good example—the *nation* is the German people; the state is the Holy Roman Empire. They were not co-extensive. Indeed, it can be argued that Germany was not a nation-state until after World War I. Statehood, like the nation, is a quality, not an absolute. Smith suggests that "history is no sweetshop in which its children may 'pick and mix'; but neither is it an un-changing essence or succession of superimposed strata...the challenge for scholars as well as nations is to represent the relationship of ethnic past to modern nation more accurately and convincingly."[26] It is also important to examine the concept of sovereignty under international law, as it too is not black and white. Sovereignty, after all, is the condition that makes a nation a state. It is useful to examine some of sovereignty's basic concepts.

The nineteenth century fashioned the constitutive model of state creation. The concept originated at the Congress of Vienna, which re-established the principle of traditional legitimacy after the horrors of the French Revolution and the offensive conquests of Napoleon I. Serving well for a *status quo ante bellum* world, a state exists exclusively by the recognition of other states in this constitutive model. It is the primary basis by which, for example, the Sovereign Order of Malta and the Holy See articulate statehood. Furthermore, recognition is absolute. One country cannot partially recognize another any more than you would fractionally recognize your grandmother. Only when the family of nations begrudgingly allowed you to join their exclusive club could you become a nation. Despite the rule of force, no state on earth can presume to take its place in the litany of nations unless some other recognized polity acknowledges it. This was hammered home in Europe in the aftermath of Napoleon at the herculean international reorganization known as the Congress of Vienna. The constitutive definition splits, however, on whether recognition demands diplomatic recognition or simply recognition of existence.

In the newer, declarative model of statehood, an entity becomes a state when it meets the minimal criteria for statehood, such as those defined by the Montevideo Convention of 1933.[27] This construct concludes that defined territory, permanent population, government, and the capacity to enter into relationships with other sovereign states are the only necessary qualifications for statehood. The Montevideo Convention was used, for example, by government-in-exile officials from Tibet to argue their national claims before the United Nations following annexation of their country by China in the 1950s. Since the Montevideo Convention was endorsed primarily by the American states, other similar agreements have been ratified elsewhere.

One can see that the declarative model of statehood supports the ideology of the University Declaration of Human Rights, which is at the core of the United Nations charter. Here all peoples have inherent rights to identity as a collective of their own making, and by implication, a sovereign state should they wish. Nothing in the declarative paradigm suggests quantification of the collective by size or population requirements, or the achievement of legitimacy through recognition.

The Montevideo Convention was more recently upheld by the European Community Opinion in the Badinter Arbitration Committee.[28] In addition to territory, population, and government, Badinter added that states come into being and disappear as facts, while recognition by other states is simply declarative. The Badinter ruling would suggest that, for example, the Empire of Manchukuo

(1934-1945) actually existed in Northeastern China, while modern nationalists in the People's Republic of China insist that the colony established in Manchuria by Japan was as fantastical a country as Tibet was ca. 1914-1950. Revisionism is the handmaiden of ethnogenesis and the process of national identity formation.

The Italian Microstates

A brief introduction to each of the seven European microstates may be useful here before plunging into the detailed narratives that follow. They may be roughly grouped into the Italian microstates and the borderland states.

The tiny enclaves of territories once scattered about the Italian countryside are the direct descendents of the old Germanic Lombard "fortress and field system" that fractured Italy (and Germany) into tiny principalities over the centuries. Those states were clearly defined through the personality and idiosyncrasy of the founding tribal leader and their successors. San Marino is an example that survives today. Many microstates and enclaves existed previously in Italy. Cospaia and Tavolara are discussed in Chapter Eight, as is the possibly still-sovereign Ligurian community of Seborga. Monaco, too, although now seemingly thoroughly French, is also an old Italian *rocca*. The Vatican, as last of the Papal States, and the Sovereign Military Order of Malta in Rome, were formed by more lateral, universalistic processes, as affiliations of elites, rather than vertically created from an ethnic community.

State of Vatican City

The State of Vatican City[29] is the sovereign territorial expression of the Papacy. Although the religious focus of nearly two billion people, it comprises only 160 acres in west-central Rome. It was given only in 1929 as partial compensation for the nineteenth century capture of Rome and the Papal States by the House of Savoy in their unification of Italy. It is the only surviving state[30] whose citizens reproduce by apostolic succession. As such it does not represent an ethnic community, but is a tiny survivor of the universalism ideal that was the early Church.

Sovereign Military Order of Malta

Now headquartered in Rome, the ancient Order of St. John of Jerusalem, of Rhodes, and of Malta is represented by hospitals, clinics, and embassies throughout the world. It is the last surviving Crusader state, having remained intact for over 900 years. Its *raison d'être* throughout is to defend Christendom and to succor the poor and the sick.

This nation of superlatives does have a territory—a whopping 1.6 acres, but an independent territory nevertheless. In secular matters, it holds allegiance to no one—SMOM is only subject to international law. It has a constitutional government headed by the Prince/Grand Master, enjoys the status of Permanent Observer at the United Nations, and issues its own passports, stamps, and coins. The Grand Master of SMOM is assisted by an elected government, the Sovereign Council, which together provides for the day-to-day government and the executive capacity of the SMOM. Two dozen or so individuals comprise the permanent population of SMOM. Most of them are dual citizens, and in keeping with male monasticism, for nearly a thousand years, all leadership has been male.

The Republic of San Marino

The sixty-one sq. km (twenty-three sq. mile) Most Serene Republic of San Marino is a landlocked enclave in the Apennine Mountains completely surrounded by Italy. It was founded in ca. A.D. 301 by Marinus of Rab, a Christian stonemason fleeing the religious persecution of Roman Emperor Diocletian. He escaped to the nearby Monte Titano, where he built a small church and founded a Christian community. Although eventually surrounded by the Papal States, San Marino has retained its independence.

During the early phase of the Italian unification in the nineteenth century, San Marino served as a refuge for the Savoyards and other unificationists. In appreciation of this support, Giuseppe Garibaldi accepted the wish of San Marino not to be incorporated into the new Italian state. Napoleon I and Napoleon III also refused to annex the country.

The country of approximately thirty thousand citizens hosts a visitor industry of over three million visitors per year. This revenue helps place San Marino among the highest GNP per capita places on Earth.

The Principality of Monaco

Monaco is perched on the cliffs where the Maritime Alps meet the sea. Its spectacular setting is reason enough for its natives to have fought hard to maintain its independence. For most of the twentieth century, Monaco, with its elite casino, its megawealthy residents, and its colorful ruling family, was known primarily through a tabloid lens. Cheap journalism has tainted the international image of this most intriguing sovereignty, a country perhaps more fairy tale-like than all other microstates in Europe.

In the early days of the Holy Roman Empire, Emperor Henry VI gave Genoa the sovereignty of the entire Ligurian coast westward to Monaco. In 1215 Genoese Ghibellines led by Fulco del Cassello laid the foundation stones for a fortress upon the rock of Monaco, marking the birth of the principality. The rival Grimaldi family, of the Guelph party supporting the pope rather than the emperor, settled in Monaco and seceded from Genoa in 1297.

The family continued building a strong relationship with France, serving in the courts of Paris and of Provence. The Monégasques were continuing to develop an identity away from Genoa and the Ligurian Coast peoples. They spoke a dialect of Ligurian, but heavily influenced by Occitan or Provençal, a French vernacular.

Monaco gave up the substantial territories of Menton and Roquebrune to France in exchange for recognition of its independence in 1861. It was left with less than one square mile of land. It remained a rather impoverished region until the tourism bug caught the French Riviera in the 1860s. Prince Charles (Carlos) III and his mother Princess Caroline helped establish the first grand casino and hotel at a beachfront hillock—Monte-Carlo. From that point Monaco's fortunes began to rise exponentially, having now, by far, the highest per capita income in the world.

Along the Marches

Principality of Liechtenstein

For millions of Euro-Americans, living in a Swiss chalet among the mountains and lakes in the fastness of Switzerland is a dream. Like being coddled by pillows of eiderdown after a frightfully thorough spa treatment or being nudged by richness of a cheese fondue and a *pot au chocolat*, this forgotten land would seem to be oblivious to the *realpolitik* of the modern West.

The Principality of Liechtenstein is only twenty-five by ten km wide (fifteen by six miles), covering 160 square kilometers (62 square miles), the same size as San Marino. It was located at the far western edge of the Holy Roman Empire, thus being quite conveniently placed to drop out of it as well. Over time, the family has become strongly identified with the people, whose members, like in Monaco, have among the highest incomes in the world.

Liechtenstein is a striking example of the artificiality of all countries—it was founded, in fact, by a foreigner. Wishing to achieve higher status at the court of the Holy Roman Empire and become a member of the Imperial Diet, Hans Adam Andrew of Schloss Liechtenstein, south of Vienna, simply bought the Demesne of Schellenberg, a direct fief of the Empire, in 1699. To round out the estate, Hans Adam purchased the adjacent County of Vaduz. In 1719 these were united to form the Imperial Principality of Liechtenstein, with imperial immediacy, under Prince Anton Florian. Unlike many of the constituent states of the Holy Roman Empire, Liechtenstein managed to steer a course clear of the empire-building policies of Napoleon I and III, and the rise of the Prussian state. It avoided the colonel, kaiser, and führer. In 1939 the Liechtenstein family finally moved to the principality, becoming naturalized within a quite homogenous nation-state.

Principality of Andorra

Andorra, in the Pyrenees, has reinvented itself with each sociopolitical upheaval throughout its history. It survived Napoleon because a provincial bureaucrat, at the point of an Andorran pitchfork "forgot" to record to annexation of the country in the early nineteenth century.

The tiny country is twenty-nine km by twenty-six km long (eighteen by sixteen miles), with a population of ten thousand. Its official language is Catalán, the only sovereign nation in the world where it is the official language. The country thrives by being a regional merchandiser, having no European Value Added Tax. Andorra is a major a ski resort in winter, and a spa retreat at all times.

The Republic of Malta

Although an island, Malta is a land between great empires, beginning with the Punic and Roman, and navigating through to the Ottoman and Holy Roman. Recently Malta was a battleground between Allied and Axis forces. The Republic of Malta is exceptional from the states presented here as it is a microstate in territory but is a "modern" state in the sense that it has passed through a long period of foreign colonialism, emerging in 1964 as a small, post-colonial independent republic. In fact, Malta had not enjoyed independence since the Bronze Age. Malta is now a member of the European Union and the Commonwealth of Nations, the latter as a reminder of its history as a British colony.

The Sovereign Order of St. John was to rule here until Napoleon seized the property of the knights, sending them all in exile. With the fall of the French Empire in 1814 the islands were officially given to Britain rather than returned to the knights. Of vast strategic importance, the British Empire would rule Malta as a colony until 1964.

The process of Maltese ethnogenesis is one of accretion, uniquely layering, throughout the centuries, many layers of Semitic and knightly cultures blended with Italian and British ones.

Notes

1. I define a microstate as being a sovereign entity so small that it is possible to en-
compass the whole state in one unaided view standing six feet off the ground. Luxembourg, stretching over the horizon, is too big. In fact it is about five times bigger than the
next largest European microstate. (2,538 square km vs. 469 square km or 980 miles vs
181 sq. miles for the Principality of Andorra).

2. Benedict Anderson. *Imagined Communities: Reflections on the Origins and
Spread of Nationalism.* (London, Verso, 1991).

3. Josep R. Llobera. *Foundation of National Identity* (New York: Berghahn Books,
2004), 179.

4. John Sack, *Report from Practically Nowhere* (Lincoln, NE: iUniverse.com, 2000
[1955]).

5. John Ryan, George Dunford, and Simon Sellars, *Micronations,* (Oakland, CA:
Lonely Planet, 2006).

6. In 2012, the winner of a shooting match in Kuwait, Maria Dmitrienko from Ka-
zakhistan was dishonored with the playing of Borat's anthem instead of the real Kazak-
histani song by mistake, much to the horror of the audience but to the amusement of the
gracious athlete. See Eric Pfeiffer, "The Sideshow," *Yahoo News,* 23 March 2012. http://
news.yahoo.com/blogs/sideshow/borat-anthem-played-during-actual-kazakh-gold-medal-
211102106.html (accessed 7 April 2012).

7. Jorri Duursma, *Fragmentation and the International Relations of Micro-states:
Self-determination and Statehood* (Cambridge, UK: Cambridge University Press, 1996).

8. Thomas Eccardt, *Secrets of the Seven Smallest States of Europe* (New York: Hippocrene Books, 2005).

9. Leonard Wibberley, *The Mouse the Roared* (London: Little, Brown, 1955).

10. Hitler speech. www.youtube.com/watch?v=S;09v9H2UrU (accessed 29 June
2012).

11. Arnold van Gennap. *The Rites of Passage* (Chicago: University of Chicago
Press, 1960 [1909]).

12. Johan Huizinga. *Homo Ludens* (Boston: Beacon Press), 1955.

13. Edward Norbeck. "Anthropological Views of Play," *American Zoologist,* 14(1)
(1971), 267-73.

14. This was indeed a widely held sentiment among American visitors and missiona-
ries to the Kingdom of the Hawaiian Islands in mid-nineteenth century. The king and his
court were often berated for "playing country" in a realm that was on the verge of being
annexed by either the British Empire or the United States. See P. Christiaan Klieger,
Moku'ula: Maui's Sacred Island (Honolulu: Bishop Museum Press, 1997).

15. Anthony D. Smith, "Gastronomy or Geology? The Role of Nationalism in the
Reconstruction of Nations," *Nations and Nationalism,* 1, no. 1(March 1995), 3-23.
http://onlinelibrary.wiley.com/doi/10.1111/j.1354-5078.1995.00003.x/,1994. (accessed 4/
23/12).

16. Ernest Gellner, *Nations and Nationalism.* (Ithaca, NY: Cornell University Press,
1983), 1.

17. Anderson, *Imagined Communities.*

18. Cited in Joseph Seymour, "The National Question in the Marxist Movement, 1848-1914," *Workers Vanguard*, 123, 125, 3 September and 17 September 1976. www.icl-fi.org/english/wv/931/national-question.html (accessed 6/21/2012).

19. Marx, Karl and Friedrich Engels. *The Communist Manifesto* (New York: Penguin Group, 1998 [1849]).

20. Morton H. Fried, *The Notion of Tribe* (New York: Cummings, 1975).

21. Elman Service, *Origins of the State and Civilization* (New York: W.W. Norton, 1975).

22. Anthony D. Smith, *National Identity* (Reno: University of Nevada Press, 1991), 37-40.

23. See Natalie Angier, "Cooperate or Die," *Smithsonian*, April 2012, a review of E.O. Wilson, *The Social Conquest of the Earth* (New York: Liveright, 2012). Also http://www.smithsonianmag.com/science-nature/Edward-O-Wilsons-New-Take-on-Human Nature.html (accessed 7/22/12).

24. Immanuel Kant. A Critique of Pure Reason. (Cambridge: Cambridge University Press, 1999 [1781]), thesis from the Third Antimony. http://praxeology.net/kant.htm (accessed 7/4/2012).

25. Robert Cooper. "The Post-Modern State," Conflict Resolution and Sustainable Peace Building. www.world-governance.org/spip.php?article86 (accessed 1 July 2012).

26. Smith, "Gastronomy." 18-9.

27. "Montevideo Convention on the Rights and Duties of States (1933)." Council on Foreign Relations. http://www.cfr.org/sovereignty/montevideo-convention-rights-duties-states/p15897 (accessed8/2/12).

28. *The Badinter Arbitration Committee* is named for its chair. It ruled on the question of whether Croatia, Macedonia, and Slovenia, which had formally requested recognition by the members of the European Union and by the EU itself, had met conditions specified by the Council of Ministers of the European Community on 16 December 1991.

29. Actually, it is the Holy See that is the sovereign entity. The State of the Vatican City is one of its territorial expressions. The Holy See's other extraterritorial possessions around Rome are enumerated in Chapter Seven.

30. The State of Tibet, which existed in various degrees of independence until its annexation by China in 1950, was also most recently ruled by an apostolic theocracy.

Chapter Two
Principality of Andorra

The Principality of Andorra is an unlikely wedge of granite, broken with stacks of gray shale, seven valleys hidden within the ramparts of the Haute Pyrenées. Its continued survival between the great kingdoms of France and Spain through to today is one of the greatest achievements of political tenacity. Andorra lives in the modern age because a provincial bureaucrat, at the point of an Andorran pitchfork, "forgot" to record to annexation of the country to France in the early nineteenth century. Like all the microstates, Andorra has a very long and unique history of improbability.

The rough-hewn, stone architecture of most of the buildings of Andorra give it a husky, rustic flavor, reminiscent of the ancient Paleolithic and even Neanderthal cultures that had made their last stands here. "Romanesque troglodyte" would be an appropriate term for the countless stacked slate arches and dour, craggy turrets seen in the valley hamlets throughout the isolated land. The tiny country is eighteen miles wide by sixteen miles long, with a population of about 85,000 and about 181 sq. miles (468 sq. km). John Sack sums up the landscape of Andorra quite well:

> Two or three gloomy, gray stone houses stood in the area like mauso-leums, and gray stone walls were like basking snakes on the hillside. On the oldest stones, I counted at least eight kinds of lichen; their colors were gray, green, gold, black, and umber, and seen at a distance they faded into a pastel green.[1]

During Sack's days in the 1950s, Andorra was a land of heavy tobacco production and consumption—a smoking Fred Flintstone would be at home. Today Andorra has the highest life expectancy in the world.

Andorra's official language is Catalán, the only sovereign nation where this language, on the Romance dialect chain from Castilian to Occitan to Monégasque, reigns supreme. The national character of Andorra developed early, apart from either the French or Spanish kingdoms. This accounts for the great differences seen in the principality today from either France of Spain. The Iberic native language persisted here much longer than anywhere else in the eastern Py-

25

renees, and Catalán was slow to replace it. The tiny state is most definitely not a hybrid of either great state, nor is Andorra co-ruled by France and Spain. It is ruled by the co-princes, the Bishop of Urgell and the Count of Foix, whose legal inheritor is the elected President of the Republic of France.   And Andorra's ethnogenesis was no doubt strongly influenced by the idiosyncrasies of its rulers. In this regard it is similar to Liechtenstein. But unlike the Alpine principality, where absentee princes ruled from afar, only taking up residence with the onset of World War II, Andorra's rulers have never lived in these lands.

There is archaeological evidence that during the Neolithic the valleys of the high Pyrenees experienced a transhumance culture, ca. 4500 B.C. Seasonal herders would move with their grazing flocks of sheep and goats from the foothills in the winter to the high pastures in the summer. This is evidenced by a period of progressive deforestation in the high country as tree and shrub saplings were consumed faster than they could be naturally replenished. The Pyrenees are still largely deforested. The first permanently settled habitations in Andorra seem to be at sites at Serra d'Englar and Roureda del Cedre, which show evidence of both Megalithic and Bronze Age feature assemblages.[2]

It is conjectured that Hannibal from Carthage crossed over the Pyrenees near present-day Andorra on his way to conquer Rome. There is evidence that the first historic tribes living in the region were Iberian speakers, perhaps related to modern-day Basque language. Iberian was written until at least the first century A.D., when it was replaced by Latin. The script, referred to as "Levantine," appears to be influenced by Phoenician and Greek alphabets.

The Andorran region became part of Roman Celtic Gaul in 123 B.C. and was known as Gallia Narbonensis. Julius Caesar completed the conquest of Gaul in the 58-51 B.C. campaign. A distinctive Gallo-Roman culture evolved, maintaining itself well even after the Roman Empire began to disintegrate under the onslaught of Germanic tribes in the fifth century of the modern era.

The Visigoths, or Western Goths, entered this region in 418 and established a kingdom at Toulouse. At its greatest extent, the Visigoth realm straddled both sides of the Pyrenees and most of the Iberian peninsula. Most of the Visigoths were Christians, but subscribed to the Arian heresy. They believed that since Christ was created by God, he must be inferior to God the Father. This is in contrast to the Council of Nicea that defined the equality of the Trinity. Nevertheless, Visigothic culture easily melded with the Gallo-Roman culture, especially in the case of Roman law. In fact, the Roman right for women to inherit and hold property was retained throughout, allowing for many queens regnant and noblewomen in their own right to thrive in this region. One of the earliest rulers of Andorra per se was Ermesinda, Vicountess of Castelbón.

Clovis I of the Franks defeated the Visigoths in 507, reducing their possessions to the Kingdom of Septimania, the old Gallia Narbonensis, centered around the city of Narbonne.

In the early eighth century a new power burst out of Arabia, spreading quickly throughout the Mediterranean world and across North Africa. In 711, Islamic Berber and Arab forces under the Umayyad Caliph, Al-Walid I of Syria landed at Gibraltar. The army, commanded by Tarq ibn-Zinad, took seven years to fight it way through the Iberian peninsula, over the Pyrenees, to Septimania. The place where he landed on Iberia was named for the conqueror (Gibr al-Tariq). The new Islamic state was proclaimed "Al-Andalus."[3] The capital of Córdoba was established roughly in the center of the conquered lands. Many Visigoths assimilated, while others fled to the highlands, including, the valleys of the Pyrenees.

Al-Andalus proved to be a difficult realm to rule, especially from distant Syria. The Umayyad caliphs were replaced by a local emir in time, whose realm was eventually transformed into an Iberian-based Caliphate of Córdoba. Some regions broke away from this state. Cerdanya, for example, was established as an independent Berber emirate immediately east of the valleys of Andorra under Uthman ibn Naissa. Cerdanya, the home of the Kerretes tribe, still spoke their Iberic language into the eighth and ninth centuries. To the west, Christians managed to establish the small kingdom of the Asturias. Still, the Muslims continued their conquest of Frankish lands on the north side of the Pyrenees, marching into Narbonne, Toulouse, and into Aquitania. The decisive battle between the Muslims and Franks occurred between Tours and Poiters in 732, when the army of Charles Martell, *de facto* king of the Franks, defeated the Arabs and Berbers, considered by Gibbons as one of the major turning points in European history.

Charles Martel's son Pepin, and grandson Charlemagne continued the Islamic retreat southward back into Iberia. The old Visigothic kingdom of Septimania was taken from the Muslims and returned to the Franks in 759. In the fateful year 788, Charlemagne drafted troops of local Christians from the valleys of the Pyrenees. Led by Marc Almugaver, five thousand men from the Andorran Vall de Carol joined Charles' growing army. The Frankish king was impressed, and after pushing the Muslims southward out of the Pyrenees, noted that the Andorrans should be recognized as a sovereign people. Charlemagne set the annual tribute from the Andorrans as "one or two trout."

The Carloman rulers helped this process by establishing a line of pocket states along the Pyrenees and down the Catalonian coast (Figure 2.1). This was a Frankish tactic to help secure the frontiers of the newly forming empire, most clearly demonstrated in the career successes of Charlemagne. The king of the Franks, made emperor of the Romans by the pope in 800, developed the *aprisco* land tenure system to encourage the settlement of the rather barren and remote mountain terrain along the border between the Christian and Muslim worlds. A populated *Marca Hispanica* served as an effective bulwark against further expansion by the Muslims of Spain. The counties of Catalonia, the kingdoms of Aragon and Navarre, were also created in this manner.

"The great Charlemagne, my father, has delivered me from the Arabs..." so goes the current national anthem of Andorra. Charlemagne created a charter

guaranteeing Andorran rights the *Carta de Fundacio d'Andorra*, and gave it to
his son Louis. This rare document currently resides under heavy security in the
Andorra National Archives. The principality is most likely (see Chapter Nine)
the last survivor of the Spanish March created by Charlemagne, which at its
height consisted of eighteen counties.[4] Over time and through strategic marriage
alliances, many of these counties would unite. Charles the Bald (823-877),
grandson of Charlemagne, specifically entrusted the Andorran valleys to Suni-
fred I, Count of Cerdanya and Urgell:

> *Tradimus namque ipsas parroquias de Valle HAndorransis id est ipsa parro-*
> *quia de Lauredia atque Andorra cum Sancta Columba sive illa Maciana atque*
> *Hordinaui uel Hencamp sive Kanillaue cum omnibus ecclesiis atque villulis uel*
> *uilarunculis earum* (We give as well the parishes of the Valleys of Andorra,
> this is to say, Loria and Andorra, and Santa Coloma, Massana, Ordino, En-
> camp, and Canillo with all their churches and possessions, big or small).[5]

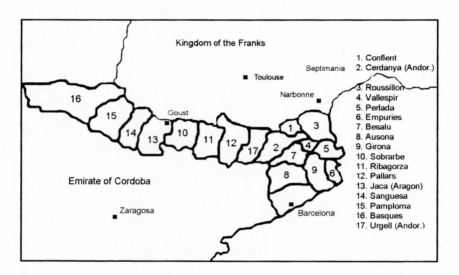

Figure 2.1 Marca Hispanica, ca. 802

Thus Andorra became part of the County of Urgell, established in 798 and given
to Borrell I, a Visigothic noble, who was also the Count of Cerdanya and Osona.
These lands were enfoefed to the County of Barcelona, which was beholden
directly to the emperor. The line continued for over four hundred years, ending
with the Countess Aurembiaix in 1231. Urgell was subsumed into Aragon when
Aurembiaix married King Peter I.

The remains of the Emirate of Córdoba continued to shrink throughout the second millennium. The Islamic state also maintained border lands on the southern flanks of the Pyrenees, known as the Upper, Middle, and Lower Marches. Muslim rule in Iberia was finally reduced to the Emirate of Grenada, when in 1492 Isabella I of Castile-Leon and Ferdinand of Aragon defeated the last emir and unified the much of the Spanish state. Most of the Marca territory, however, remained distanced from the Castilian unification.

In 988, the Count of Urgell, Borell II, exchanged Loria, Santa Coloma, and Ordino valleys of Andorra with the diocese of Urgell for the adjacent lands of Berga and Cerdanya to the east. The former Berber state had been given to the Church, and now the Church ruled the Urgell highlands, the valleys of Andorra.

In 1095, however, Bishop Bernard de Villemar of Urgell, became anxious that the present Count of Urgell and Cerdanya, Ermengol VI, was interested in reclaiming the Andorran estate at the expense of the diocese. Subsequently, the bishop made a defensive agreement with a local noble, Lord Arnau de Caboet, offering to share Andorra as co-princes in exchange for protection. The Caboet interest in Andorra was inherited by the lord's daughter, Arnalda, who married Count Arnald de Castellbó in 1185. Their daughter Ermesinda I married Roger II, Count of Foix , passing her Andorran inheritance on to Foix. Unlike most of the Frankish world, the *Marca* was not party to the Salic Law—women could and did inherit tiles and property.

From the Arianism of the Visigoths, through the Albignesian heresy, and the Protestant Hugenouts, the region from which Andorra developed was an area quite defiant of the Catholic Church and of the two Catholic empires, France and Spain, developing around it. No doubt the deeply rooted love of freedom and the stubborn refusal to give in must account for Andorran sovereignty today. Remarkably, the population of Andorra in 1176 was only 2,298 souls.

From the eleventh to thirteenth centuries, the Pyrenees, Béarn, and most of Languedoc were embroiled in a break-away religious movement, the Albigensian Heresies. The Albigens, also known as the Cathars, had a great zeal for their religion and their tenacity provided the Roman Church with one of the greatest challenges to its authority ever encountered. This movement seems to have had its origins in Thrace, Armenia, and Bulgaria among the Bogomils, areas then subject to the Byzantine Empire.[6] Arriving on trade routes, many Albigens settled in the Occitan-speaking region of what was the southern mark of the Frankish empire. Their strongholds were at Carcassonne, Saint Felix-Lauragais, Agen, and Foix. The Albigens are also known as the Cathars. The heresy was finally rooted out in the early fourteenth century, after a crusade, inquisition, and the death of tens of thousands.

The Cathars were perhaps most distinctly known for their rejection of the priestly community of the Roman Catholic faith, rejecting most sacraments, including the efficacy of sacerdotal confession. The Cathars believed that the Church had fallen into error with the Donation of Constantine (which was still believed to be genuine at that time), the making of the Papacy into a secular power. Similarly, they did not believe in the transubstantiation of the Holy Eucharist. They had but one sacrament, the *consolamentum*, which was to purify sins; it was only given once, thus was usually given just before death.[7] There were elements of Arianism and belief in a single God with multiple modalities.

In an attempt to root out the heresy, Rome even sent Saint Dominic to the region in 1203 to convince reprobates to refute their errant beliefs. He felt by showing sanctity, humility, and asceticism, the Cathars would be able to restore their confidence in the Roman faith. Dominic did not succeed in acquiring many converts, but he did found a most successful order that maintained those ideals.

The local rulers in Languedoc were not only tolerant of the Cathar settlers, the *bons hommes* as they called themselves, many actively took up their cause, often in an attempt to wrest political power away from the Church. Raymond-Roger of Foix (d. 1223) was a defender of the Cathars, as was his son, Roger II Bernard. This evolved into profound difficulties, as Roger II's wife, Ermesinda I, was co-ruler of Andorra with the enemy, the Catholic Bishop of Urgell.

The Albigensian heresy was considered such a threat to Rome that Pope Innocent III, with the help of Philip (II) Augustus of France, called for a crusade to destroy the heresy. Forces were led under Simon IV de Montfort. The decisive battle occurred at the Battle of Muret, in which the Cathar rulers of Toulouse, Aragon, Foix (with Andorra), and Carcassonne, their forces and their people, were destroyed. The Kingdom of France was now able to annex Toulouse and most of Languedoc under the Treaty of Paris. Simon de Montfort was given Foix for a time, but as Roger II eventually recanted, the latter returned to Foix where he died in 1241.

To further root out the heresy, the Inquisition was established immediately after the Treaty of Paris, in 1229, which succeeded in burning hundreds of non-repentants. Still, Cathar ideas persisted in the region. Tenacious Cathar life in the village of Montaillus in Foix was brought to life in LeRoy Ladurie's solidly researched history.[8] And it was not the only non-Roman Christian movement in the region. In ca. 1160, another anti-ecclesiastical movement was founded, perhaps by a Peter Waldo. They practiced their own ordinations, and held strongholds in the Piedmont and in Provence. Pope Lucius declared the Waldensians schismatic in 1184, and they were proclaimed heretics in 1215 by Innocent III. But despite the oppression, they have managed to survive to the present day.[9]

Roger II and Ermesinda's grandson, Roger Bernard III, Count of Foix and Lord of Andorra, married Marguerite, heiress of the wealthy Viscounty of Béarn to the west of Andorra. Their son, Gaston I, signed the first peace treaty regarding the See of Urgell and Foix over Andorra in 1278, under the sponsorship of Aragonese King Pedro III. This is known as the first *pariétage*. The treaty was followed by a second in 1288 signed by the rulers of Catalonia/Aragon and the former combatants, and was endorsed by Pope Martin IV. The *pariétages* consecrated the joint rulership of the sovereign Principality by the Bishop of the See of Urgell on the Iberian side and the Count of Foix in France. These are among the documents that modern Andorrans consider as establishing their state. In the treaties, Andorra would pay an annual tribute or *questia* to the co-rulers consisting of four Serrano hams, forty loaves of bread, and a quantity of wine.

The grandson of Gaston I, Gaston III Phoebus, Vicomte of Béarn, Count of Foix, and Prince of Andorra, was known for his handsomeness and the beauty of his prose referencing the hunt, *Livre de chasse*. His life (1331-1391) seems to be a cultural high point in the late Middle Ages. He was the last ruler of the House of Foix-Béarn. Dying childless, he was succeeded by a collateral branch of the family, the Foix-Grailly. In 1419, the Andorrans asked permission to create a representative counsel, and the bishop and the Count of Foix agreed. The *Consell de la Terra*, the General Council, gave the right for heads of households of the valleys to elect representatives. The little, but growing, kingdom between France and Iberia became quite powerful, much more so when Gaston IV (1422-1472) of Foix-Grailly married Leonora I, heiress of Navarre.

The configuration of the Marca Hispanica, established as borderlands to prevent the incursion of Islam into the Frankish empire had some unintended results. The marginality of the Marca must have contributed significantly to Andorran national sentiment, as it had in the rest of Catalonia. Ferdinand IV of Aragon managed to defeat the last Muslim emirate on the peninsula, Granada. The newly unified Spanish state was solidly Roman Catholic. So too was the emerging Kingdom of France. Not so loyal to Rome were the old counties of the Marca. Especially independent from the Most Catholic and Most Christian majesties were the inhabitants of the Pyrenean valleys, the lands of Navarre and Béarn to the west, and Foix to the east.

While Foix had become the center of the Albeginsian heresy, and the Cathars were wiped out by the early fourteenth century, some of their ideas still lingered, especially in Occitania. Many of the proto-Reformation ideas were carried forward by the Waldensians, although they too were severely persecuted by Rome. Occitania and the northern Pyrenees remained an area in defiance of the power of the Papacy and the Catholic Church in general.

Catherine, a granddaughter of Leonora I, became Queen of Navarre in 1483. She married Duke Jean d'Albret of Gause. Navarre split in 1513, with the southern half uniting with Spain. Still, French Navarre was a kingdom of considerable power and wealth. Jean and Catherine were succeeded by their son, Henri II, in 1517. Henri developed considerable sympathies with the teachings of John Calvin, even though he had married Marguerite, sister of Francis I of France. Their daughter, Jeanne, would become the most famous of all the rulers of Andorra. She was a woman of high principles and steadfast determination. When forced to marry at age twelve the rather plain Duke of Cleves (brother of Anne) she had to be physically dragged to the altar, attired in golden crown and crimson silk.[10] Succeeding the throne of Navarre in 1555, she and her husband, Antoine of Bourbon, were crowned at Pau in an elaborate Catholic ceremony. But she had been influenced greatly by her mother Marguerite toward humanist thinking, reform, and liberal ideals. She turned to Calvinism, and in 1560, declared it to be the official religion of her realm. Her followers were called the Huguenots. The Bible was translated into Basque; nuns and priests were banished. This made her the nemesis of the power behind the French throne, the very Italian and Catholic Catherine de Medici. Aloof and arrogant, Jeanne d'Albret referred to the emotional French queen mother as the "Florentine grocer's daughter."[11]

Thus ensued the French Wars of Religion, fought between the Huguenots and the Catholics (1562-1598). Jeanne had become the spiritual and political leader of the movement. She was the mirror image of her contemporary to the north, Elizabeth I of England and Ireland. The pope tried to intervene, summoning Queen Jeanne to Rome under the triple threat of deposition, confiscation, and excommunication—she simply never appeared. The wars continued until she met with Catherine d'Medici. The two queens met and agreed on a marriage contract between Jeanne's son Henri and Catherine's beautiful daughter, Marguerite. It was clear that France and Navarre would soon be one kingdom, and the Huguenots were losing. Jeanne d'Albret died soon after making the pact with the French queen.

Of glorious succession, King Enric III of Navarre, Vicomte of Béarn, and Comte of Foix, Co-prince of Andorra, now became Henri IV of France, as the senior male descendent of Hugh Capet. Henri became the first Bourbon king of France. Although he remained a Protestant for the first four years of his reign, he had to convert from Calvinism to receive the sacred anointing and coronation of Clovis. Upon securing Paris, he is known for uttering the famous "*Paris vaut bien une messe.*"[12] The Huguenot cause was essentially dead, and Andorra's fortunes were now strongly tied to France.

Initially, however, Henri wished to secure an inheritance for his sister Catherine, since she could inherit the thrones of Navarre, Béarn, Foix, and Andorra but not France due to the Frankish Salic Law. He drew up letters patent to that extent in 1590 and 1591. By 1607, however, Catherine had died without heirs and Henri revoked the patent. He gave Andorra and the other southern realms to the French crown. The process was finished by his son Louis XIII who did not wish the Kingdom of France to lose the non-French states of France due to the differences in the inheritance laws. France became a united kingdom of several sovereign states rather than a merged kingdom. In the edict of 1620, Louis proclaimed:

> By this our perpetual and irrevocable Edict, we have united and incorporated, and we unite and incorporate said Crown and State of Navarre, and our State and Sovereignty of Béarn, Andorre and Donesan, and all lands appertaining thereunto and which have customarily depended thereon, to our Crown and Domain of France, to be hereafter members thereof, and of the same Nation, rank and status as the other members of our Kingdom, Crown and Domain, without however infringing on the franchises, freedoms, privileges and rights belonging to our subject of said Kingdom and State of Béarn.[13]

In 1793, the French revolutionaries refused the tribute of hams and trout and renounced Andorran independence. The Revolution placed the Andorrans' fortunes again in the sole hands of the Bishop of Urgell. Not willing for his Andorran lands to be absorbed by Spain, the bishop continued playing the game of playing Spain off against the French. With the gamesmanship of five hundred years, an Andorran delegation convinced Napoleon to continue the status of the co-principality. The nation had been reproduced. But Napoleon was co-prince for only six years. When he annexed Catalonia in 1812, the emperor specified that the Vall d'Andorra be included. This time the mountain men from Andorra marched to the headquarters of the Prefect of the Department of the Eastern Pyrenees, who promptly "forgot" to include the tiny principality in the department. By then Napoleon was busy with greater matters. Finally, he accepted the tribute of 960 *francs*, its pre-1789 value. Inflation being what it is, to this sum was added twelve cheeses, a dozen chickens, twelve partridges, and six hams. The syndic of Andorra promptly made its oath to Napoleon. At this downfall, the *status quo ante bellum* of Andorra was respected by the Congress of Vienna.

The restored king, Louis XVIII, King of France and Navarre, Vicomte de Béarn, became co-prince of Andorra, all technically sovereign states. And with the fall of the French Bourbons and Bourbon-Orleans kings in 1848, the *de jure* title passed to the elected President of the Republic, to Emperor Napoleon III, and to the Republic again. The French co-prince is the only monarch in the world popularly elected by citizens of another country. The hams, cheese, and chickens continued to flow from Andorra to the French president until 1993.

The years 1933-1934 were particularly eventfully for sleepy Andorra, including two occasions where the ultimate authority of the Co-princes was tested. In 1933, the viceroys of the Co-princes ordered the General Council dissolved and exiled the Head of Government, Andres Masso. Both representatives of the co-princes were disturbed by the Council's using the title "Republica de Andorra" in official documents, including passports and automobile registrations. The government seemed to be submitting to young rebels. A provisional government was then appointed pending general elections. The Council, however, refused to resign. Many Andorrans objected to the dismissal in the belief that the sovereign rights of the Co-princes exclude interference in the country's internal affairs. The French Government reacted by proclaiming an embargo on the country in an attempt to reestablish the authority of its president as co-prince. The Superior Council of Justice upheld the unseating of the Council.[14]

In August, France dispatched a force of sixty French gendarmes who promptly occupied the principality, disarmed the country's six constables and thirty-six citizen police, arrested six officials and installed a permanent representative of the President.[15]

No sooner did things die down than the little country was thrown into an intrigue involving the other co-prince. In 1933, an adventurer, Boris Skossyreff of Vilnius, arrived in Andorra, stayed for awhile, drew up a few plans for administrative reform, and declared himself King Boris I under a regency of the Pretender to the throne of France, Henri, the Count of Paris. The real count quickly disavowed any knowledge of Boris or his plans. In 1934, Boris declared war on the hapless Bishop of Urgell, whereupon the former was arrested by Spanish authorities. It was great fodder for a novel by Catalán writer Antoni Morell i Mora.[16]

Through sheer cunning the Andorrans wrested themselves from external control as feudalism ended and European nation-states grew. One of the last threats to Andorran sovereignty occurred in World War II when the Germans were persuaded from invading at the insistence of Spanish dictator Francisco Franco.

Despite this love of independence, before 1993 Andorra acted not so much like a sovereign country as a jointly owned property of France and Spain. Its red, yellow, and blue flag is a combination of its two neighbors' colors; the post and telephone are managed jointly, with the France-bound mail operated by the Postes et Télégraphes and the Spanish by Caja Postal de Ahorros. Domestic Andorran mail is carried free. The churches are run by Spain and the country's foreign affairs are handled by France. There are French schools and Spanish schools. And there are now Andorran schools. The dual nature has not run that smoothly—in the 1860s, half the country leaned to the south and half to France in the north—a civil war was the result. After two years of bickering, the Treaty of Pont dels Escalls was signed, the war having had but one fatality.

The year 1993 was a time of change in Andorra. In March, the citizens adopted a constitution for the first time in their history; on 28 July, Andorra became the 184th member of the United Nations. With renewed confidence in its success in nation-building, it sent its first ambassadorial delegation to the United Nations. This diplomat is also the ambassador to the United States. The impetus for the constitution was pressure from the broader European community to insure basic rights for non-citizen residents and guest workers.

The constitution retains the co-princes as heads of state, but assigns the executive to the Head of Government. The princes do not have veto power over acts of government, but do have the sole power to enter into foreign treaties, establish diplomatic relations with other states, maintain territorial integrity, and enjoy most of the usual functions as a head of state. The French president is represented in Andorra by a resident delegate. In this regard, the government of France officially participates in Andorran affairs. This is defined more clearly in information from the Andorran Government, in Catalán:

> *Els Coprínceps són símbol i garantia de la permanència i continuïtat d'Andorra, així com de la seva independència i del manteniment de l'esperit paritari en les tradicionals relacions d'equilibri amb els Estats veïns. Manifesten el consentiment de l'Estat andorrà a obligar-se internacionalment, d'acord amb la Constitució.*[17] (The co-princes are the symbol and guarantee of the permanence and continuity of Andorra as well as its independence and the spirit of maintaining parity in the traditional balance of relations with neighboring states.

They express the consent of the Andorran State in honoring its international obligations, in accordance with the Constitution).

No such direct participation is seen on the Spanish side, as the co-prince is a bishop who acts according to Canon Law without influence from the Spanish government. In many regards he is in the same position as the old bishoprics of the Holy Roman Empire, e.g. Mainz, Salzburg, etc., but without a secular suzerain. This is not a coincidence, as many of these old realms were elevated as Church-held imperial marches under Charlemagne and his successors in the Empire.

The present co-princes of Andorra are Joan Enric Vives i Sicília, Bishop of Urgell and François Hollande, President of France. The president is currently represented by Sylvie Hubac in Andorra (2012). The bishop is represented by Nemesi Marqués (2012).[18]

Representative government is realized in Andorra with the twenty-eight member General Council. The members are elected to four-year terms. In turn the body nominates a president of the council, called the Sindic General, and a deputy.[19] Four members from each of the seven parishes were traditionally seated in the Council. To correct the imbalance between populous and sparely populated parishes, half of the members are now elected from nationwide lists. The Council in turn elects the Head of Government to a four-year term, and that officer appoints an Executive Council of eight ministers. The current Head of Government is Antoni Marti, a member of the Democrats for Andorra Party.

Justice in Andorra is handled by a triple system of courts, and is based on Roman and Catalán law. The lowest court consists of four judges chosen by the co-princes. An appellate court hears appeals; the Superior Council of Justice exists above the appellate court.

In 1997 the University of Andorra opened, offering undergraduate degrees and graduate degrees in nursing, computer sciences, and business administration.

With a population now of about 89,000, and a GDP of $3.9 billion, Andorra, in line with most of the other European microstates, has a very high standard of living. Tourism is by far the largest industry, offering year round VAT-free shopping and spa resort life to an astounding nine million visitors per year. With no railroads or airport, and just a two-lane highway in and out, no wonder the traffic is often bumper-to-bumper on weekends from Toulouse and Barcelona. Skiing in the winter is matched with mountaineering and hiking in the summer. Surprisingly, Andorra is still a major tobacco grower. Other natural resources include hydroelectric power, mineral water, timber, iron ore, and lead. In the capital, commerce and banking are important.[20]

In March of 2009, the then Co-prince Nicholas Sarkozy, President of France, threatened to renounce the co-princely title unless Andorra revised its secretive banking laws.[21] The laws were changed, as they were in Switzerland and Liechtenstein, to keep in line with standard European practice. This is a major reversal among the extant microstates of Europe.

Andorra, since its constitutional reform of 1993, has continued to establish diplomatic relations with the world. It currently maintains diplomatic relations with Austria, Belaruss, Belgium, Brunei, Estonia, France, Georgia, India, Mongolia, Spain, Portugal, and the United States. The U.S. representative, located at the United Nations, also serves Canada and Mexico.[22] Switzerland is represented by a Consul General. This activity has grown exponentially in recent years, with totals being around 122 countries with bilateral representation. It is an enclave within the EU, not a member, but uses the euro as currency.

In 2010, the two co-princes made a state visit to their principality, a strong show of support that all is well in this Catalán nation[23] of gray slate and lichens.

Notes

1. Sack, *Nowhere*, 50-51.
2. "Andorra history." www.andorramania.com (accessed 3/3/2012).
3. Andalus has uncertain etymology. It might be an Arabic pronunciation of Atlantis, or it could be the Visigothic term for "Gothic land lots," theorized as *landahlauts*, a reference to Septimania. See Heinz Halm, "Al-Andalus und Gothica Sors," *Der Islam* 66 1989, 252–63.
4. The French term *margrave* is a *comte* of the borderlands, from the Frankish *markgraf*, a ruler of a border region protecting the central state.
5. "Andorra history."
6. Mark Pegg, "On Cathars, Albigenses, and good men of Languedoc," *Journal of Medieval History* 27, no.2 (2001): 181–90.
7. Bernard Gui, *The Inquisitor's Guide: A Medieval Manual on Heretics*, translated by Janet Shirley (Garden City, UK: Ravenhall Books, 2006).
8. LeRoy Ladurie, *Montaillou: The Promised Land of Error* (New York: George Braziller), 1978.
9. "Waldensese." *The New Advent Catholic Encyclopedia.* http://www.newadvent. org/cathen/15527b. htm (accessed 8/2/12).
10. Nancy Lyman Roelker, *Queen of Navarre: Jeanne d'Albret* (Cambridge: Harvard University Press, 1968), 55.
11. Mark Strage, *Women of Power* (San Diego: Harcourt Brace Jovanovich, 1976), 150.
12. "Paris is well worth a mass."
13. "Navarre." www.heraldica.org/topics/france/navarre.htm (accessed 3/3/2012).
14. "The World at War—Andorra 1866-1957." www.schudak.de/timelines/andorra 1976 (accessed 3/1/2012).
15. "The World at War."
16. Antoni Morell, *Boris I, Rei D'andorra.* (Barcelona: La Magrana, 1984).
17. "La Constitució del Principat d'Andorra." Article 44, 1. http://www.andorra-mania. ad/constitucio-principat-andorra.php (accessed 4/24/12).
18. "Representación de los Copríncipes," *Govern d'Andorra.* http://www.exteriors. ad/index.php?option=com_content&view=article&id=223&Itemid=59&lang=es (accessed 7/22/12).

19. "U.S. Department of State, Background Note—Andorra." http://www.state. gov/r/pa/ei/bgn/3164.htm (accessed 3/19/2012).

20. "U.S. Department of State."

21. "France's Sarkozy to Andorra: Behave or I quit as co-prince." *Today's Zaman.* 29 March 2007. http://www.todayszaman.com/news-170741-frances-sarkozy-to-andorra-behave-or-i-quit-as-co-prince.html (accessed 4/25/12).

22. "Addresses of the Andorran diplomatic missions." *Government of Andorra—The Ministry of External Affairs.* http://www.exteriors.ad/index.php?lang=en (accessed 8/3/12).

23. It is an interesting oversight that nationalism scholar Josep R. Llobera, in his *Foundations of National Identity*, which is largely based on the study of the Catalonian ethnonation, never acknowledged the continued existence of a completely independent Catalán state, Andorra, which he merely places as part of a Greater Catalonia. He implies that the Barcelona-based Catalonia is the *principat* and locus of the national discourse. See Llobera, *Foundations*, 59.

Chapter Three
Principality of Liechtenstein

While many of the other nations of Europe derive their name from the tribe that settled it (e.g. France, Belgium, Sweden), Liechtenstein (Figure 3.1) is named for its founding, ruling family similar to Saudi Arabia. Liechtenstein's national creation is a sterling example of the artificiality of state formation, since its founders were foreigners. The House of Liechtenstein purchased their territory in a region of central Europe already undergoing significant ethnogenesis.

Seventeenth century Prince Hans-Adam I von Liechtenstein had a premonition of the future of the tiny German states of the Holy Roman Empire—one by one they would lose their sovereignty and be swallowed up by various *reich*. The House of Liechtenstein's grand game of national pinball, has lead it to the formation of a state far from its own homeland, one which has continued its independence to the present day. In Liechtenstein, the histories of the ruling family and the state are cut from the same cloth. It can be tightly summarized:

- In 1699, Prince Hans-Adam I of Liechtenstein secures the fief of Schellenberg on the Rhine, one with imperial immediacy, from the Holy Roman emperor. This was followed by the addition of the County of Vaduz, and the creation of the principality from the two.
- Napoleon grants Liechtenstein sovereignty for leaving the Holy Roman Empire; but the principality does not join the Confederation of the Rhine.
- Liechtenstein eventually snubs Napoleon and the Confederation of the Rhine breaks up, but the principality retains its sovereignty at the Congress of Vienna in 1815.
- Liechtenstein joins the German Confederation, but chooses not to participate in the Prusso-Austrian War of 1869. Thus, the tiny state was not mediatised as punishment by victorious Prussia, as were pro-Austrian German allies.
- Liechtenstein remains neutral in World War I—thus unique among German states, the ruling Prince Johann II does not lose his throne at the defeat of the Axis Powers. In addition to Kaiser Wilhelm II,

the august kings of Bavaria, Baden-Wurttenberg, and Saxony, and all the minor princes of the Second German *reich* are forced into exile.

- Liechtenstein remains close to Switzerland and remains neutral in World War II, avoiding Hitler and the Allies, too. The state is untouched by war, giving its economy a jump-start in the post-war years.

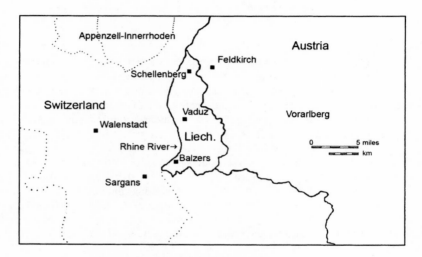

Figure 3.1 Liechtenstein

These alliances are not coincidences—they underscore the amazingly consistent ability of the Princely House of Liechtenstein to change with the vicissitudes of political fortune, and, incidentally, to choose the winning side each time.

The Liechtenstein family were consummate builders, avid collectors, accomplished property managers—they were very ambitious; they thought in terms of centuries, not generation to generation as your run-of-the-mill noble family might. With their wealth and success, they not only created their own country but insured that it remained independent by siding with the right European force at the right time. In that regard, it has never made a mistake. Of the hundreds of princely states that constituted the Holy Roman Empire of the German Nation, Liechtenstein is the only German survivor. The Grand Master of the Order of Malta, the Prince of Monaco, and the *fürsten* of Liechtenstein are all imperial princes who are current heads of state.

The oldest settlements in the fairy-tale land are two loess-rich hills, Gutenberg in the south and Eschnerberg in the north. On the castle mound of the ruins of Schellenberg, archaeological finds reveal a probable religious site. Bronze human and animal figures dating from pre-Christian times, apparently Etruscan, were found at Gutenberg Castle in Balzers. These figures, including especially that of the "Gutenberg Mars," point to the mound having been a sacred locale. Place names such as Schaan, Eschen, and Bendern indicate a movement of Celts through the valley.

The first named people to settle in the valley were the Rhaetians. Augustus Caesar's stepsons Drusus and Tiberius subjugated the alpine Rhaetians. The infamous future Emperor Tiberius himself became the first well-known historical figure to enter the land when he crossed the Julier Pass. A road was constructed by Augustus between the Splügen and Julier passes in the Grison Alps. The ruins of Roman villas can be found in Schaanwald, Nendeln, Triesen, and at Gutenberg Castle. The land became part of the province of Rhaetia, named after the mother goddess Rhaea (Cybele). When the German tribes were again on the move at the end of the Roman Empire, the Alemanni settled in the land. Theodoric, King of the Ostrogoths, allowed the Alemanni to settle around Lake Constance and up the Rhine valley. After Theodoric's death the Franks conquered the land, becoming part of the ecclesiastical state of Central Rhaetia. The Rhaeto-Romansch language, descended from vernacular Latin, predominated until 1100, when German finally took a solid hold. Being a Frankish land, Charlemagne's empire ruled the region, as the County of Rhaetia—the count's title eventually becoming hereditary. Imperial estates were noted in Schaan and Balzers.

In 1300, the Walsers, a mountain-dwelling Alemannic speaking group from Valais in Switzerland, entered and inhabited modern eastern Switzerland, Liechtenstein, and Vorarlberg, Austria. The mountain village of Triesenberg is a modern preserve of the Walser people and their dialect.

The powerful counts of Bregenz in Lower Rhaetia were important feudal lords—as their lands were parceled out to descendents over the years, two brothers Hartmann and Rudolf of Werdenberg-Sargans divided their land into eastern and western portions at the Rhine. The possessions on the east became Hartmann's County of Vaduz. He moved into the extant Vaduz Castle, built on an escarpment overlooking the Rhine. The counts of Vaduz succeeded in acquiring letters-patent from King Wenceslas in 1396 that provided for that rare gift of Imperial Immediacy, making Vaduz a direct fief of the emperor. This became a key for the national sovereignty that Liechtenstein enjoys today. The last male heir of the Werdenberg-Sargans-Vaduz line was Bishop Hartmann of Chur, who gave his lands to relatives, the Barons of Brandis from the Bernese Oberland. In 1434 the current baron acquired the Lordship of Schellenberg, the rich farmlands on the Rhine floodplain. Schellenberg thereupon became also directly enfeoffed to the emperor. The Brandis barons were given special privileges, including capital powers of life and death and the right to delegate judicial and administrative functions. These are known as the Brandis Privileges. This evolved into the elective position of *landammann,* the chief magistrate of the court of twelve other judges. There was one *landammann* in Vaduz and the other in Schellenberg.

In the fifteenth century, Vaduz and Schellenberg experienced a time of war. During the Appenzell War, the castles of Old and New Schellenberg were destroyed. At the Battle of Triesen in 1499, Vaduz Castle was burnt down and Count Ludwig was taken prisoner. In 1510 the last Brandis sold the two estates to his nephew Rudolf of Sulz, who oriented his lands closely with Austria. Count Rudolf kept the Reformation away and suppressed a peasant rebellion. The rule of the Sulz dynasty was generally a time of peace. At the end of the dynasty, Count Charles Ludwig, ridden with inherited debt, had to sell Vaduz and Schellenberg to Count Caspar of Hohenems in 1613.

On the other side of the German-speaking world, the House of Liechtenstein of Austria dates back to the twelfth century—their family seat being at Liechtenstein ("bright stone") Castle near Maria Enzersdorf, just south of Vienna at Weinviertel in the Wienerwald. One of the oldest European noble families, the first recorded member is Hugo, who appears in 1136. Heinrich I (d. 1265) obtained the lordship of Nikolsburg in South Moravia. By 1394, Johann I of Liechtenstein rose to the ranks of Chamberlain of the Habsburg Duke Albrecht III. The family slowly began to accumulate estates in Lower Austria and South Moravia.

The Catholic Teutonic knights and the Franciscan Minorites had been expelled from Lutheran Bohemia in the late sixteenth century, giving rise to the Thirty Years War. The Bohemian supreme commander was the Protestant John George von Hohenzollern of Jägerndorf. In 1620, brothers Karl and Maximillian von Liechtenstein stood by the Habsburgs in victory against the Protestant Bohemians. The House of Liechtenstein was given John George's duchies of Jägerndorf and Toppau.

Always close to the Habsburgs, the Liechtensteins had been created "regular" princes 1608, and by 1623 were raised to the rank of hereditary Imperial Princes. The arms of Liechtenstein record the early achievements of the house. Consisting of six escutcheons, it describes the arms of the Kuenring, the Earldom of East Frisia, and the duchies of Jägerndorf and Troppau in Silesia.

The immediate ancestors of all current living members of the House of Liechtenstein are Prince Hartmann III (1613-1686) and his wife Princess Sidonie Elisabeth zu Salm-Reifferscheidt who had twenty-four children. Their primary residence was Schloss Liechtenstein in Wilfersdorf.[1]

Out along the western marches, the reign of the Hohenems family in Vorarlberg in the Tyrol was characterized by warfare and the movement of troops through the land—even the Swedes had entered by the end of the Thirty Years War in 1647. The land was also raked by plague and witch hunts. The latter saw the deaths of three hundred people out of a total population of three thousand. It ended only when a group fled the country and petitioned the emperor.

He promptly deposed the Count of Hohenems and appointed Prince-Abbot Rupert of Kempten to rule instead. The prelate immediately realized that the count had also left the County of Vaduz and the Lordship of Schellenberg bankrupt. The abbot took drastic action, offering the land and its titles for sale.

In 1699, in order to earn a seat in the Imperial Diet and move up a notch in the social hierarchy of the Empire, Prince Hans-Adam Andrew of Liechtenstein started shopping for a particular type of estate. He bought the Demesne of Schellenberg, which was a direct fief of the Empire (*unmittelbar*) for 115,000 *florins*. On 16 March 1699, the people of "the Lower Country" of Schellenberg swore their oath of fealty before the elders at Bendern. But Schellenberg by itself was too small to be raised to the dignity of a principality, so Hans-Adam continued hunting. In 1712 the prince purchased the adjacent County of Vaduz. Like Schellenberg, Vaduz had no superior lord save the emperor.

Basel Hoop of Blazers, representing the people, then received an assurance from the representatives of the Liechtenstein family that the office of the *landammann*, and the rights of the communes, and other traditions under the old Brandis Privileges, the medieval pact with the people, would be respected. On 9 June 1712, all the men and boys over sixteen in the two polities swore allegiance to Prince Hans-Adam I. The "father" of his country died a short time later, but one of the long ambitions of the wealthy Liechtenstein family was finally achieved. Unfortunately for the people, the representative, Commissioner Harprecht, came into conflict with the clergy and the communes, and abolished the *landammann* constitution.

The focus of the life of the Liechtenstein family at the time, however, was not the two estates in the Alemannic west, but the brilliant Imperial Court in Vienna. Here, Prince Eusebius (1611-1684), an architecture scholar, began his family's long-term occupation with building palaces. His visions were put into stone by his son, Prince Hans-Adam I (1657-1712). As a result, the brilliant Liechtenstein palaces in Vienna are still among the most significant examples of Baroque architecture. Their style is distinctly Italian.

Hans-Adam I was the leading figure in the history of the country, having started the process of carving out a principality from the family fortune. Liechtenstein to a large extent can be considered a product of the close relationship between the family and the co-ascendant Habsburg family. As the emperors consolidated their realm in Vienna, the Liechtenstein family became one of the most prominent and influential components of the Imperial Court. Supported by his valuable estates in Moravia, Silesia, and Austria, Hans-Adam I acquired a plot of land in front of the Viennese city gates, at Rossau in 1687. The following year the great architect Johann Bernand Fischer of Erlach arrived and was commissioned to build a Baroque belvedere, or viewing pavilion-palace, following Roman and Venetian designs. The belvedere was located at the end of a magnificent garden. The first complete design for the palace was presented to the prince by Domenico Egidio Rossi in 1690. He was joined by Domenico Martinelli in 1692. The latter finished the town palace, while construction of the

Rossau estate continued in earnest after 1699. When Hans-Adam I died in 1712, the Rossau exterior had been constructed, but not the interior.

Hans-Adam was succeeded by his brother Joseph Wenzel (1712-1718), then by his younger brother, Anton Florian (b. 1656). Anton also had been very close to the Habsburgs, becoming primary aide d'corps of the young Archduke Karl, in charge of his education. During the War of the Spanish Succession, Karl took Anton with him to Spain to be his prime minster. In 1711, Karl was elected Holy Roman Emperor as Charles VI and returned to Vienna. He kept Prince Anton in the position of chief intendant, and made him chairman of the Secret Council of the Empire. For his long service to the emperor, Anton was admitted *ad personam* to the Imperial Council of Princes of the *Reichstag* in 1713, his family having previously obtained the necessary feudal immediacy (c.f. *reichsstand)* with the emperor through the estates of Schellenberg and Vaduz.

Finally in 1719, the emperor unified the two estates and elevated them to the position of an imperial principality. The two residences in Vienna became Anton's *pied de terre* in the imperial capital. Initially there had been no direct contact between the Liechtenstein family and the people of the principality. In fact, the princes did not reside in their country until 1938. Instead, bailiffs were appointed and sent to the country to keep the princes in Vienna informed of matters, but even these bailiffs lived, not in Liechtenstein, but just across the border in Feldskirch, near Hohenems in Vorarlberg, Austria!

Prince Anton was succeeded by Joseph Johann in 1721. Like his predecessors, he continued to work on the construction of the Rossau Palace in Vienna, helping to create a confectionary of plasterwork putti amid gilded mirrors and panels to rival both the Schönbrunn and Versailles.

The office of the *landammann* was finally reinstated in 1733, with modifications. The officer was no longer to be chairman of the court, but a non-voting assessor with certain administrative duties. The princes' main representatives were still the bailiffs. Of note was Bailiff Menzinger of the late eighteenth century who seemed genuinely concerned for the people of Liechtenstein. He introduced compulsory schooling, and pioneered the growing of potatoes as a boon to subsistence farmers, as it had been in his native Swabia. With the addition of maize, first grown at the beginning of the eighteenth century, the people were beginning to have some control over the spectre of famine. Menzinger tried to convince the prince to abolish serfdom, but the chancery in Vienna would not listen.[2]

Prince Johann I (b. 1760) reigned from 1805 to 1836. Like Prince Wenzel he chose a military career. Napoleon made Prince Johann commander in chief and field marshal over the Austrian army, and was placed in charge of the peace negotiations between France and Austria. He remained loyal to the Holy Roman Emperor. Winning the decisive Battle of Austerlitz in Moravia against the Russian and Austrian armies, Napoleon defeated the ancient Holy Roman Empire.

In 1806, the Habsburgs, having for centuries held together the ghostly and feudal Holy Roman Empire of the German Nation, finally saw the handwriting on the Hofburg's Baroque walls. On 1 August the Confederation of the Rhine was established. Napoleon admitted Liechtenstein and fifteen other states into the Confederation and granted each independence under his protection. On 6 August, Francis II first declared himself Emperor of Austria, then abdicated as Holy Roman Emperor, releasing all the bonds of fealty between it and the non-hereditary lands, such as Liechtenstein. After nearly fifteen hundred years, Caesaropapism had completely faded from the European political scene, giving birth to several modern nation-states. Liechtenstein would become one of these entities.

Establishing the Confederation of the Rhine with member sovereignty proved to be irresistible to many German princes, and for Napoleon's sake, tied the league to the fortunes of the French Empire. The Prince of Liechtenstein did not sign, yet the principality was given its independence nevertheless. Napoleon had come to respect Prince Johann at the Battle of Austerlitz and his through his negotiating skills at the peace talks representing Austria. Of all the members of the Rhenish Confederation, i.e. Hesse-Darmstadt, Anhalt-Bernburg, Anhalt-Dessau, Anhalt-Kothen, Hohenzollern-Hechingen, Hohenzollern-Sigmaringen, Isenberg, Leyen, Mecklenburg-Schwerin, Mecklenburg-Strelitz, Ebersdorf, Gera, Greiz, Lobenstein, Schleiz, Saxe-Coburg-Saalfield, Saxe-Gotha-Alternburg, Saxe-Hildburghausen, Saxe-Mengingen, Schaumburg-Lippe, Schwarburg-Rudolstadt, Schwarzburg-Sonderhausen, Waldeck-Pyrmont, Erfurt, Frankfurt, Westphalia, Duchy of Warsaw, Cleve-Berg, the kingdoms of Bavaria, Baden, Wurttemburg, and Saxony, only Liechtenstein has retained its sovereignty into the modern era. Indeed, the other states are now largely forgotten outside of Germany.

One prominent factor in the sustainability of the microstates of Europe is their good fortune of keeping out of harm's way. The last fighting on Liechtenstein territory was in 1799, when Switzerland was first overrun by the French Army. Its General Massena, on his way to occupy the Austrian Vorarlberg, crossed the Rhine at Blazers and took Luziensteig. Advancing on to Feldkirch, his army was repulsed back to Switzerland after three weeks. Then the Austrian army moved through, followed by the French again. The billeting of soldiers plunged the tiny principality into debt.

Liechtenstein was supposed to provide Napoleon with forty soldiers as a condition for membership in the Confederation. However, Liechtenstein was able to hire enlisted men from the Duchy of Nassau downstream for five thousand *florins* per year to satisfy that contingent.[3]

In several decisive moves, Prince Johann outfoxed Napoleon. Whereas the pitchfork-brandishing Andorran peasants had stormed the local Napoleonic magistrate when the great general was distracted, Prince Johann confronted Napoleon directly. Despite being adversaries, the French general had a particular admiration for Field Marshal Prince Johann, Supreme Commander of the Austrian Army, with whom he became acquainted after Johann's cavalry command of the Battle of the Three Emperors at Austerlitz in 1805. No doubt as a tribute, Napoleon included Johann's princely state as a member of the Confederation of the Rhine, despite the prince's continued loyalty to Austria. Although the charter establishes Liechtenstein's independence, and this action was verified at Vienna, there is no signature of the prince or his representative on the foundation charter. This brilliant move for Liechtenstein built a certain political capital that paid off later. After Napoleon's defeat, Liechtenstein could cast off the Confederation without penalty and keep the sovereignty it had been given by Napoleon. In 1808, the tribunal was abolished. In 1810 the absolutist Johann, having been criticized for poor diplomacy, retired to build the Princely Art Collection. He named his son Alois II governing prince. Johann lived on until 1836.

Johann can also be credited with taking a personal interest in the principality. In 1808 he sent an inspection team to Liechtenstein. Their report provided a dour glimpse of the condition of the state—huge debts, an illiterate population, antiquated agricultural systems, no tradesmen or merchant class, and that bane of Germanic land tenure—the fragmentation of lands into smaller and smaller units to attend to the needs of multiple heirs. As a result of this dilemma, a capable bailiff, Joseph Schuppler was appointed in 1808. First duty: abolish the feudal office of *landammann*. This was justified by the fact that the office operated in accordance with the ancient laws of the County of Sulz, which were quite obsolete. Second, the tribunal and the *landammann* never had any legal training. Some were, in fact, illiterate.[4] Then, with the age of feudalism clearly being over, serfdom was finally abolished in 1808.

When Napoleon invaded Russia, many of the states of the confederation had finally become disillusioned and disaffected with the Corsican upstart. With the Allied victory of Leipzig in 1813, several of the states, including Liechtenstein, changed sides, formed the "Little Alliance," and liberated Germany from the French. In 1815, at the Congress of Vienna, the German Confederation was signed, Liechtenstein becoming a full member. The little principality had, in a few years, steered from loyalty to a declining Holy Roman Empire, to an ascendant but unsustainable Napoleon. It sailed through the end of the French Empire and the Confederation of the Rhine by becoming a full member of the German Confederation at the Congress of Vienna in 1815. Like during the times of the Rhenish Confederation, Liechtenstein would become the only member that retained its independence after its dissolution.

Prince Alois II (b. 1796) became interested in agricultural production and botany, an interest that benefited the various lands of the House. He also continued to add to the family art collection. In 1842 he became the first prince to visit the country, after nearly 140 years of ownership by the Liechtenstein family. These visits (the second in 1847) actively promoted the economic and political development of the principality. In 1852, a customs treaty was signed with

Austria. Alois saw to the building of protective canals and weirs along the Rhine as a means of flood control.

In the republican fever of 1848 that swept away the French King Louis-Philippe, revolution was felt throughout Europe. In Austria, conservative Emperor Ferdinand was forced to abdicate in favor of his young nephew, Franz Joseph. In Liechtenstein, too, the population demanded a liberal constitution. Prince Alois acted by revoking a set of old taxes and granting some political liberties. In 1852, with the revolutionary spirit dying down, he rescinded all reforms. His death in 1858 ended the reactionary regime, and the populace moving steadily towards lasting constitutional reform.

The foundation of the great banking institutions that would make the principality one of the wealthiest states in the world occurred in 1861, with the establishment of the Zins- und Credit-Landes-Anstalt (Saving and Loan Bank), which is now the giant Liechtensteinische Landesbank.

In 1862, Prince Johann II promulgated the first Liechtenstein constitution, with a representative Diet, giving the people the right to construct a state budget, and the right of initiative.[5] Prior to this time the state was essentially an absolute monarchy, since the prince quite literally owned the country. The Redemption of Tithes Act abolished the payment of in-kind dues to the authorities that originated in the Middle Ages. Also during this decade, industry began with a cotton mill. Unfortunately during this time many men had to journey to Switzerland as seasonal workers in the building trades.

With the rise of Prussia, the creation of the North German Confederation in 1866 following the Austro-Prussian War, and the 1871 declaration of the Second Reich, Liechtenstein's perpetual alliance with Austria served it well. The former principality of the Holy Roman Empire chose not to join the new German Empire. In addition, Bavaria, which had been a border state to Liechtenstein, lost its Tyrolean and Vorarlberg provinces to Austria at the Congress of Vienna. Thus, the principality no longer bordered German territory and most likely the new Prussian dominated government did not relish having to govern a discontinuous territory, a factor for weakness in the erstwhile Holy Roman Empire. Prince Johann II had sent a handful of soldiers to help Austria in the war, against the Prussian ally. After six weeks of non-engagement in the Alps, they were sent home, and disbanded forever.

In the last half of the nineteenth century the principality modernized rapidly. Four bridges were constructed over the Rhine linking Switzerland with Liechtenstein, and roads were constructed from the heretofore isolated communities of Schellenberg, Triesenberg, and Planken and the Rhenish plains.

The Twentieth Century

In 1918, the Austro-Hungarian Empire broke up and the Emperor Karl went into exile. The Republic of Czechoslovakia was established, and all noble families of the new nation lost their lands. Austria also became a republic, hostile to the former ruling family of Habsburg. The duchies of Jägernsdorf and Troppau were eventually lost to the Liechtenstein family.

The Principality of Liechtenstein, wisely, had been neutral in World War I. However, the end of the war saw the state destitute. It had since 1852 used the Austrian currency, which was nearly worthless in late 1918. People's life savings evaporated. In an act of great generosity, Prince Johann II bestowed a loan of 550,000 *francs* upon his people for the purchase of food in Switzerland. Five years later he tore up the note.

In 1920 the Liechtenstein Global Trust was established, which has now become the largest private bank and wealth management institution in Europe. In 1930, its shares were purchased by the princely family.

In a further move away from now non-Habsburg Austria, Liechtenstein requested Switzerland to represent it diplomatically. In 1923 it established a customs union with its western neighbor and in 1924 adopted the Swiss *franc* as the official unit of currency in Liechtenstein, dispensing with the Austrian *schilling* whose worthlessness had plunged many citizens into poverty. Vexed with little arable land, and a wartime collapse of the textile industry, Liechtenstein was hard pressed. It was this time that the tiny country developed a small source of income through the sale of postage stamps. A casino company also presented a rescue scheme, similar to that which revived sister microstate Monaco, but neither the prince nor the Diet were interested in the latter scheme. To add to the general misery, the Rhine flooded in 1927, inundating much of the arable land of the principality.

In 1929, having reigned for an unprecedented seventy years, Prince Johann II died.[6] His younger brother Franz succeeded. Prince Franz, who ruled 1929-1938, was married to Elizabeth von Gutmann of Jewish descent. Both Johann and Franz had politically moved the principality away from Austria and aligned themselves more closely with Switzerland. With the rise of Nazism, Franz abdicated rather than subject his wife to embarrassment and the country to a possible invasion. Like Johann II, he had no children—the throne passed to the son of his first cousin twice removed, Franz Joseph.

Throughout the 1920s the Liechtenstein economy slowly improved. Tourism had a tenuous beginning, and many skilled laborers in the building trades found employment across the Rhine in Switzerland. This was all to set back during the worldwide Great Depression of the 1930s. The state responded by providing infrastructure projects such as the Inner Canal of the Rhine, which helped heal the lands damaged by the flood of 1927.

Liechtenstein became one of the few European states that did not recognize the Munich Pact and the occupation of Czechoslovakia by Nazi Germany. Shortly afterwards Germany annexed Austria. Fleeing Hitler, the new ruling Prince Franz Joseph and his family left Vienna and settled permanently in Liechtenstein. The family moved into Schloss Vaduz, an ancient castle and former tavern that had been rebuilt during the 1920s. Unlike the Baroque family palaces of Vienna, Schloss Vaduz is a snug stone castle precipitously perched on a cliff overlooking the town of Vaduz and the Rhine.

Liechtenstein, now firmly aligned with Switzerland, remained neutral throughout World War II. The state projects of the 1930s were paying off—agricultural production increased dramatically, and was tied with the Swiss markets. Employment rose.

In the immediate post-war period, Liechtenstein began a rapid change from an agrarian economy to an industrial and service-based one. This would prove to be the basis of its great wealth that is seen today. For example, industrial products exported rose from 13 million Swiss francs in 1946 to 894 million francs in 1982.[7] The great increase in the standards of living also increased the princely family's political capital and their own private fortunes, despite setbacks elsewhere.

In 1989 Prince Franz-Joseph II passed away and was succeeded by his eldest son, Hans-Adam II. The new prince's mother, Princess Georgina, also passed away that year. Hans-Adam is married to the former Countess Marie Kinsky von Wchinitz und Tettau, and they have three sons and a daughter. He has had a most successful reign.

A Claim to the Czech Lands

The post-war Czech government confiscated the Liechtenstein estates in Moravia and Bohemia that had been the old duchies of Jägerndorf and Troppau—over nineteen hundred square kilometers, twelve times larger than the Principality itself and about the size of Luxembourg, even though Liechtenstein had been a non-adversary in the two world wars. The decrees issued by the President of the Czechoslovak Government-in-Exile, Beneš, justified the confiscation of the ancient South Moravian properties of the princely family on the grounds that Franz Joseph was a German and that he had benefited by purchasing stolen Jewish lands from the Nazis.[8] Of the ninety-nine-odd estates in Moravia and Silesia, the lands of Feldsberg (now Valtice, Czech Republic), Eisgrub (Lednice), and Nikolsburg (Mikulov), were the most important, forming a considerable portion of the real estate base of the family since the fifteenth century. Feldsberg Castle was the administrate center of these Liechtenstein estates.

In the early twenty-first century, sovereign Prince Hans-Adam II filed claim in the World Court for the return of the seized estates. A certain amount of misunderstanding has occurred, presuming that the Prince is seeking to expand his principality by this move. Unlike the Lordship of Schellenberg and the Country of Vaduz, however, the Moravian and Silesia estates were not immediate imperial fiefs—Nikolsburg, for example was suzerain to the Bohemian king Premysl Otakar II. Thus, no similar sovereignty could be attached to these lands as it had with the passing of the Holy Roman Empire. The claim, therefore, is based on an interpretation of these lands as private property of the Liechtenstein family, and not of the state. The princely family also retains its ancient properties in Austria, which were never nationalized. Perhaps because of this misunderstanding, the governments of the Czech and Slovak republics have refused to recognize the Principality of Liechtenstein. As such, Liechtenstein sued Germany in April 2001 at the International Court of Justice in the Hague. It was triggered over a Dutch painting loaned by the Czech government to a museum in Germany in 1998. Prince Hans-Adam II requested that it be given back to him instead of returning it to the Czech Republic. The issue of the duchies lies before the International Court, having grown to nineteen hundred square kilometers of property considered illegally given to the Czechs by Germany as war reparations.[9] This represents about four percent of the entire land area of the Czech Republic.

The World's Wealthiest Per Capita Country

Banking continues to be a major service in the Liechtenstein economy. In 1970, the profits of the Liechtenstein Global Trust were given over to the Prince of Liechtenstein Foundation. The bank changed its name in 1996, becoming the Liechtenstein LGT Bank in Liechtenstein. It went public in 1986, and has branches throughout the world. Germany had conducted several audits of deposits of its citizens in 2008, suspicious of Liechtenstein as a tax haven. The Prince of Liechtenstein foundation manages a complex portfolio of Vienna real estate, and the principality's two museums, the Landesmuseum and the famous Vaduz Museum of Art. Prince Hans-Adam II had been the head of the bank and the foundation, and was succeeded upon his elevation to the throne by his nephew Prince Maximilian and brother Prince Erasmus, respectively.[10] Other members of the family are well-connected with numerous business and charitable enterprises throughout Europe. Prince Andreas, a resident of Sweden, is president of the Scandinavian Association of the Order of Malta.

Liechtenstein maintains direct diplomatic relations with Switzerland, Austria, the Holy See, Belgium, and the Sovereign Order of Malta. It is a full member of the United Nations. It is otherwise represented internationally by Switzerland. Liechtenstein and Switzerland have open borders, with no permanent border stops. The frontier with Austria is manned with Swiss custom agents, and beyond represents a different economic zone and road toll region of the Eurozone.

Prince Hans-Adam II is the wealthiest head of state in Europe, with a family fortune in excess of $7 billion. He owns the Liechtenstein LGT Bank and is heir to the famous Liechtenstein art collection. The success of Liechtenstein is phenomenal—in 2008 it jumped significantly over Monaco to become the wealthiest country per capita per GDP in the world.[11]

In 2003, Hans-Adam promulgated a new constitution which gave the ruling prince sweeping powers. In the true spirit of a microstate, it also has provisions by which any of the tiny country's parishes may secede from the principality. In fact, although Liechtenstein is a solid monarchy, it also practices direct democracy. The people have significantly greater freedoms to participate in the life of the nation than in most western democracies. The Diet, or Landtag, consists of twenty-five deputies who represent the people. They are elected by proportional representation by the electorate. The executive officials are appointed by the reigning prince, on advice of the Landtag. The head of government and two other members belong to the majority party, whereas the deputy and one other government official belong to the minority party. The judiciary is represented by a lower, high, and supreme court. By tradition, Swiss and Austrian judges sit on Liechtensteiner courts. Only the seven Lower Court judges are full-time. An administrative court attends to matters against the government; the State Court of Justice deals with constitutional rights. Suffrage for female citizens over twenty was only available after 1983. Citizens hold the right to initiative and referendum.[12]

Although the princely family, the state, and much of the population are Roman Catholic, the nation guarantees religious freedom. Local government is enacted through the government of eleven communes representing the main towns of the principality. Six communes comprise the Upper Country (the old County of Vaduz), while five communes form the Lower Country (the old Lordship of Schellenberg). The electorates of each commune elect a mayor.

In 2004 Prince Hans-Adam named his eldest son Alois regent, and Alois has taken over the day-to-day running of the country while his father remains the formal head of state. Prince Alois is married to Princess Sophie, nee Duchess in Bavaria, of the ancient House of Wittelsbach. They have four children. Sophie is the Jacobite heiress of the centuries-old claim of the Stuart family to the thrones of England, Ireland, and Scotland.

Liechtenstein Institute of Self-Determination

For the House of Liechtenstein, the principle of self-determination has been the family business—most successfully turning its estates between the Tyrol and the Swiss Confederation into a nation-state surviving confidently into the twenty-first century. It is only natural then for reigning Prince Hans-Adam II to establish an institute to study the application of the principles of self-determination on the world stage. In 1995 the Liechtenstein Institute on Self-Determination (LISD) was established at Princeton University in New Jersey to support research on self-determination and educate and publish on the topics of state sovereignty, boundaries, and autonomy. International law and policy are examined, as well as economic matters, and the characteristics of international organizations such as the UN and NGOs in search of greater autonomy or independence.

In many ways LISD represents and reflects the hopes and dreams of peoples around the world whose ethnogenesis is in its infancy or has somehow been arrested through war and occupation. The success of Liechtenstein as a nation is used as a standard and an inspiration for many disenfranchised peoples, and LISD provides a forum for discussion at an international level.

Struggles over self-determination and sovereignty, autonomy, and independence are among the most contentious of sociopolitical issues in the postcolonial world. Endless conflicts have arisen over groups forcing themselves upon others. Recognizing the nature of societal fissioning as well as the fusing of other groups in the process of nation building, LISD was established as an autonomous institution within the Center of International Studies of the Woodrow Wilson School of Public and International Affairs at Princeton. It is designed to further the study of the prevention and peaceful resolution of intrastate and international conflicts that are born from the search for autonomy and independence by various communities.

The principal benefactor of LISD is Prince Hans-Adam II; the institute is currently (2012) directed by Dr. Wolfgang Danspeckgruber, a lecturer in public and international affairs at Woodrow Wilson School. The program is designed to create an objective and non-polemical environment for the discussion and dissemination of issues related to the pursuit of self-determination. Fellows, representing both the academic and the diplomatic world, spend a year in residence at LISD. The institute sponsors conferences and supports research fellowships for undergraduates and graduates.

Several projects have been initiated since the founding of LISD. Its first program was devoted to basic research on issues emanating from the search for greater self-determination. Two international conferences were held in 1995 that examined the notion of self-determination and global interdependence. Edited volumes were published as a result of the conference.[13]

Phase II began in 1996 and focused on the decentralization of India coinciding with its fiftieth anniversary of independence. In 1997 two conferences were held in Vaduz bringing together scholars from ten countries to discuss democratization and decentralization in India. In 2000 LISD began to examine the autonomy, decentralization, and borders of the lands occupied by the former Soviet Union. Concepts of ethnicity, migration, regionalism, trade, energy and natural resources, and the emergence of organized crime were discussed under the chairmanship of Stephen Kotkin, associate professor of history and director of the Russian Studies program at Princeton. In 2000, LISD hosted a conference at Princeton to discuss the crisis in Chechnya with forty experts on the subject. A publication was also published based on that meeting.

LISD has also focused on the problems in the Balkan states, especially the recent situation in Macedonia, Kosovo, and Montenegro. Several international conferences have been held on the Balkans, including diplomatic roundtables and workshops. In June 1999 LISD organized the Sixth Liechtenstein Colloquium on European and International Affairs entitled "The Future of the South Balkins" held in Triesenberg, Liechtenstein. A report of that meeting was submitted to the General Assembly and UN Security Council.

With his interest in self-determination, Prince Hans-Adam II has a great concern with the plight of Tibet, the Himalayan region occupied by China in 1950. He has granted audiences with several board members of the Committee of 100 for Tibet to discuss aspects of Tibetan self-determination. These discussions were carried further at a meeting of the Association for Asian Studies in Atlanta where there was a presentation of a scenario envisioning the re-establishment of the Tibetan state in exile in the manner inspired by Liechtenstein and the SMOM.[14]

In the process of nation-building, the Liechtenstein family itself became naturalized. Over several generations they transformed themselves from professional Imperial courtiers to sovereign rulers of their own state. They now identify and are identified by the people as Liechtensteiners and fathers of the country. This nationalization is quite similar to the transformation the Habsburg family underwent, somewhat unsuccessfully, from divine rulers of the Holy Roman Empire to *pater familias* of the nation-states of Austria and Hungary. I am tempted to suggest that currently the nexus of Liechtensteiner identity lies with the founding family rather than Walser or Rhaetian antecedents.

First millennium sources seem to indicate that the Roman Rhaetians and the German Alemannic tribes were highly independent people. They were later joined by the Walsers from the west, but all seemed to co-exist. In a sense, the *longue durée* of ethnogenesis was most likely happening in the canton-like domain when the Liechtenstein family took an interest in the region. Surely the raising of the lands to a state was felt by the people to be in their interest, too, as states are all-powerful. The Liechtenstein family, graced by wealth, intelligence, and good luck, in the *courte durée* catalyzed the formation of the independent realm from which residents were perhaps building a strong sense of nation.

Of all the microstates of Europe, Liechtenstein presents the clearest example of the single-minded determination of one family to create a polity free of the constraints of excessive alliances and military deployment, rich in traditional particularisms, graced with direct democracy, dedicated to social welfare, and above all, framed with the recognized right of self-determination for all its people.

Liechtensteiner Cuisine

Cuisine and national identity go hand in hand. While Luxembourg may have its stuffed cow's udders and jellied pig trotters, little Liechtenstein has similar culinary delights that reify the notions of shared identity and uniqueness. In many countries, survival foods have taken on the aura of national icons. Used in times of national crisis, such foods become symbolic of the struggle. It is patriotic to prepare these dishes, even though better times are often at hand. Every culture has one or two—Norway has its trembling *lutefisk*, a lye-soaked jellied cod. Liechtenstein has its *rebi* or *ribl*, a mush of cornmeal and semolina sometimes garnished with gravy, vegetables, meat, or elderberry puree. A variant of the Swiss *rosti* is seen with bacon or ham and Gruyere cheese, topped with a fried egg. In Liechtenstein it is called *alperrosti*.

As could be expected, Liechtenstein dishes have much similarity with its neighbors Austria and Switzerland. Most of these specialties emanate from home kitchens, handed down from generation to generation, but a few are beginning to appear on restaurant menus. According to Robinson, national dishes could include *saukerkas*, a local cheese, *hafalaab*, a concoction of cornmeal and wheat dumplings in ham broth, various schnitzels, sauerkraut stews, and fondues. *Spatzl* or *knöpfli* are dumplings with ham or bacon and cheese served in soup or with sauces as in Austria. Beef consommé with liver dumplings is common.

A unique dessert in the principality is the Snowball, a vanilla flavored meringue with custard and berries. In Schaan, watercress soup is made. The Walser up in Triesenberg claim a unique noodle dish flavored with sour cream, cheese, and bacon. In the Eschen highlands one may enjoy the locally caught trout. In Blazers on the Rhine one can sample *geshnetzltes*, thinly sliced meat in sauce, as well as Blazers split pea-sausage stew. In Ruggell you can try the cheese and mushroom pudding. In Schellenberg, one may try the local *kasknöpfli* and a head cheese known as *schwartenmagen*.

From the princely kitchens come such confections as *Braganzer eisbombe* made of orange ice and Grand Marnier flavored whipped cream, and *zitronenpalatschinken*, composed of lemon crème filled ravioli. Published by the princely chef by the Prince of Liechtenstein Press, the desserts clearly show the Liechtenstein family's Viennese origin.[15]

Notes

1. "Schoss Liechetenstein." http://www.liechtenstein-schloss-wilfersdorf.at/eng/eng_02. html (accessed 2/20/12).

2. Otto Seger. *A Survey of Liechtenstein History.* (Press and Information Office, Government of the Principality of Liechtenstein, Vaduz, 1984). 14.

3. Seger. *Survey.* 16.

4. Seger. *Survey.* 18.

5. Seger. *Survey.* 20.

6. In Europe, only Louis XIV reigned longer.

7. Seger, *Survey.* 29.

8. Ladislav Kahoun. "Liechtenstein Prince Hans-Adam II: I want my property back." http://www.blisty.cz/art/17123.html (accessed 3/15/2012).

9. Olga Szantova. "Liechtenstein sues Germany over Czech property." Radio Praha. Http://www.radio.cz/en/article/10871 (accessed 3/10/2012).

10. "LGT History." http://www.lgt.com/en/lgt-group/history/index.html (accessed 8/3/12).

11. "CIA World Facts." https://www.cia.gov/library/publications/the-world-factbook rankorder/2004rank.html (accessed 7/8/12)

12. Press and Information Office, *Liechtenstein—Principality in the heart of Europe* (Vaduz: Press and Information Office, 1996), 10-12.

13. For example see W. Danspeckgruber, ed., *Self-determination and Self-Administration: A Sourcebook* (New York: Lynne Rienner Press, 1997).

14. P. Christiaan Klieger, 2008 "Envisioning a Tibet outside Tibet." Paper given at the panel, *Who's Afraid of China's Tibet?* Association of Asian Studies, Atlanta, Georgia. April, 2008.

15. Lix Buchmaier, *Fürstliche Desserts* (Vaduz: Fürst von Liechtenstein-Stiftung, n.d.).

Chapter Four
Sovereign Military Order of Malta

It was very early in the morning on Sunday 25 April 2005 when I sat in my bedroom watching the inauguration of the new pope, Benedict XVI live from the colonnade of St. Peter's Basilica. The scene panned down the front row of heads of state, beginning with King Juan Carlos and Queen Sofia of Spain to the Grand Duke and Grand Duchess of Luxembourg. Further on, between Prince Albert II of Monaco and King Carl XVI Gustav of Sweden, sat the venerable Frà Andrew Bertie, Prince and Grand Master of the Sovereign Military Hospitaller Order of St. John of Jerusalem, of Rhodes, and of Malta. As the world looked on, he sat there, a crowned head of state among his peers. In the row *behind* sat President G.W. Bush of the United States. Who, then, was this most unusual head of state?

Of all the diminutive countries of the world, perhaps the most extraordinary and most opaque is also the smallest. With the exception of Vatican City, it is the only one with a mission statement, as it were, defining itself more as what it does than where it is. In fact it is, like the Holy See, everywhere. It would seem on the surface to be the most anachronistic and implausible of all tiny survivor states, were it not for a mission that was generally unassailable in the western world—to defend Christendom and to succor the poor and the sick throughout the world. For these noble reasons it has survived nine centuries, wending its way through inconceivably labyrinthine passages in the history of the West. Like the phoenix, it rose from the ashes from at least three annihilating defeats, moving, as a truly international body, from its origins in Jerusalem, through Cyprus, Rhodes, Malta, Russia, to present-day Rome. Of all the microstates of Europe, it presents the clearest historical structures of the *longue durée*, resources that have successfully reproduced the institution for over nine hundred years.

So prestigious has its name become that much of its energy has been spent over the last few centuries keeping its legitimate lineage away from imitators who would wish to benefit from its burnished entitlement. This nation of superlatives does have a territory—a whopping 1.6 acres, smaller than most Walmarts, but an independent territory nevertheless. In secular matters, it holds allegiance to no one. The smallest country also has the longest name: the Sovereign Military Hospitaller Order of St. John of Jerusalem, of Rhodes, and of Malta

(SMOM). The name is really more of a short history of the country, indicating some of the major transformations incurred over its eventful history. It is more commonly known as the Order of Malta, its "citizens" the knights and dames of Malta. Here in the SMOM, the black and white definition of nationhood breaks into a noble gray. Many geographers and political scientists do not recognize the SMOM as a country, but the 104 nations who do not recognize these scholars' verdict exchange embassies as concrete proof of the Order's sovereignty. One can assume, however, that all 104 ambassadors and their staffs occupy offices and residences elsewhere in Rome than within those precious 1.6 acres of terra firma.

SMOM is presently headquartered in Rome, its sovereign status making it, with the Vatican and the Republic of Italy, the third country of the Eternal City. With San Marino, it is the fourth independent entity still existing on the Italian peninsula—a backhanded salute to the Garibaldi and the unification movement of the nineteenth century. And, like the other Italian sovereignties, SMOM is a Roman Catholic country. The Order, in fact, is the last existing order of knighthood that was founded as both a military and religious order. Its first mission is the *obsequium pauperum*, the honoring of "our lords the sick." Second is its military vocation, *tuitio Fidei*, the defense of the faith. Popularly known by their near oxymoron, the "warrior monks" established and maintained hospitals in the Holy Land for the benefit of poor and sick pilgrims. However, due to their actually historical circumstances, it would be more accurate to call them "monk soldiers." Early in their hospitaller mission, the lay brethren of the Hospital were called upon the defense of their mission. And they were called on for their leadership and military prowess during the Crusades of the twelfth and thirteenth centuries. To this day, the Order maintains its twin mission to defend the faith and minister to the sick and poor. The hospitallers did not start as an order of knights—early on they were primarily lay brothers who were conscripted to take on the role as warrior knights to protect pilgrims during the Crusades. Then the Rule was pronounced and they became an order of religious with the triple vows. As noblemen of inherited wealth and ancient lineage, it was quite a sacrifice to assume the vows of poverty and chastity. As born leaders, it was dear for a prospective knight to take on the third vow of obedience.[1]

No ritualistic mummery, the professed knights are authentically ennobled by the sovereign power vested in its head of state, the Grand Master, who additionally holds title of an Imperial Prince of the Holy Roman Empire,[2] that ghost of a unified Christian empire that harkens back to Charlemagne and Constantine. Imperial and papal favor even granted powers beyond mere kings—the knights for a time had the power to legitimate the illegitimate.

Due to its inherent humility, very little of the outside world knows about SMOM, which has led to the hatching of much unfortunate misinformation about the Order, with the implication that an apparent secrecy must obscure some sort of misconduct. Books on the Order are often egregiously misclassified with Freemasonry in many bookstores. Where little information exists, conspiracy enthusiasts, and quite legitimate authors included, conjure up the ghosts of the Knights Templar, beplumed Knights of Columbus, Shriners driving about in clown cars, and a host of others, inventing sinister connections to decipher the passage of history. These writings have little relationship to the true Order of Malta, which now operates through the world quietly and piously. The SMOM is serene primarily because it is a religious organization dedicated to the service of the poor. In this sense it is as so many of the major orders of the religious of the Catholic Church. Secondly, the Order has fought its battles: it is sovereign and now has little need to defend territorial borders. It does battle, however, with those that would appropriate its heritage to their own devices.

As an independent entity, SMOM is subject only to international and Canon law in religious matters. It has a constitutional government headed by the prince-grand master, enjoys the status of Permanent Observer at the United Nations, and issues its own passports, license plates, stamps, and coins (the *scudo*). The International Red Cross, of which the Order often bears comparison, has few sovereign abilities in the fulfillment of its mission, and none of the prerogatives of a state. The grand master is assisted by the Sovereign Council, which together provide for the day-to-day government and the executive capacity of the SMOM. The Sovereign Council consists of four Great Officers (the Grand Commander, Grand Chancellor, Grand Hospitaller, and Receiver of the Common Treasure), and six others. The legislative duties are ensconced with the Chapter General, which represents the grand assembly of knights.

Unlike most other countries, SMOM has few commoners—the eleven thousand members of SMOM, or "SMOMians," as John Sack has written,[3] are all knights and dames. Auxiliaries abound, but these members generally are not invested with the promises contained within the Order. While a handful do hold SMOM citizenship and even carry red SMOM passports, most keep the exclusive citizenship of their native countries. The international order is arranged along two parallel lines, the *langues* or tongues, and the newer national associations. The ancient *langues* reflect the knightly organization in the Holy Roman Empire, the ideal of Christian political unity from the times of Charlemagne. Before the modern creation of nation-states, the knights were organized by linguistic affinity, Aragonese, Provençal, German, English... They now have been recognized as Grand Priories (with three subpriories). The national associations historically represent the creation of the modern nation-states and the divisions within them. The U.S. has three national associations and two sub-priories.

It is difficult to summarize a political sovereignty that has persevered nearly a millennium. At the heart of it is perhaps the clearest idea of nationhood of the microstates of Europe. The project to protect the pilgrims to Jerusalem from all of Christendom, to care for their illnesses, has developed into an entity whose dedicated members volunteer their fortunes, skills, and hearts to alleviating suffering across the world. "Our lords are the poor," the words of the Order's founder, the Blessed Gerard. But for practical purposes, the current ruler is the His Most Eminent Highness, the Prince and Grand Master, Frà Matthew Festing of Northumberland, England. He is the son of Sir Francis Festing, Chief of the Imperial General Staff. He assumed office on 11 March 2008, following the death of Frà Andrew Bertie, a Scottish aristocrat with bloodlines descending from the legendary Catholic Stuarts. Frà Matthew is the third British grand master, of the seventy-nine men who have ruled the order.

The grand master is the monarch of a powerful organization that operates hospitals and clinics in all corners of the world, and is the largest private landowner in all Italy. In papal protocol the grand master enjoys the rank of cardinal, and is symbolically placed in precedence exactly between the ecclesiastical and secular nobility, no doubt reflecting the twin missions of the Order to defend Christendom and attend to the needs of the poor and sick.

Origins

Since the seventh century the Holy Land had been under the control of Muslims despite continued claims of the Byzantine Greek Empire to the homeland of Jesus Christ. Yet for most of this time pilgrims were allowed to visit the Holy shrines. There even had been a Christian hospice in Jerusalem in the sixth century, when St. Gregory the Great had one established.[4] But times changed and Jerusalem became a dangerous place. In 614 it was taken by the Persian Empire, and taken back by Byzantine Emperor Heraclius ten years later. In 636 it fell to the leaders of the new faith of Islam. Persecutions abated somewhat under Caliph Harun al-Rascid, and Frankish King Pepin sent an embassy to the Saracens. Pepin's son Charlemagne, by the late eight century, was allowed to build churches in the holy city, including Santa Maria that was home to Latin monks. Attached to that was a hospital, or hospice.

This was all to change—by the early eleventh century the Fatimid Caliph Hakim Biamrillah destroyed the Holy Sepulchre, Santa Maria, and other Christian property. After Hakim's death in 1021, the Holy pilgrimage cautiously returned, underscoring the need for protection of Christian pilgrims. While Emperor Constantine IX rebuilt the Church of the Holy Sepulchre in 1048,[5] it was also the beginning of a strong Latin influence in the Holy Land and its neighborhood. In 1054, a papal legate placed Pope Leo IX's Bull of Excommunication upon the high altar of Hagia Sophia for Patriarch Michael Cerularius and all his followers—the eastern and western apostolic churches were separated.

With the division of Christianity, the Latin Church had to go its own in maintaining representation at its ultimate source in Palestine. And to back its charitable and religious missions, it would soon need defenders—an army whose knightly officers were drawn from the noblest families of Medieval Europe. It appears at this time that the new Latin canons of the Holy Sepulchre were also in charge of the Hospital of Santa Maria of the Latins.[6] On a different mien, the Crusades can be thought of as an important episode in the long-term movement of Germanic tribes—first from the Indo-Aryan origins along the Caspian Sea region, moving steadily across the steppes to Western Europe; as Franks and Teutons, Lombards and Goths, eventually taking the *imperium* of Rome; and having run out of lands to conquest and settle (1066 Battle of Hastings, England, being among the last of the westward push of the German tribes), turned upon itself at headed for the Levant in one case, and to the wilds of Prussia in another.[7] This was particularly true of the upper classes, the knights of the sword who had run out of lands to conquer, rather than the land-holding and land-working classes who were fettered to their lands.

The Order of St. John traces its roots back to 1050 when merchants from the Italian republic of Amalfi received permission from an agreeable Caliph of Egypt the right to establish a foundation, hospice, and "hospital" for tired and sick pilgrims of any faith—with a church and abbey in Jerusalem. A refuge was built by the Amalfi community on the traditional site of the Annunciation of the Conception of St. John the Baptist. The hospital, named after the saint, was constructed under the direction of the Blessed Gerard, completed in 1063, and primarily run by lay brothers. It may have been established on the site of St. Gregory's hospital, being adjacent to St. Maria of the Latins. Built in the Christian Quarter, the Amalfi merchants also rebuilt the church of St. Maria Latina in association with its hospital. Pilgrims began to flock to the hospice on their way to the Holy Sepulchre.

From the very beginning, the Hospital had begun to establish an independent existence, relying as it did on the contributions of the nobility of Catholic Europe. Very soon after the founding of the hospital, the Seljuk Turks went on the ascendancy, placing the members of the Hospital of Jerusalem in somewhat of a difficult position. The anathematized Byzantine Empire called upon the West to save them and the Holy places in Palestine from the battering they were receiving from the Seljuk Turks. Pope Urban II and princes of Europe heeded the call, in a blaze of chivalric passion, sent armies in 1095-1097, the first Crusades to attempt to free the Holy Places from the Turks. When the warriors had conquered Jerusalem in 1099, they turned their concern to the Hospital, upon whom their illnesses and wounds had been so carefully attended. Godfrey of Bouillon and his brother Baldwin I, king of Jerusalem, led the triumphant princes in bestowing riches upon the Hospital then led by the Blessed Frà Gerard. This date marks the official establishment of the Order. The recognition allowed the Order to expand and establish branches in several places in Europe, ports of embarkation where pilgrims could sail directly to the Holy Land. Finally in *Pie postulation voluntatis* in 1113 Pope Pascal II recognized the Order of St. John of Jerusalem as an exempt religious and chivalric order, independent of any diocese, with the right to elect its own leaders, and under the direct protection of the Holy See.[8] Further privileges were granted by the popes until by mid-century, the Order was essentially free from the jurisdiction of the patriarchate of Jerusalem, its bishops and parishes. The Order became directly answerable to the papacy, which was reaching the zenith of its powers over the Church. It also helped steer the Order on a course of self-sovereignty that it has enjoyed to the present day.

In the defense of its hospitals, its sick and wounded, the monks of the Order of St. John were called upon to become militaristic from the beginning. When the Crusaders took Jerusalem in 1099, having fulfilled their vows, they soon returned to Europe leaving much of the new Christian kingdom without defenses. This led to the rise of three great military orders: the Knights of St. John, the Knights of the Temple (of Solomon, i.e. the Templars), and the Knights of St. Mary of the Teutons (Teutonic Knights).

The image of the monastic knight, in this secular age, might strike one as incongruous. However, the ideals of the early Middle Ages followed from the Roman Empire of Constantine and the unification of the "two swords" of God, the secular and ecclesiastic, in the figure of the emperor. All that was noble was both pious and powerful in defense of all Christendom. This caesaropapism flowed through the *baselius* of the Byzantine emperor, through Charlemagne, and the establishment of the Holy Roman Empire of the Germans. It was also manifest in the *imperium* seen at the height of Papal power. Only much later, with the development of modern nation-states in Europe did the chivalric orders of knighthood drift away from their religious vocation and the defense of the Faith, becoming vows of service to a particular prince. While immensely prestigious, the orders of the Garter of England, the Golden Fleece of Burgundy, and the Holy Spirit of France were essentially secular and headed by the sovereign of their respective state. The knights of St. John, of the Temple, and of St. Mary of the Teutons represented the original, dual-vocation concept within an undifferentiated, universal Christendom.

The second master of St. John, Raymond du Puy (1120-1160), bound the members to the vows of chastity, obedience, and poverty under the Benedictine Rule. He perhaps chose as the Order's emblem the eight-pointed Cross of St. John, representing Christ's Eight Beatitudes and the four arms representing Prudence, Temperance, Fortitude, and Justice.[9] To help protect his hospital and the arriving pilgrims, he enlisted knight crusaders to form an armored, heavy cavalry, and local Palestinians, or Turcopoles, to serve as light cavalry. The first dignities of the Order thus came into fashion, the marshal to command the knights and the turcopolier to lead the light cavalry. In 1136 King Fulk granted to the Order its first fortress-hospital at Bethgibelin. Others followed, including Crac in Tripoli, Belvoir in 1168, Margat in 1186, and Mount Thabor in 1255.[10]

Only a hundred years after its founding, a pseudo-history of the Order and its origins arose. Like the Donation of Constantine allegorically linking the Papal States to the gift of the fourth century Roman emperor, the Hospital was credited with a much longer history. In fact, it was mentioned that it was attended by Judas Maccabaeus (ca. 160 B.C.), John the Baptist's parents, and even Christ Himself, who is credited as performing many miracles there.[11] Endorsements of the Order from the popes and kings often used these revisionist embellishments to gild an origin of the Hospital that was cloudy at best.

Throughout the early years of the Latin kingdom of Jerusalem, the Knights of the Temple generally formed the first line of defense. Inevitably, there rose disputes between the two great military orders in Jerusalem, the Templars and the Knights of St. John. The Templars disputed a pre-emptive strike on Egypt, which St. John supported to prevent Egypt and the Emirate of Damascus from unifying and driving out the Latin kingdom in the middle. The two Moslem states united under Saladin of the Ayyubid Dynasty. The Hospitaller knights, including the Order of St. Lazarus, of the Latin kingdom came together at the decisive Battle of the Horns of Hattin, 4 July 1187, when they were soundly defeated by Saladin. The Muslims retook the Holy Land. The remaining Knights of St. John retreated to Margat in Tripoli. After the Third Crusade under Richard the Lionhearted of England, the new capital of the Kingdom of Jerusalem was established at Acre in 1192.

The Knights of St. John had even a greater need to take up arms to protect pilgrims under their care. The Order became one of knighthood in addition to its religious profile. Two classes formed under the ninth Grand Master, Alfonso of Portugal (ca. 1200), the secular knights (the externs) and the professed knights. To this was added a third, the religious chaplains. The three classes attended to military affairs, the hospital, and divine service, respectively.

In 1258, despite their great differences, the Templars, Knights of St. John, and the Teutonic Order banded together for mutual assistance in the war against the Saracens. Thirty-three years later, Acre, the last major Christian bastion on the Holy Land, fell to the Saracens. Only seven Knights of St. John survived.

The remaining members of the Order, King Henry of Jerusalem, and other refugees floated away to Cyprus in 1292, formerly the stronghold of the Knights Templar. The Knights of the Temple on Cyprus and their commanderies in Europe had become the debit holders of many notable Europeans, and were becoming resented. They also developed a reputation for secret initiations and the practice of Freemasonry, which went against the ideals of the Order of St. John and most Christian propriety. In France, Philip IV (the Fair) was covetous of the Templars' property and power, and was heavily indebted to them. He had them arrested on trumped-up accusations of idolatry and other crimes. Under torture, the knights were forced to confess—in 1312 the Pope Clement V decreed the suppression of the Order of the Temple. Grand Master Jacques de Molay was burned at the stake. Their property was given to the Hospitallers, who also adopted surviving Templar knights into their fold.

The Knights of St. John realized that Cyprus was not the ideal base wherein they could restore their Order. Indeed, the same fate might have awaited them as the Templars. In fact, in 1308 Grand Master Foulques de Villaret had discovered the Byzantine island of Rhodes. Nominally a part of the crumbling Greek Empire, it had been partially occupied by the Turks, and a line of Genovese governors. Pope Clement V recognized their hold of the island, just a few weeks before King Philip IV of France destroyed the Templars.[12]

The new island seemed an ideal place—green and fertile, with good quarries and precipices for fortresses. With the field clear, they could attract the sons of nobility without the spectre of the ill-regarded Templars, restoring their mission to attend to the poor and sick and to defend the Faith. This ability to reinvent itself is one of the reasons the SMOM is still around. Sire writes:

It is due to [Villaret] that in the age of Francis I and Henry VIII all Europe continued to take it for granted that the Order of St. John should be preserved as an independent military and naval force, and that even today the same Order pursues its international hospitaller tasks with the freedom and advantages of a sovereign body.[13]

The knights were, in fact, given much of the former property of the Templars on Cyprus and elsewhere.[14] With the move to Rhodes, Villaret assumed the role of a sovereign prince, nominally subject to the ghostly Byzantine Greek emperor. Forced to abdicate in 1317 due to his authoritarian rule, Villaret was succeeded by Hélion de Villeneuve,[15] who spent much of his time in Europe trying to digest the Templar properties and re-establish the credibility of military orders in general. De Villeneuve, the legend went, spent his youth in Rhodes rescuing maidens from a ravenous dragon. Here flourished an Arthurian ideal of chivalry in its own rosy realm, garden-like, surrounded by the sea.

Through the move to Rhodes, the knights had been transformed from hospitaller monks, to mounted knights, to corsairs. Their great duty was to protect Christian seaborne commerce from Moslem piracy. From the fall of the Holy Land it was evident that Christendom needed a great defender, a navy—and this was to be provided by the Order. While the great European nations could often be unreliable in defense of Christian interests, it was the knights of the Order of St. John, whose very mission included the defense of the Faith, who could be directly relied upon by the papacy. Their aggressive attacks on Muslims include a raid on Smyrna in 1341, and a rather ill-fated expedition to Egypt in 1365, considered the key for any reconquest of Jerusalem. Alexandria was taken by a combined force from Cyprus, Venice, and the Knights of St. John, but quickly fell to looters. The alliance broke up over the destruction, and had no further success in the Levant.

The Order was organized around seven *langues*, in order of precedence: Provence, Auvergne, France, Spain, Italy, England (with Scotland and Ireland), and Germany. To these "pillars" were accorded one of the seven great offices of state, now including the Admiral and Turcopolier.[16] Each was headed by a bailiff, and was subdivided by priories, which were in turn composed of commanderies. In the fourteenth century there were 24 priories and 656 commanderies. The head of each priory had the right to receive new knights. Each of the seven nations had an edifice in Rhodes, and knights belonging to each *langue* lived communally within. Like a mini-empire, it was held together by the Grand Master, now Prince of Rhodes. The knights soon fanned out and acquired several islands near the Turkish coastline: Castelrosso, Carqui, Simie, Episcopia, Lango, Calamo, and Lerro, effectively protecting the other islands of the Aegean possessed by Genoese, Venetian, and other Latin colonial powers. Outside of the Aegean, the Order defended Armenia from the Mamelukes until it fell in 1337.

Throughout the fourteenth century the Order on Rhodes was dominated by the three *langues* of France: Provence, Auvergne, and France proper. From

1296 to 1374 there was an unbroken lineage of Provençal grand masters. This was partly because of the ascendancy of the Bourbons to the throne of Naples, then as Angevin kings of Hungary, Wallachia, Navarre, and Poland.[17] Finally, the Chapter-General of the Order broke the monopoly and in 1374 a French grand master was elected. On Rhodes, the Greek Orthodox Church was reconciled to the authority of the pope, and a Uniate metropolitan served the archdiocese alongside of a Roman archbishop. The Order did much to foster a reunion of the two churches, but the peasantry of Rhodes withheld support. Eventually, this undermined the Order's power on the island—the populace easily accepted the surrender of the island to the Turks in 1522.

The fourteenth century was the height of medieval chivalry, characterized most clearly through one individual. Juan Fernandez de Heredia. The High Middle Ages was also the century of the great schism of the Roman Catholic Church, the exile to Avignon, the Black Death, and the era of anti-popes. Heredia was an Aragonese nobleman, closely attached to King Peter, who appointed him Castellan of Amposta.[18] This brought him the former assets of the Templars in Aragon. Heredia was a great scholar, a lover of the Greek classics, and lifelong patron of universities and establisher of great libraries. Early on he became involved in the affairs of the papacy at Avignon. Innocent VI sent him to Rhodes. In 1354 he became prior of Castile and then prior of Saint-Gilles, two of the most powerful offices of the Order.[19] Soon he also became the Captain-General of the Papal Army.

Heredia's great skill at diplomacy and management brought him in great demand by both the pope and the king of Aragon. Heredia thrived at the Avignon court, then the most brilliant in Europe. Building up scholarship throughout Europe, supporting projects to translate and copy the classics, Heredia was helping to lay the groundwork for the Renaissance. But despite his influence in Spain and within the Papacy, Heredia was unable to win election as Master of the Order in 1365. Raymond Bérenger of Provence instead was elected. Heredia gave up his two priories and retired to the court of Aragon. Here he was able to settle the claims of the Templar lands in Castile, and to obtain the commanderies of Aragon and the Priory of Catatonia in exchange for giving up the old claims.

When Gregory XI succeeded to the Avignon papacy in 1370, Heredia was restored to his military command. Gregory, influenced by St. Catherine of Sienna, was returned to Rome in Heredia's fleet in 1376, after seventy years of exile. The next year, when the Master of Rhodes died, Gregory undid the rules of the Order and appointed Heredia. This unprecedented step was due to dire urgency: A new power was on the ascendancy in the East—the Ottoman Turks. By this time they had penetrated as far as the Adriatic coast. Taking the offensive against West, the new Turks were felt a direct threat to all Christianity.

Pope Gregory XI planned a new crusade with Heredia to form a bulwark in Western Greece led by the Order. But due to the death of the pope and other misfortunes, Heredia was taken prisoner by the Despot of Arta in Albania. The ransom quickly raised by the Order, Heredia returned to Rhodes in 1379. But the election of the new pope once again broke open the Great Schism. Urban VI now ruled in Rome while Clement VII wore the tiara in Avignon. Europe divided its loyalties: France, Spain, Scotland, and Scandinavia gave its allegiance to Avignon; England, the Empire, with Greece and Italy, supported Rome.[20] Heredia's loyalties were obvious, his Order being predominantly French and himself Spanish. The Order of St. John sided with the anti-popes in the Great Schism. This was not to their advantage in the Greek islands, many of which were Italian colonies.

When in 1383 Heredia returned to the papal court in Avignon, the Roman Pope Urban VI declared the Master of Rhodes deposed. In his place he appointed Riccardo Caraciolo, Prior of Capua. Ultimately, no knight would put his obedience to any pope higher than that to the Order, and the coup failed—although Urban VI and successors continued a line of pro-Roman lieutenants for nearly twenty years.

Upon his retirement to Avignon, Master Heredia continued amassing his great library, and corresponded with the early leaders of the Renaissance movement beginning in Florence.[21] In 1393 the Turks conquered Bulgaria, forcing King Sigismund of Hungary to ask for assistance from the western princes. Heredia sent a contingent of knights up from the mouth of the Danube, joining western armies. It was the last international crusade fought against the Muslims. Heredia did not experience the end of the campaign, dying in 1396 at age ninety.[22]

The knights and the western armies lost the war at Nicopolis on the Danube, and managed a retreat back to Rhodes. Philibert de Naillac, Prior of Aquitaine and leader of the knights in the war, returned to Rhodes having already been elected Master. By 1400, the knights, having made peace with the Turks, abandoned most of their possessions in Peloponnesia. The Turks were occupied with the incursions of the Mongol khan Tamburlaine, who was laying siege to Anatolia, Syria, Smyrna, and Egypt. At Tamburlaine's death, quarrels within his family allowed the Turks to regain Egypt and part of Turkey. Master Naillac took advantage of the peace and was allowed the right to rebuild the hospital in Jerusalem, and build a fortress of St. Peter on the Turkish mainland across from Arco and close to Rhodes.[23]

Naillac, like Heredia, became deeply involved in papal politics. He reconciled the Roman division of the Order by recognizing the anti-Lieutenant Carafa as Prior of Rome.[24] Naillac took part, unique for a layman,[25] in the Church Council of Pisa in 1409 that provided the world with three popes simultaneously: Avignon's Benedict XIII, Rome's Gregory XII, and Pisa's new Alexander V. While Pisa declared Benedict and Gregory heretics and schismatics, thus deposed automatically, Avignon and Rome refused to accept the decision. This resulted in a unique spectacle of the three popes grimly excommunicating one another, and Bridget of Sweden canonized three times to be absolutely sure she became a saint.[26] Alexander V died after only ten months, and was replaced by the Pisan Balassare Cossa as (the first)[27] Pope John XXIII. Of rather notorious character, John garnered only a weak following as well. Finally, Emperor-elect

Sigismund called another Council, to "reduce the number of popes consistent with the Gospel."[28] When the Council met at Lake Constance in 1414, Sigismund arrived Christmas morning and ordered Pope John to resign. The Council proceeded to determine that it derived its authority directly from Christ, and that Benedict XIII and John XXIII were deposed. Finally, having led the Council through months of turbulence, the remaining pope Gregory XII abdicated. Cardinal Deacon Oddo Colonna was elected by the Council, and was crowned Pope Martin V by the hand of Master Naillac himself.[29] The new pope immediately confirmed Naillac in his office, further reuniting the Order.

The crowning of a pope underscores the immense political reputation, power, and esteem the Knights of St. John held throughout the Middle Ages. The Master of the Order was now the equal to any monarch in Europe, and having saved Christianity from an impossible schism, added even greater luster to the eight-pointed cross.

By the mid-fifteenth century, the Provençal dominance of the Order had subsided. The Kingdom of Naples was lost to Aragon. Eventually, the Langue of Provence was reduced to one vote from two in the Chapter General, and Spain the ascendant was divided into the *langues* of Aragon and Castile, reflecting the political realignment.[30] Aragon maintained a strong influence with the Order until the papal-guided election of the Italian Giovan Battista Orsini in the middle of the fifteenth century.

During the next hundred years, the Order of St. John would reach the height of its military achievements, "three feats of arms worthy of an empire."[31] The Ottoman Turks recovered from the disruptions caused by Tamburlaine, and in the hands of the young, aggressive Sultan Mahomet II Fatih. One by one he conquered the Greek isles, and then the mainland—Venice itself was made a tributary. A thousand years of Christendom was destroyed in 1453 when the heroic Emperor Constantine XI Palaeologus died defending the walls of the doomed Constantinople and Mahomet rode his horse up to the very altar of Hagia Sophia. In 1479 this sultan prepared his troops to destroy the thorn in the palm of the Ottoman Empire on the verdant island of Rhodes. Unlike the defeated Italian merchant states, the knights had maintained their presence in Rhodes all these years expressly to destroy the Turks.

The defending army was small—only six hundred knights and sergeants at arms and 1,500-2,000 soldiers, plus the regular inhabitants of the islands. They were led by the Grand Master Pierre d'Aubusson. In 1480 the fleet of Mesic Pasha, the Turkish commander, rounded the northern coast of Rhodes and attempted to take the Tower of St. Nicolas guarding the harbor of Mandraccio. Twice he was repelled by the knights. However after nearly two months of bombardment from the land, the Turks opened a breech in the eastern wall of the outer city. Before the tide could be stopped, the Master was wounded in the chest by an arrow. The knights prevailed, and pursued the Turks out of the city. Mesic not only gave up the siege, and also abandoned the attack on Italy. The consequences of its opposite being all too clear: the Order had saved Western Christianity, now beginning to blossom in the first flower of the Renaissance.

D'Aubsson, who had recovered, was showered with laurels. He was given a cardinal's hat by Innocent VIII, and treasure flowed. For keeping his rival brother Zizim under guard at Rhodes, the new Sultan Bajazet II sent him relics from Constantinople—the right arm of St. John the Baptist and a thorn of the Crown of Thorns. At this time the Vice-chancellor of the Order published a florid, illuminated history of the Siege, marking perhaps the height of the prosperity of the Order and the summit of chivalry.

During this time of recovery, the walls of the city of Rhodes were increased from about two to five meters and then to twelve, making it the strongest fortress in the West. In 1521, two great adversaries had come to their respective throne—each would go down in history and among the great rulers of their respective realms. Suleiman the Magnificent of the Ottoman Empire now faced the former Grand Prior of France, Phillippe Villiers de l'Isle Adam. By 1522, the second siege of Rhodes had begun.

Forgoing a sea-launched attack that was the undoing of Mahomet II, Suleiman concentrated on the land battlements to the south of the city. The battle became one of subterranean intrigue as the Turks bore into the walls and the knights reburied them by digging transverse tunnels. The city remained under siege for five months—at the end, with supplies running out, l'Isle Adam accepted Salesman's offer to leave with honor. The knights sailed away to Civitavecchia in the Papal States. Here l'Isle Adam was made guardian of the Papal Conclave that elected Clement VII. Clement, a Knight of the Order, gave l'Isle Adam a residence at Viterbo.[32]

The knights being defeated, the Ottoman Turks continued their aggression towards the West. Since the line of defense had shifted far to the west of Rhodes long before that island's final capture, it was a necessity for the western states to re-establish a strong line of defense. In 1526 Suleiman won the Battle of Mohacs and became master of Hungary, staring down at the gates of the capital of the Holy Roman Empire at Vienna. Charles V, due to the dynastic alliance of his predecessors, was now not only ruler of the Habsburg lands in Central Europe, but also a united Spain and its associated kingdoms and territories, including the New World. By now Spain had amassed territories through the western and southern Mediterranean, including the Kingdom of Sicily and Tripoli.

The great Emperor Charles V, grandson of Ferdinand and Isabella, nephew of English Queen Catherine of Aragon, stood face to face with the encroaching Turks on the Empire's eastern mark. Providing the now landless Knights of St. John with a strategic territory to help bulwark the Mediterranean southern flanks of the Holy Roman Empire became essential. Malta was the ideal choice, a tiny 120 square-mile slab of rock and scrub, but located in the middle of the Mediterranean and possessing a fabulous harbor. The knights at Malta would be enormously important to the defense of Europe. Malta would provide for the second resurrection of the Order, preventing it from becoming useless ornamentation. Malta was also the oldest continuous Christian community anywhere, its inhabitants having been converted by St. Paul himself in A.D. 59-60.

The islands of Malta, Gozo, and Comino, plus the northern African city of Tripoli, were formally offered to the knights in 1523 by Emperor Charles V, and accepted by the Chapter General of the Order in 1527. Unlike the Principality of Liechtenstein, which was an imperial principality directly under the emperor, Malta was a fief of the Aragonese throne that included Naples and Sicily. But that kingdom was inherited by the Habsburgs, then headed, of course, by Charles V. The feudal arrangement between the knights and the emperor was symbolized with the yearly presentation of a falcon to the emperor's viceroy at Naples, the root of the famous "Maltese Falcon" story. A great officer of the household bred the birds—in time they were sent as gifts to other sovereigns.[33]

It was not a smooth transaction. The French knights resented the symbolic suzerainty of Malta under the Spanish Habsburgs, France being then at war with Spain. Bit by bit, however, the French opposition was overruled, and the documents enfeoffing the Order with Malta and Tripoli were signed in 1530. Charles V had, as a final incentive, granted the right of the Order to coin money. This right provided yet another symbol of national sovereignty to SMOM that is entertained to this day.

For his capital, l'Isle Adam brushed aside the ancient Maltese town of Notabile in the center of the island for the fishing village of Birgu and immediately built up the fortress of Sant' Angelo there. He was still preoccupied, however, with thoughts of recapturing Rhodes from the Turks. After an expedition to Modon, Greece, failed with its recapture by the Turks, L'Isle Adam returned to Malta where he passed away in 1534.[34]

In this year the High Admiral of the Ottoman Navy, Chaireddin the Barbarossa, captured Tunis and added it to the Ottoman Empire (as had Algiers in 1516). The new Grand Master Pietro del Monte joined other European forces lead by Charles himself and arrived at Tunis. A rebellion within the city broke out, and Barbarossa fled. The emperor restored the Tunisian king under his vassalage, guarded by the Order's garrisons just to the east at Tripoli and Malta. About this time, one of the Spanish knights, Ignatius Loyola, founded the Society of Jesus and innocently established the Holy Inquisition to root out heresy.

With this victory, the French influence in the Order continued to decline in favor of the Spanish. This was noted with the election in 1536 of Juan de Homedes of Aragon as grand master. France had also made a treaty that year with Turkey, which must have humiliated the French knights, their country at complete odds with the knights' profession to defend Christendom. Homedes quickly set upon fortifying the Castel Sant' Angelo. But the knights were not convinced that Malta was to be a permanent home. In 1548 the Chapter General voted to slowly abandon Malta for Tripoli. Homedes reacted to this by sending only the French knights to Africa, thus eliminating the most vexatious element of the magistral court. Although Turkey was allied to France, Dragut, the Turkish admiral in succession to Barbarossa, seized Tripoli in 1551. The French knights were sent back to Malta; their men captured by the Turks. This defeat made the necessity of the fortification of Malta top priority to the Order.

In 1557 Gascon Jean de la Valette Parisot was elected Grand Master. One of his first acts was to attempt to recapture Tripoli. By this time, however, Spain had been defeated in most of North Africa, and was reluctant to support the expedition. Their subsequent annihilation by the Turks made de la Valette realize the imminent threat to Malta itself. The Turks now ruled the Mediterranean seas.

In 1564 the Viceroy of Sicily, Don Garcia de Toledo, asked Philip II for an army to help defend the inevitable attack on Malta. The siege of Malta was one of the most legendary battles in history—when it began in May 1564, only 540 knights, 400 Spanish troops, and 4,000 able-bodied Maltese faced a force of upwards of 40,000 Turks. The knights had two advantages that Rhodes lacked—Malta was barren, thus not able to sustain an invading army, and the supply lines leading back to Istanbul were much longer. The strategy for the Order was to endure the siege until the bulk of the Spanish troops arrived from Philip II. La Valette concentrated his defenses on the Fort St. Elmo, which on the Sciberras Peninsula guarded the entrance to the Grand harbor. The Turks had landed to the north at Marcamuscetto. In the ferocious battle that followed, La Valette galvanized the knights into holding on to St. Elmo, whatever the costs, until the promised reinforcements could arrive. Just as the force from Sicily arrived, St. Elmo fell. The knights had lost fifteen hundred men, the Turks six thousand—at least one-fifth of the invading force. Dragut himself was killed.[35] When the Turkish general displayed his victory by nailing dead knights to crosses and floating them across the Grand Harbor, La Valette responded by shooting Turkish heads out of cannon aimed at the other side. But the Knights of St. John held on. By September, the defending force was down to only six hundred, but Notabile still stood. Garcia de Toledo finally arrived with the Spanish force of sixteen thousand. The Turks fled, retreating all the way back to Constantinople, the greatest defeat in the history of the Ottoman Empire.

Surviving the Great Siege of Malta not only saved the Order, but all of European Christendom, a point that cannot remain understated. It catapulted the knights right back into the forefront of European glory and a place of honor that remains to this day.

The great naval battle of Lepanto (1571), with the forces of the West pitted against the Turks, changed forever the balance of power in the Mediterranean. At long last realizing the important of the Order, great wealth flowed from Europe, enough to build a great city on the Sciberras. Francesco Laparelli, a student of Michelangelo, was sent by the pope to perform this task. On 28 March 1566 the cornerstone of the city was laid by La Valette, and named after him. The city was designed with the latest in fortifications, and all houses had water tanks and sewers.[36] La Valette died two years later and was succeeded by Pietro del Monte, who continued the building program with zeal. When Laparelli left Malta, he assigned the work to his student Girolamo Cassar, who is now credited with much of the building of Valetta. Each of the seven Langues built *auberges* and churches for themselves. An enormous amount of wealth flowed into Malta, transforming a marginal population into a thriving international community. It was also a time when the international Order of knights took on an even greater national character

The religious and secular nature of the Order is reflected to this day in the title and styles of the office of grand master that flowed from that period. In the late sixteenth century, the grand master was accorded precedence of a cardinal deacon of the Church.[37] With the waning of feudalism, the ghostly Sicilian and Aragonese suzerainty over Malta was replaced. The Order became a sovereign principality in 1607 when Grand Master Wignacourt and his successors became Princes of the Holy Roman Empire under Rudolf II. The Order now stood on the same footing as other imperial principalities, such as the German *fürstentum* of Waldeck-Pyrmont and the still-extant Liechtenstein. Grand Master Manuel Pinto da Fonseca (r. 1741-1773),[38] borrowing the styles of the powerful Prince-Archbishops of the Empire who had become cardinals, replaced "Serene" with "Eminent," becoming uniquely a "Most Eminent Highness" reflecting the hybridization. Pinto added a closed crown to the arms of the Order to symbolize its sovereignty. During his reign, the Order's ambassadors received the right of royal privilege in their reception at the Sala Regia of the Vatican and Quirinal palaces. Pinto bestowed titles on the Maltese, creating bonds to the Order while ignoring the ancient nobility of the island.

At the height of their power, the Order was overwhelmed by the desire of the young nobility to enter it. Hence, a balancing act was performed to adjust the demand for the prestigious accolade with the source of its appeal: allow too many knights and one could destroy the exclusive blue-bloodedness that was one of the sources of appeal; exclude too many, and one could strangle the flow of wealth and talent that made the twin missions of the Order and its building projects possible. As the concept of knighthood grew in the period of feudalism, the qualification for the proofs of nobility grew as well.

In the modern world, dominated by secular societies and achievement-based awards, it is easy to forget the basic principles of the now archaic notion of the hereditary principle of rulership, which is generally the same around the world. In Polynesia, for example, the ruling caste was physically and socially separated from the common stock by an elaborate system of *kapu* (taboo). Over the generations, this artificial selection was felt to help pass on and concentrate desirable genetic gifts to their noble successors, such as skill in warfare, physical prowess, all reflections of the sacred power of the gods or *mana*. Indeed, when the first Westerners visited Hawai'i in the late eighteenth century, observers remarked on the notable size differential between the commoner and the *ali'i* or nobles, the latter being considerably taller and far heavier. We know now that much of this differential is due to the superior nutrition, access to medical care, and other resources that elites are generally afforded. But from Polynesia to Western Europe, the folk eugenics ethos of the warrior caste, was taken literally.

In the early years of the Order of St. John one could qualify as a knight-aspirant if one was legitimately born to a knightly family. But by the fourteenth century, one qualified only if both one's parents were noble. In those early years, this simply meant the land-owning class, the gentry. What we would today call a real estate closing was then an enfoeffment of land from a ruling sovereign, usually through intermediary lords, to an individual. In addition to tax obligations, an enfoeffment contained explicit social obligations, including military ones, in exchange for a title, an entitlement to the land. That title would then be recognized by society with a term of style and address granted to that particularly individual. The personal style and the title to the land were meshed together, and because of the landed aspect, both could be inherited as any property. In most countries of Europe, the old nobility, then, were descendents of those warriors who together with their king had been successful in the wars of conquest. Highest families of all were those Frankish rulers that succeeded to the rule of the old Roman Empire in the West.

By the time of the High Middle Ages and the creation of many orders of chivalry by the rulers of newly emergent nation-states, the balance tilted. To keep an accolade prestigious in competition with those of others orders, especially those of the new national orders (the Garter, Golden Fleece, St. Esprit, etc.), greater and greater qualifications of nobility were required. By the fifteenth century, an aspirant for Knight of Justice in the Order of St. John had to prove nobility in the male line for four generations. In the sixteenth century, the "four quarters of nobility" proof from both parental lines was the rule of most sovereign orders--all four grandparents had to be of noble stock. In Germany, ancient rules of inheritance partitioning estates to all sons equally had greatly inflated the numbers of eligible gentry. Over the centuries, inherited properties in the German lands and the titles that devolved from them became physically smaller and smaller while qualifications for eligibility in the highest order became ever greater. In the Holy Roman Empire of the German Nation, a postulant eventually had to prove all sixteen great-grandparents to qualify for most noble orders, including the Order of St. John. At the pinnacle of pedigree lay the specifications for entry into the Teutonic Knights, which required a stunning thirty-two quarters of nobility in a postulant's background. It is easy to see how close this rarefied membership stood should-to-shoulder with its own extinction.[39]

Another means of admission into the Order was through a novitiate of the "Knights of Majority," youths between sixteen and twenty years of age. Younger boys were brought in as pages and squires, knights-in-training as it were. The novitiate for professed knights was twelve months, as is the modern provisional period for all entering members of the Order. After five years they were eligible for a commandery, and with additional service could rise through the ranks, commanding a ship, or becoming a Pilier of the Langue. The latter came with the Grand Cross of the Order and was a platform from which the ambitious could often seek the magistral throne itself.[40] In addition to the professed knights, there were professed conventual chaplains and the serving brethren. Qualifications for these classes were much less stringent.

Early on in the history of the Order, a parallel system of noble achievement and service was available for women—lay and religious alike. In the times of the Blessed Gerard there was already a hospital for women. In the fanciful writings about the Hospital in the twelfth century, it was stated that the Virgin Mary herself lived there.[41]The nuns of the Order wore the eight-pointed cross and took vows of obedience to the Master of the Hospital.[42] The great women's convents of Sijena, Alguaire, and Beaulieu also required their nuns to have full proofs of nobility. Others required less of a pedigree. Lay sisters worked in these convents, as did their counterpart serving brethren.

Recruitment into the Order was challenged with the wholesale dismemberment of the three great European empires after WWI, Russia, Germany, and Austro-Hungary, and the decline of monarchy in Portugal, Spain, the Balkans, and Italy. Without kings and emperors creating new patents of nobility, and fewer colleges of heralds to record older claims of noble blood, the "nobility of the spirit" and the *noblese de robe* began to achieve greater significance, especially among the second and third classes of knights.

The right to enfeoff or grant titles of nobility, then as now, was the exclusive privilege of a reigning sovereign. One reason that the Sovereign Military and Hospitaller Order of St. John has for nine hundred years vigorously demanded the recognition of their sovereignty by generations of popes and emperors was that a sovereign was needed for the creation a legitimate knighthood. And indeed a sovereign needed his or her nobles and knights to support the throne. Today, the knights and dames of the Order are bestowed a genuine knighthood by a sovereign Grand Master, in contrast to members of many charitable and fraternal organizations whose claim to sovereignty does not go beyond a Section 501 (c) 3-like non-profit status given by a central government. Although the form may seem archaic, the charismatic substance, the care of the sick and poor and defense of the Faith, is universal, omnipresent, and a founding principle of Christianity itself.

With the death of del Monte in 1572, the knights elected the French chevalier Jean l'Eveque de La Cassiere.[43] He began to build the great Church of St. John in Valletta, the "Valhalla" of the knights, according to Cassar's designs. His difficulty lay not with a lack of resources, not with an enemy out to sea, but within his own Order. A certain lassitude had crept in, perhaps due to the final great victories of the last few years. La Cassiere partly responded by reaffirming the knights' hospitaller role by beginning construction of the Sacred Infirmary of Valleta, which was to become the greatest in the world for its time.[44] The best of foods, meats, chicken, fish, and fresh vegetables were served to patients of all classes on silver plate. The silver had the distinct benefit of being antibiotic.

The great Church of St. John was consecrated in 1578, becoming the Conventual Church of the Order; La Cassiere continued on with the building of the Palace of the Grand Masters in Valletta.

Still, the knights were restless, and La Cassiere was anxious, perhaps due to the unsettling times of the Great Reformation now underway in most of Europe. Some knights were leaving their *auberges* without permission, scuffling with brother knights, pillaging cargoes, and even insulting the Grand Master himself. When La Cassiere sent a knight to Rome to consult with the Pope on routine matters, the latter sent an Inquisitor back with him. The rouge knights responded by impeaching La Cassiere and appointing one of their own as Lieutenant Grand Master. The matter was ultimately settled in Rome, with La Cassiere winning and subsequently forgiving the usurpers. The Grand Master passed away while in Rome (1581). Although there were a total of sixty-nine inquisitors sent to Malta, the knights and grand masters were not intimidated—they often took matters of conflict directly to the Pope, and often prevailed.

La Cassiere's comrade Hugues Loubenx de Verdalle (Verdala) of Provence was put forth as candidate for the grand magistral position by his friend Pope Sixtus V. Upon his election, the pope made Verdala a cardinal.[45] This was quite useful, as Verdala was now a senior hierarch over the Malta Inquisitor. He was the first and only grand master to wear the scarlet robes of a cardinal. Verdala established an elaborate court on Malta, and built a country retreat in the mountains, the fortified castle of Verdala Palace. So spectacular was the castle's garden setting and furnishings that it is still used for Maltese state occasions. The historian Attard makes much to-do about Verdala taking part in privateering on the high seas with his fleet,[46] but in fact it was a common practice among princes of the day, including England's Queen Elizabeth I and her courtier Sir Francis Drake.

Verdala had a pious streak and patronized the Capuchin Order, whose establishment was the precursor to the University of Malta. He established an Ursuline Convent for nuns under the rule of the Grand Master, and they follow the same Benedictine Rule as do the knights to this day. The nuns were given estates to provide revenues, and were entitled to a portion of the booty captured in the line of Verdala's privateering enterprises.[47]

In general, many of the knights became disaffected by the worldliness of Verdala and his quest for riches—in fact, they impeached him and brought him before the Holy Office of the Inquisition. While the charges were eventually dropped, Verdala was broken-hearted by the treatment of his knights, and he died soon after, in 1595. He left all his vast property to the Order.

After a brief reign by the Spaniard Martin Garzes, the French knight Alof de Wignacourt assumed the magistral throne in 1601. One of the first great works Wignacourt put in place was an aqueduct that extended from Mdina to Valletta. He continued, providing grain for a country that had been seeing times of scarcity, and rebuilt the navy that had been languishing since the Great Siege.

In the spirit of the Renaissance, the Order began to embellish their properties and buildings. The painter Michelangelo Amerigi Caravagio was brought to Malta. Finishing two portraits of the Grand Master, Caravagio began his masterpieces, "The Beheading of St. John" and "St. Jerome." While the painter was made a Knight of Obedience, Wignacourt learned that Caravagio was wanted in Italy for murder. He was arrested, but escaped to Sicily.

After so many years, the peace of Malta turned, and the Turks were reassembling forces in what seemed to be another siege. Yet after a minor landing, the Turks retreated and left the islands forever. Malta had been greatly fortified over the years, and had become prosperous.

In 1622 Wignacourt passed away and was succeeded by Portuguese Luiz Mendez de Vascancellos. Reigning only one year, he was succeeded by the French knight Antoine de Paule. He built San Anton Palace, which has been the official palace of the rulers of Malta ever since. And it was during the tenure of de Paule that the pope permanently gave the position of Grand Master the precedence of a cardinal.

The Order now had been on Malta a century, the population having quadruped during that time.[48] Many knights were now Maltese—an honor long denied the indigenous population. Still, births were arranged to take place in Sicily, and the sons joined the Italian Langue. By now the inhabitants of Malta, knights and indigenous alike, were forming a national culture. The Order was even developing a distinctive cuisine, which included dishes such as *imbuljuta* (chestnuts, coca, and citrus), *pastizzi* (cheesecake), and special sausages.

From the Pharmacopoeia

It is widely believed that the Knights of St. John, having been in contact with Arab physicians in the eastern Mediterranean, and being primarily involved in running hospitals, became the conduit by which ancient medical knowledge from the Romans and the Greeks was retransmitted to Europe after the "Dark Ages." That they were leaders of the medical profession in the western world at the time is not in dispute.

An example of one drug that was pioneered by the Hospitallers on Malta was the cynomorium "fungus." Cynomorium is obtained mainly from the East Asian species, *Cynomorium songaricum*, though the similar *C. coccineum* is sometimes used.[49] The plant is also harvested for Tibetan and Chinese medicine, and grows at high altitude in Tibet. In China it is used to tone the *yang* (treat impotence and backache), strengthen the tendons, and nourish the blood to alleviate a blood-deficiency constipation (typically occurring with old age).

The value of cynomorium or tarthuth was described in many eastern cultures. In sixteenth century Europe, it was known as the Maltese mushroom, though it is a parasitic plant rather than a true fungus. The plant was so highly regarded that the Order often sent samples of it to European monarchs as presents, as it grew in profusion on a rock off the coast of Goza. Known to the Maltese as Gebla tal-General, General's Rock, after a Hospitaller naval squadron commander credited with discovering it, it is now called Fungus Rock. To protect Fungus Rock, the Grand Master posted guards around the area and ordered the sides of the outcropping to be rendered smooth to eliminate any footholds and prevent access from the sea. The rock, rising to a sheer height of sixty meters (two hundred feet) from the rough sea, became virtually inaccessible.

The medicinal uses of tarthuth are cited by Ibn Masawayh (777-857), a Persian Christian who directed a hospital and served as personal physician to four caliphs at Baghdad, and by Maimonides, the celebrated twelfth century Sephartic Jewish doctor and philosopher who was court physician to Saladin in Egypt. Ninth-century Chaldean scholar Ibn Wahshiya, wrote a toxicological treatise called the *Book on Poisons* that includes tarthuth as a key ingredient in several antidotes.[50] Knowledge of the medicinal value of tarthuth was passed to Europe through the Order of St. John on Malta. It was in Palestine that Hospitaller physicians first learned of tarthuth from their Muslim counterparts and began using the plant in their treatments. When the knights finally moved to Malta, they were delighted to find tarthuth growing on a tiny islet.

The knights quickly took control of Fungus Rock, placed guards on the mainland and barred access to any but their own. They hacked all ledges from the sides of the islet to keep people from climbing the cliffs. Trespassers who tried anyway were imprisoned and made galley slaves, according to Dharmananda.[51] Thieves who managed to steal Maltese mushroom were reportedly put to death. The only way to reach the island's top was by a primitive cable car rigged on ropes and pulleys and connected to poles on the mainland. A version of that survived into the early nineteenth century, when English traveler Claudius Shaw made the dangerous crossing in 1815:

> It is not a very pleasant sensation to be suspended some hundred feet above the water, and if there is any wind, the movement of the box is anything but agreeable, and all that can be obtained are a few pieces of fungus. I was well pleased to be back again, and made a determination never to risk my precious carcass in that conveyance again.[52]

The knights harvested the precious plant and stored it in a watchtower on the mainland. This structure, Dwejra Tower, was built in 1651 to guard Fungus Rock and protect the island of Gozo from pirate raids. Once harvested, the spikes were dried, pulverized and preserved in various liquids. Hospitaller doctors used it to cure dysentery and ulcers, to stop hemorrhages and prevent infection. The plant was a favored treatment for apoplexy and venereal disease, and was used as a contraceptive, as a toothpaste and as a dye to color textiles. It was also prescribed in Malta to treat high blood pressure, vomiting and irregular menstrual periods. It also seems to show promise as an HIV treatment.[53]

In 1565 Grand Master Jean de la Vallette was wounded by a grenade blast during the Great Siege by Ottoman Turkish forces. His wounds were dressed with tarthuth and he recovered and returned to battle.[54] Upon losing Malta in 1798, the use of tarthuth also was eclipsed. By the nineteenth century, the old herbal remedies of the Middle East, plant extracts known as galenicals, were largely replaced in the West by new, mineral-based drugs.

Today Maltese mushroom survives atop Fungus Rock, drawing its nourishment from the roots of tamarisk or sea lavender. The Maltese now call it *gherq is-sinjur*, which may derive from the Arabic *'irq al-sinja*, "bayonet root." A species of reptile found nowhere else, the Fungus Rock wall lizard, *Podarcis filfolensis generalensis*, seems to have a special affinity for the plant and can often be found climbing the succulent red spikes.

Into the Baroque Era

Another Frenchman, Jean Paulede Lascaris Castellar, succeeded Grand Master De Paule in 1636. Although already elderly, he nevertheless set out to continue building fortifications on Malta, took heed at maintaining discipline for the knights, and built a new hospital for the isolation of infectious patients. When the Order's galleys captured a Turkish galleon with high-ranking members of the Sultan's court aboard, Lascaris began to prepare for Turkish vengeance. He began to melt down silver plate and coin money to pay for the battle. But the war never materialized. Thoughts of expansion of the Order's realm into the Caribbean were introduced in this time. In 1653 the Order purchased the islands of St. Croix, St. Bartholomew, and Tortuga, and part of St. Kitts and St. Martin from Louis XIV.[55] It remained to be seen how the Order could rule such a distant place, then a land of sugar plantations worked by African slaves and haunted by pirates.

Lascaris died in 1657 at the aged of ninety-six. After two brief reigns, the Spaniard Raphael Cottoner became grand master. The Order now at peace, he is credited in the introduction of the glory of the Renaissance to the islands. But first he remodeled the hospital, establishing separate wards for surgery, mental illness, and internal medicine, the further isolation of infectious patients—all of which were innovations in Western medicine. Cottoner brought over the painter Mattia Preti who painted the Baroque frescos that can still be seen in St. John's Church. Frà Raphael Cottoner was succeeded by his brother Nicholas in 1663. Preti continued his painting at various churches and secular palaces throughout Malta.[56]

By 1665, the folly of the Order's West Indies empire was seen and the Caribbean islands were sold at a loss to the West Indies Company. More energies were focused at home. When money wasn't being spent for art, it went for continued fortifications. Cottoner built an elaborate system of bastions, gates, towers and other state-of the-art defenses. By now all the wealth flowing into Malta raised the standard of living considerably above the European mean. Throughout, the grand masters had been accorded the position of equal to all other European princes, as can be attested in correspondence with the Holy Roman emperors, the English and French kings, and the sovereigns of German and Italy.

The Cottoner brothers were succeeded by Gregorio Caraffa, an Italian. He too preferred building the arts of the Renaissance rather than remodeling the fleet. But the forces of the Reformation were also changing the appeal of the Order, and many English and German knights resigned to support their faith at home. When Caraffa passed away in 1690, he was succeeded by Adrien de Wignacourt, nephew of the previous Grand Master. In 1693 a great earthquake struck Malta that destroyed the cathedral of Notabile, built on the site of one of Christendom's first houses of worship established by St. Paul himself. The Grand Master chose to rebuild it rather than tackle the problem of the now rapidly decaying navy. It was left to Grand Master Ramon Perellos y Roccaful to build the first set of new ships, and he did so at his own expense. But the continued maintenance of Malta as the fortress of Christian Europe had begun to decline. The Western Powers were busy making treaties with the Turks and the military mission of the Order was becoming obsolete. It was a common saying at the time that the Order "had become smothered under wigs and powder."[57]

In 1722 the Portuguese Antonio Manoel de Vihena was elected grand master,[58] who was adept at conceiving ways to spare the decline of the Order. He envisioned providing missions for the young knights and engaging their elders; he revived ideas of attacking the Turks and filling the rapidly emptying coffers with Barbary booty. But the Ottoman Empire was at peace with Europe, and while Vilhena built the great Fort Manoel, the focus of his reign was to be the centralization of civil government and the establishment of the University. One of the knights captured the Turkish capital ship *Sultana* in 1732, but this was the last action of its kind. There was even talk of establishing a peace treaty with the Ottomans, but nothing came of it.

Under Vilhena's reign, the magistral state finally removed the flag of Spain from its staff in Notabile, which had represented the suzerainty of Aragon over Malta for over four hundred years.[59] This was followed by Vilhena refusing to receive a representative from the Sicilian viceroy.

Vilhena, like his predecessors, continued to build and enrich Valletta and other cities. He built a grand theatre and for the first time the knights and the populace could enjoy plays and comedies. When Vihena died in 1736, popular legend suggested that his spirit haunted Fort Manoel, as the "Black Knight."[60] The knight was seen after restoration work began on the chapel that had been destroyed by German bombers in World War II!

In 1741 another grand master of prodigious ability was elected—the Portuguese knight Manoel Pinto de Fonseca, Vilhena's vice-chancellor. During his colorful reign a serious plot was uncovered involving a Turkish-inspired slave revolt intent on assassinating Pinto and overthrowing the Order. But the Grand Master Pinto caught wind of the plot, and dealt swiftly with the conspirators. During much of Pinto's reign he harbored a hope to annex the island of Corsica. Belonging to Genoa, it was much larger than Malta, and had a mild climate where olive and mulberry orchards could provide revenues. Pinto also befriended an adventurer known as Count Cagliostro, who dabbled in alchemy. This is the same Cagliostro who later went to France and became involved in the infamous scandal of the Queen's Necklace which rocked the entire kingdom. Cagliostro was imprisoned for the alleged theft, but eventually released.[61]

Pinto went on raising the prestige of the Order. He became friends with the Prussian king Frederick the Great, and received a stack of honors from Pope Benedict XIV. This was useful in the great game, as France steadfastly refused to grant the Order Corsica. Pinto was clever, but antagonized the pope and the grand inquisitor by demanding that the Jesuits leave, and leave their property to the University. He adamantly refused attempts of annexation of Malta by the new Bourbon king of Naples and Sicily, Charles VII. Refuting the feudal arrangement once and for all, he closed the arches of his coronet, now become a royal crown.

Despite the proclamations Maltese sovereignty, Europe seemed to be going its own way, occupied by the Seven Years War (1756-1763) and other international dramas. Russia, however, began to court the Order. Catherine II was building her navy and needed to build upon the good relations with the Order started by her grandfather-in-law, Peter the Great. She had her naval officers train on the Order's ships, and sent two of the grand master's bailiffs to reorganize her Baltic fleet.[62] But Catherine's influence was accentuated with the ideas of Voltaire and Rousseau, the concept of the essential rights of man, which were making their way into Malta. Pinto had become quite authoritarian in his old age, further removing the civil rights belonging to the majority of the Maltese while bestowing titles and creating a new local nobility with others. Many knights sided with the populace, and looked forward to the time when Pinto would be gone. The end came in 1773 to the ninety-two-year old Grand Master—a symbol of absolutism had vanished on the eve of the American rebellion and the French Revolution.

After a short reign by Ximenez, the Frenchman Emmanuel de Rohan de Polduc succeeded to the magistral throne. A nobleman of noblemen, descended from the ancient kings of Brittany, Rohan was very well connected to most of the courts of Europe. One of Rohan's first acts was to summon a Chapter General to put forth needed reforms, in the fateful year 1776. Thoughts of secularizing the Order were overruled. The treasury was desperately in need of reform, and the changes were successful. The Order rose out of debt, so much so that it greatly increased its possessions, overcoming much of the loss it incurred during the Reformation. Even the Protestant knights of the German Order were convinced to make their contributions to Rohan. The Order, after a long period of decline, was rebounding. In a sense, the magistral civilization had reached its apogee—prosperous, prodigal, industrious, and refined.

Like the pinnacle of courtly life noted at Versailles, the knights of Rohan had developed an exquisite system of manners and refinement. The intricate code of behavior, as Elias has elaborated, was designed as a system of ideal behavior from which criteria of courtly affiliation and mutual support could be regulated by the sovereign in support of the crown.[63] It was not merely mummery but integral to keeping their Order in the highest stratospheres of European aristocracy. Not having families of their own, professed knights often attached themselves to Maltese families, especially the middle class and the new magistral nobility. The mores of the court of the Order were no more or less than those shared in royal courts throughout Europe. Discretion ruled over strict interpretations of the three evangelical counsels of poverty, obedience, and chastity.

The French Revolution was not quite as difficult as it could have been for the French Langue. Although technically neutral, the knights were seen as royalist. In 1789, the National Assembly abolished all feudal rights and tithes, meaning that the dues of all French knights to the Order were suspended. In

1791 the knights were stripped of their French citizenship, but initially kept their commanderies in the country. When Louis XVI was returned to Paris from his escape to Varennes by the mob, Rohan promptly had a stroke. In 1792, the Order's property in France was confiscated, eliminating 60 percent of the Order's source of revenue. In karmic irony, Louis XVI, descendent of Philip the Fair, and his family were kept prisoner in the very Tower of the Templars his ancestor had seized.[64] For a time Rohan continued to accredit the royalist ambassador to Malta, but by 1796 gave up and recognized a representative from the Republic. But the Revolution invoked a Corsican general whose impact upon the Order would be devastating: Napoleon Bonaparte.

The sole glimmer of light during these troubled times came from the Orthodox east, where Paul I had succeeded to the Russian throne following his mother, the great Catherine II. Paul had a fascination with the knights, and was an admirer of Bailiff Litti, the Order's officer that Catherine had sent to build her navy. Paul lavishly patronized the Grand Priory of Poland, a Catholic kingdom that had passed to his rule. The Polish priory now became one of the Order's most significant sources of revenue, fortunes dwindling as it were.[65]

At this most inopportune moment, Rohan passed away (1797). It seemed as if only the Empire could offer a candidate—France and its allies could not offer a grand master to the officially neutral Order. Thus, the only significant candidate to appear was the Imperial Ambassador to Valletta, Ferdinand von Hompesch. As Sire writes, "a malign convergence of circumstances focused the choices of the Order on the one man who could be trusted to dishonour it."[66] Hompesch, while maintaining the image of business as usual, did nothing to shore up the defenses of Malta against expansionist, republican France. In a sense he could not, for the knights had an obligation not to take up arms against fellow Christians. France was planning on being masters of the Mediterranean, in addition to carving up the Holy Roman Empire and annexing the Papal States. Hompesch was notified of the French plan in June 1798, a few days before Napoleon arrived on his way to Egypt. Hompesch did nothing until the fleet was sighted off the coast. It consisted of 500-600 French vessels with 29,000 men in contrast to 300 knights and 7,000 soldiers on Malta.[67] At that moment, lightning broke out throughout the archipelago.

Notabile was surrendered without resistance by the Maltese citizens, and Gozo was taken. When Hompesch sent an embassy to negotiate a compromise with Napoleon, the general sent back a document for the Grand Master to sign surrendering Malta. The French knights would be given pensions; the Grand Master would receive a principality in Germany.[68] Hompesch refused, but then received Bonaparte in Valletta on 12 June 1798. One of Napoleon's aides remarked "it is well, General, that there was someone within to open the gates to us."[69] Hompesch was sent packing, receiving only the relic of the Hand of St. John and the icon of Our Lady of Philermo. The rest of the Order's vast treasure was loaded onto the flagship. That ship was quickly sunk by Admiral Nelson at Aboukir Bay.

Out of two hundred French knights, fifty accepted Napoleon's offer to sail to Egypt with him. Many of the latter went into exile in Russia, where Emperor Paul I received them with open arms. The knights issued a manifesto declaring Hompesch deposed. Then the proceedings took on ever-more bizarre twists: On 7 November, the Russian Priory elected the Tsar Paul grand master. The over-joyed emperor, dreamily imbued with the glory of the Crusades, created a second grand priory for his Orthodox nobility. The difficulty was soon obvious—the Romanov-Holstein-Gottorp sovereign was not a professed knight; he was married and not even a Catholic. When the pope indicated his disapproval, his Russian nuncio was dismissed by Paul. However, the message from other European leaders was mixed: Louis XVIII in exile instructed his knights to recognize Paul, as did the kings of Naples and Portugal, and reluctantly, even the kaiser in Vienna.[70] But Paul did not send his fleet to Malta to recapture the islands—Admiral Nelson did in 1800. Soon, however, the Russian emperor became increasingly unbalanced and was murdered on 23 March 1801 by his courtiers, including four of his knights of Malta. He was succeeded by his son Alexander I.

Young Emperor Alexander I renounced the Grand Mastership and the Maltese claim, and appointed a lieutenant. With the terms of the 1802 Treaty of Amiens between Britain and France, Malta was to be returned to the knights. Pius VII then appointed Giovanni Tommasi, living at Messina, grand master in 1803. Hompesch died in Montpellier in 1805. Matters seemed to be improving. However, there was considerable delay in the papal appointment, and international climate changed quickly—the Order of Malta idea lost favor. Britain, wishing to keep Malta, re-declared war on France. When it appeared that France would invade Messina in 1805, Tommasi fled to Catania, were he died. The Convent there elected Guevara Suardo as lieutenant and proposed Giuseppe Caracciolo di Marchesi di Sant'Eramo as grand master. Pope Pius refused this request, being now under Napoleon's control. But Tsar Alexander recognized Caracciolo.[71] In 1806, peace negotiations between England and France proposed giving Malta permanently to the former. At this point, Lieutenant Suardo tried to remove his knights to Rome, but was blocked by Sicily, which had confiscated the Order's remaining treasury (it was never returned).

The fall of Malta and the debacle in Russia were perhaps the two most serious crises faced by the ancient Order—and the plummet was not over. The Order of St. John stood to fall into insignificance as had most other chivalric orders whose time had long passed. To some a paramount symbol of the *Ancien Régime*, the once invincible eight-pointed cross of St. John seemed to become just another bejeweled ornament to exchange between ruling princes. As the Napoleonic Wars raged throughout Europe, the knightly commanderies throughout were wiped away. The German, Italian, Bavarian, and Russian priories disappeared between 1805 and 1810. The great, eternal secular patron of the Order, the Holy Roman emperor, abdicated and became the first emperor of Austria. Disaster upon disaster reigned, until only the Priory of Bohemia remained, quietly protected by the ever-loyal Habsburgs.[72] But even here there was even thought of absorbing the Order of St. John into the Habsburg Order of Maria-Theresa. The *langues* of Aragon, Castile, and Portugal were annexed to their respective monarchs. When Lieutenant Suardo died in Catania in 1814, the local knights ignored Caracciolo and elected the Sicilian Andrea di Giovanni Lieutenant. Russia had by now withdrawn its recognition of Caracciolo.

Restoration

In 1814, Napoleon's regime collapsed. The three *langues* of France soon formed a Commission, one that was recognized by the restored king, Louis XVIII. When the Congress of Vienna set out to restore legitimacy after the fall of Napoleon's empire, the Order was represented by delegates from newly restored *langues* in Spain and the Commission of France, plus the a new lieutenant, Andrea di Giovanni y Centelles. The latter proved to be inept—he had not developed a united front to put forth the claims of the Order, and any gains anticipated at the Congress for SMOM proved to be fruitless. With the 1814 Treaty of Paris, Malta became a British colony. With no grand master, no money, little papal support, and a divided state of affairs, the Order had sunk to its lowest depths and was clearly on the road of becoming strictly a papal order. But despite di Giovanni's incompetence, the French knights had showed some signs of strength at the Congress under their leader Camille de Rohan; thus all was not as gloomy as it could have been. In 1816, the Grand Priory of Rome was reestablished.[73]

Prince Metternich, the strongman of the post-Napoleonic Austrian Empire, offered Elba (Napoleon's first isle of exile) and Austrian islands in the Adriatic to the knights under the control of the Habsburgs. This was refused. In 1821 the Austrian Antonio Busca was appointed Lieutenant at Metternich's insistence. But Busca, despite opportunities to present the Order's case for sovereignty at the Congress in Verona, let matters drop into disaffection. In 1827, Busca attempted to resurrect the *langue* of England, but that group ran into trouble by trying to enroll Protestants. Since this went against the statutes of the Order, the English *langue* transformed itself into the Venerable Langue, with Rev. Sir Robert Peat elected as Grand Prior in 1831.

Busca ignored the Commission of French knights, who were seriously contemplating becoming involved in the Greek war of independence from the Ottoman Turks. Not only were there plenty of islands to go around, there was the mythical possibility of recovering Rhodes. In fact, a treaty was signed in secret between the Greeks and the French Commission of knights in 1823.[74] The Order was to immediately receive a few islands off the Peloponnese—upon liberation they would receive Rhodes. The knights were to raise a loan of ten million *francs* and to outfit a naval squadron. The word got out, however, and France, fearing Metternich, distanced herself from the knights. Rather than support his French *langue*, Busca expelled the Commission from the Order. In 1827, hav-

ing found British, French, and Russian support, the Greek nationalists were successful—the Order was not present to receive Rhodes. Matters moved from bad
to worse, when in 1830, with the forced abdication of Charles X from the French
throne, the influence of the knights in France came to an end. In 1834 Busca
died—he had held no Chapter General, established no novitiate for training
young knights, and supported no hospital.

At this nadir of the Order, only the pope, whose own sovereignty was under
increased scrutiny throughout the nineteenth century, and the Habsburg emper-
or, whose authority as the second sword of Christ was severely eroded by secularism and the French Revolution, recognized the Order of St. John as a sovereign power. It was fitting, in a sense, as the Order had always existed between
and for those twin institutions of Universal Christendom. Like the Papacy and
the Holy Roman Empire, the Order of St. John was in service to the ideals of a
unified faith, a representation of Christ's kingdom on Earth. The supranational
Order would rise again.

After Busca's death, Pope Gregory XVI appointed Carlo Candida as Lieutenant. Candida had been a commander before the fall of Malta. The pope ordered the Convent to leave Ferrara and take up residence in their old embassy in
Rome, the Villa Malta on the Aventine, and at the Malta Palace at 68 via Condotti, the old Grand Priory (Figure 4.1). Both properties were graced with ambassadorial extraterritoriality within the Papal States.

Two developments happened in the mid-nineteenth century that the Order
seized upon. They would be the keystone for the resurrection of Order from its
defeat at Malta to its current success in the twentieth-first century. First, once
settling in Rome, Candida immediately asked Pope Gregory XVI for a hospital,
re-activating its first charisma, the care of the poor and sick. The Order was returning to its roots, always the source of its universal appeal. Candida was given
the hospice of Cento Preti at Ponte Sisto in Rome in 1841. The convent itself
moved to the villa on the Aventine.

The second development was the Marian apparitions at Lourdes, beheld by
Bernadette Soubirous in 1858. This phenomenon became an opportunity to additionally practice the Defense of the Faith by organizing and protecting pilgrims
visiting the shrine established in southern France. Although not a major component of the Order's activities until the mid-twentieth century, the pilgrimage to
Lourdes with *malades* from around the world is a major ritual by which the Order annually revives itself. The two primary structural components of the Order,
of the *longue durée*, were reorienting themselves to new circumstances.

The pope led the way in creating family commanderies to replace those that
had fallen. In 1839, the Grand Priory of Lombardy-Venetia was restored by
Austria, with support from Parma, Modena, and Lucca.[75] Also a priory of the
Two Sicilies and five commanderies under the king of Sardinia were established. While the pontiff was anxious to restore the title of grand master, Metternich still wanted to install Habsburg Archduke Frederick in the position, and
this had again to be rejected. Pope Gregory's own nephew took his vows as a
knight. Despite this strong Roman rekindling, the succession of indifferent Pius

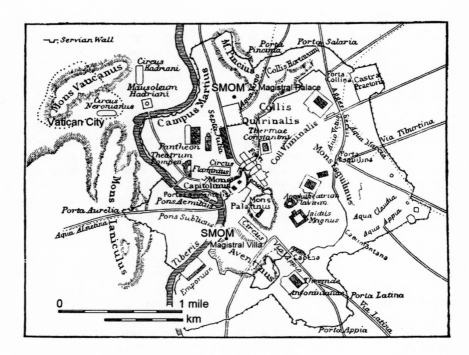

Figure 4.1 Vatican and SMOM Territories over Ancient Rome.

IX made a clear test of the fledgling restored Order. Colloredo succeed as Lieutenant of the Order in 1845. It was under his command that the second rank
Knights of Honor and Devotion began to outnumber the Knights of Justice.
This was yet another stroke of genius that allowed the Order to revive and
thrive. Without diluting the sixteen quarters of nobility qualification of the professed Knights of Justice, the easier qualifications of the second rank knights
allowed representation from emerging social and political classes of the nineteenth century—the meritocracy, the *noblese du robe*.

In 1869, Austrian and German knights took the lead in the revival of hospitaller ideals, establishing a hospital at Tantur, near Jerusalem. Its leader, August
von Haxthausen of the German Priory, had great difficulties with the ascendant
Protestant state of Prussia. The Knights of Malta of the Silesian Association
created field medical units during the Prusso-Danish War of 1864, with physicians, nurses, military chaplains serving on the line. The International Committee of the Red Cross had been developing along similar lines, and the Order was
represented at the second International Conference of the Red Cross in 1869.[76]

Another key development leading to the revival of the Order was the creation of national associations, often in Protestant-dominated countries such as

Britain and Germany. The English Langue had split from the Sovereign Order in the eighteenth century through an Irish knight of the French Langue. Upon eventually receiving recognition from the British Crown, it became the Venerable Order of St. John, known today mainly as the St. John's Ambulance Association. The Catholic Order of St. John was re-established in England by convert Sir George Bowyer, who supported the work of the Sisters of Mercy of the Hospital of St. Elizabeth. They were given the privilege of wearing the Maltese Cross. Another convert, the seventh Earl Granard established the British Association of SMOM in 1876.

In Italy, a national association was formed in 1877 that was parallel to the still-extant Grand Priory. The Spanish *Langue*, a royal order since 1802, was restored to SMOM in 1855. The Order's revival in France was hampered by another Napoleon (III), even though his wife Empress Eugenie was a Dame of Honor and Devotion. But the revival continued with great vigor—in 1879 Pope Leo XIII restored the title, grand master, and bestowed it on Lieutenant Ceschi a Santa Croce. Throughout the latter nineteenth century the Order continued to revive its Protestant affiliates as well. The Protestant Order of St. John was established in Prussia under the patronage of Frederick William IV. It remained in close communication with the Catholic Sovereign Order.

During the Italian-Libyan war over Tripoli in 1912, the Italian Association commandeered the hospital ship *Regina Margherita* that later cared for twelve thousand wounded. During World War I, German knights operated two hospital trains, nine hospitals and numerous infirmaries; Austria maintained five trains, three hospitals, and other facilities. The French Association was similarly pressed into hospitaller service. During the war the Austrian Grand Master Galeas Thun Hohenstein had to retreat to neutral Switzerland. The fall of the German and Austrian empires deprived the Order of many new knights from those countries. However, Thun Hohenstein was able to quickly re-establish relations with the Austrian Republic and the Hungarian Regency, despite the fact that one of the Order's most illustrious and loyal supporters, the Habsburg family, had retreated into a humiliating exile from their former realms.

When Hohenstein returned from Switzerland in 1920, he worked hard to maintain and develop excellent relations with the Kingdom of Italy, which are noted in the recognition of SMOM sovereignty in documents of 1869, 1884, and 1923.[77] Continued positive relationships were enhanced with the Lateran Treaty of 1929, the Kingdom of Italy and Vatican City recognizing each other's sovereignty. Thun Hohenstein retired that year, leaving the Order to Lieutenant Pio Franchi de'Cavalieri. The latter was also able to forge a similar treaty with the Kingdom of Italy.

On Hohenstein's death, de'Cavalieri passed over the grand mastership in favor of Prince Ludovico Chigi Albani della Rovere, a member of the Black Nobility of Rome and Grand Marshal of the Church. When Italy turned Ethiopia into a colony, the Order was able to open a hospital for patients with leprosy at Adowa.[78]

Throughout the twentieth century, the importance of Lourdes as one of the principal loci of Catholic pilgrimage in the world, continued to grow. The Knight Hospitallers are in their element here. Every spring, the Catholic nobility of Europe and from around the world escort the poor and sick to the Shrine of Our Lady of Lourdes, feeding and washing their charges in a classic rite of reversal. The Lourdes pilgrimage contains its own structural of liminality, being a place set apart, holy, and transformative. Miracles do occasionally happen, but many express a feeling of renewal. The nobility, through their willful *noblesse oblige* at Lourdes, are thus reaffirmed in their social statuses back home. This is most important, as the secularization and formation of republican forms of government have made the maintenance of the noble class difficult ever since the disestablishment of feudalism. In this regard, the Lourdes pilgrimage continues to enact the ancient act of riding off to the Crusades.

Like most of the aristocracy of Europe, the Order was demonstrably anti-Nazi during World War II. Knight Grand Cross Cardinal von Galen was an outspoken critic. The failed conspiracy against Hitler resulted in the execution of twelve knights from the Bailiwick of Brandenburg.

The horrible destruction of World War II in Europe was a great challenge to the Order, but provided a stimulus, as ever, for reinventing itself. The Silesian Association, losing everything in the post-war Soviet occupation, was pivotal in the formation in 1953 of the Malteser-Hilfsdienst, one of the greatest international aid organizations in the modern world. It was also a time where the Order was faced with serious challenges to its integrity and sovereignty, the likes of which had not been seen since Napoleon.

It was at this time, around 1949, that Argentinean first lady Eva Perón, the champion of the poor of her country, sought recognition from SMOM for her charitable works as a Dame of Honor and Devotion, in exchange for a favorable export price on grain. This highest non-professed honor, requiring the proof of sixteen quarters of nobility, never came—the Order kept its integrity.[79]

A greater challenge came from the Vatican itself, and with two ambitious cardinals. Pius XII had given Nicola, Cardinal Canali great latitude in running the finances of the Holy See; Canali was named the Major Penitentiary of the Church, becoming the most powerful man in the Holy See after the pope. He had also been made grand master of the Equestrian Order of the Holy Sepulchre of Jerusalem, heretofore an honor the pope himself held. The EOHSJ was an order entirely under the protection, and authority, of the Roman Church. Cardinal Canali was also made the Order of Malta Grand Prior of Rome under Prince Chigi; thus he was intimate to the great differences in prerogatives and relative authority between each order.

The second vexatious cardinal who provided a challenge to the Order surfaced in the United States—Francis Spellman, the archbishop of New York. The cardinal saw developing membership in the Order as a cash cow for his archdiocese. The "passage fees"[80] collected by the cardinal ultimately rose to astronomical heights relative to what the Grand Magistry usually collected. Much of this was diverted to the Vatican, to Cardinal Pizzardo, who sat on the Congregation of the Religious with Cardinal Canali. An astonished Grand Master Chigi had known nothing of this.

Perhaps the ambitious Canali was jealous of the sovereignty that the Order of Malta held, especially in comparison to the Order of the Holy Sepulchre. Regardless of the motivation, a cardinalitial commission was established with the stated purpose to reform SMOM and to assure that the "sanctification of its members" remained in the forefront. The commission, to the dismay of SMOM, was headed by Canali and Pizzardo. Canali was really attempting to reel the Order of Malta in and transform it into a papal honor, as the Order of the Holy Sepulchre had become. This would have caused great difficulties for the Sovereign Order of Malta. By placing the members of SMOM under the Congregation of Religious, even heads of state with the honor of Grand Cross would become subject to the Congregation, an impossibility under international law. In November 1951, the Vatican actually threatened to invade the Magistral Palace to place seals on all its records—the Holy See was thwarted. The Order successfully achieved a delay in the commission's pronouncement by appealing directly to Pius XII. This had the effect of cooling the argument and allowing the pope and more objective minds to eventually prevail.

In 1953 the cardinalitial Tribunal privately released its findings.[81] The Order won the challenge generated by the Canali and Spellman party, retaining its independence. The judgment essentially forms the basis upon which the modern secular and religious nature of SMOM is based. The issue of the continuance of the Order's sovereignty was continued, but with the understanding that SMOM's political independence was based on its function as an international organization, not upon its territorial possessions. That judgment in no way diminished the status of SMOM's extraterritorial possessions in Rome—those properties are, in all respects, independent of both the Vatican and the Italian Republic. And its sovereignty is not based on these tiny possessions. The tribunal underscored the Order's essential religious nature, and thus confirmed its subordinate nature in religious matters. The religious subordination only practically applies to professed knights, not to the secular knights of the third class (second class knights hold obedience to a regent, who is usually but not always a religious). Due to its continuing sovereign nature, the Order maintained the right to address the pope directly through the Secretariat of State, as it had recently exercised in 1951, an action that blocked the "great siege" of the cardinals.

This exercise in sovereignty helped clarify both the positions of SMOM and the Holy See vis-à-vis the world in international law. As such, it is not a coincidence that the SMOM holds its sovereignty in the same manner as does the Holy See. During the troubles of 1951-53, the Vatican clearly maintained a memory of the times its own sovereignty was abrogated under the unifying Italian kingdom. The *largess* finally agreed upon by the kingdom to the pope in the Lateran Treaty must have been fresh in the mind of the great diplomat Pius XII and his Curia as they finally reasoned with the Order in 1953. Since this time, the relations between SMOM and the Vatican have grown steadily stronger. In recent years, Pope Benedict XVI has entrusted the Catechism of the Church to the Order, as well as the "poor and sick of Jesus Christ." By these acts, the Church reconfirms the twin charisma of the Order.

Cardinal Spellman's power-brokerage in the Vatican led to great embarrassment within the American Association, and alienated many of the members. In partial response to this awkwardness, a small group of knights on the western coast of the United States petitioned Rome for a new national association. On 24 June 1953, the Western Association—USA was formed, headquartered in San Francisco and serving the western states. The old American Association was divided again in 1973-74, the southern states becoming the Federal Association headquartered in Washington, DC. In the United States, ladies were first admitted by the Western Association in 1975 as Dames of Malta.

The Spurious Orders

Subversive challenges to the sovereignty of the Order continued throughout the remainder of the twentieth century. The motivations and structure for the construction of counterfeit orders most likely had always been there—indeed, even the accounts of the origination of the Hospital of St. John had been clouded by the embellishment histories of a century later. But the technology of the modern age, and the lack of an enforcing authority, the lack of heraldic authorities with real power, seems to have spawned the proliferation of spurious orders claiming affinity with SMOM.

Imitation being the sincerest form of flattery, the organization and symbols of the Order of St. John of Jerusalem had been copied for centuries. An eight-pointed red cross on a white field became the emblem of the Order of Santo Stefano, formed by the Duke of Tuscany in 1562. Like the Knights of Malta, they were active in privateering along the Barbary Coast of North Africa and the Levant, capturing Moslem ships and bringing their cargoes, crews, and vessels back for sale and redistribution.[82] Another example is the simple white cross of St. John, which is the prototype of the International Committee of the Red Cross and many other agencies of this nature. The Hospitallers, active helping the Danes defeat pagan Estonia, adopted the Dannebrog as their own.[83]

While some counterfeit orders are no doubt outright frauds, appropriating the Order's insignia and mission for their own personal gain, some of these organizations have developed during time of weakness within the Order itself and are artifacts of factions that have split off and gone their own ways. One good example of the latter is the branch that traces its lineage from the treaty between the Order and the Russian Empire by which the group of knights in exile from Malta during the Napoleonic Era were placed under the protection of the tsars. This organization styles itself "The Sovereign Military and Hospitaller Order of Saint John of Jerusalem Ecumenical Knights of Rhodes and Malta, O.S.J."

With the assassination of Tsar Nicholas II in 1918, the "Ecumenical Knights" came under the magistry of Grand Duke Alexander in exile. Upon his passing in 1933, a lieutenancy was created that was first given to Grand Duke Andrew (1933-1956), then Count von Zeppelin (1956-1960), and Colonel de Cassagnac (1960-1962). De Cassagnac ran into some opposition among the knights, and was forced to resign in 1962. The Ecumenical Knights then elected former King Peter II of Yugoslavia, hereditary protector of the Order, who was living in exile in England. Peter gave a new chapter and constitution to the Order on 21 June 1965. The royal grand master died in 1970. This gave occasion to question the legitimacy of the succession in the United States under the sponsorship of the Polish Priory. After debating the issue for over ten years, an international grand council was called by some Ecumenical priories and hereditary commanders, in opposition to others in the Order. The former elected H.R.H. Prince Alexis d'Anjou de Bourbon-Conde, Duke of Durazzo, son of the pretender to the Neapolitan throne.

The mission of the Ecumenical Knights is charitable and chivalrous, not dissimilar to SMOM of Rome. But to add to the general confusion, the Ecumenical Knights even have diplomatic representation—with one country, the Democratic Republic of Sao Tomé e Principe. Negotiations were being made for recognition with five other countries! A few years ago, Crown Prince Alexander of Yugoslavia, son of Peter II, renounced his hereditary claims as protector of this Russian splinter group to Grand Master Andrew Bertie.

During the Reformation, several priories or small groups of knights split from the Catholic Order of St. John and formed their own Protestant orders under the patronage of their respective rulers. The Most Venerable Order of the Hospital of Saint John of Jerusalem in Great Britain, the Swedish Johanniter Order, and the Johanniter orders of Germany and the Netherlands are examples of these Protestant royal orders. The Venerable Order in England continued to function as if it was a part of SMOM, even acknowledging Candida and the pope as its spiritual head. It all became most confusing until 1858, when the Venerable Langue declared sovereignty and became in time the Most Venerable Order of the Hospital of St. John of Jerusalem, descending upon modern times primarily as the St. John Ambulance Brigade. It is now a British order under the queen.

Due to the fact that not everyone is a historian or herald of arms, or has one on staff, it has been notoriously easy for a group to establish themselves as the Knights of Malta without any claims to legitimacy. The great problem with the spurious orders is that their existence can potentially confuse the interpreters of international law and ultimately threaten the sovereign prerogatives of the legitimate order.

There is not a general consensus as to the actual number of spurious orders, although SMOM accounts for about twenty-five. This is no doubt due to the mutagenic nature of these organizations—perhaps starting with a grain of legitimacy, such groups change and reorganize with the tides, and most fade away to be replaced by others. Various branches of the legitimate Order (SMOM and its Protestant affiliates) have issued disclaimers on the illicit association of numerous spurious orders. The four Protestant orders recognized by SMOM, collectively known as the Alliance Orders of St. John, have issued the following list of unrecognized "Orders of St. John of Jerusalem." It is appropriate to appreciate the entire list above in order to get a sense how subtle and confusing the methods of historical revisionism can be.

1. Sovereign Order of St. John of Jerusalem, Knights of Malta. Royal protector, King Michael of Romania. Prince Grand Master: Capt. Joseph Frendo Cumbo, Ontario, Canada.

2. Sovereign Order of St. John of Jerusalem, Family Commanders and Hereditary Knights of St. John. Prince Grand Master, Dr. John L. Grady, Tennessee, USA.

3. Sovereign Order of St. John of Jerusalem, Knights of Malta, Knights of Rhodes, Hospitallers of Jerusalem. Imperial Protector, Prince Aleksei Nicholievich Romanoff. Lt. Grand Master, Savatore T. Messineo, Reading, PA, USA.

4. Sovereign Order of St. John of Jerusalem, Knights of Malta, the International Order. The Hereditary OSJ Prince Grand Master, Baron Kenneth B. Benefield of Palmonova, Gzira, Malta.

5. Order Souverain de Saint-Jean de Jérusalem, Chevalier de Malta, OSJ. Principal, Baron Yves Galouzeau de Villepin, Paris, France.

6. Order of St. John of Jerusalem, Knights Hospitaller (OSJ). Patron, Prince Karl-Wladmir Karageorgevitch. Lt. Grand Master, Prince Serge Troubetzkoy, Middlesex, England. Grand Priories, UK, Ireland, Australia, Netherlands, USA, Malta. Dependent Order, Russian Grand Priory of Malta. Lt. Grand Master, Anthony Zammit, Valetta, Malta.

7. Sovereign Order of Saint John of Jerusalem, Knights Hospitaller, Under the Constitution given by King Peter II of Yugoslavia; Patron: HRH Prince Karl Vladimir Karageorgevitch; Lt Grand Master: Anthoney Zammit, GCSJ; Grand Prior of Australia: Bailiff Robert Halliday, OAM, GCSJ. It consists of two sections: OSJ Grand Priory of Australia | OSJ Priory of Victoria | OSJ Geelong Commanderie, and OSJ: Ordine di San Giovanni di Gerusalemme, Gran Priorato Russo di Malta e d'Europa, under Victor Xuereb as Lieutenant Grand Master.

8. Order of Saint John of Jerusalem, Belgium Roman Catholic.

9. Order of St. John of Jerusalem, Knights Hospitallers (The Sacred Orthodox Order of St. John of Jerusalem). Grand Prior and Grand Chancellor, John Wilkinson de Batemberg, Houston, Texas, USA. Administrative Headquarters at Zug , Switzerland.

10. The Imperial Russian Order of St. John of Jerusalem, Ecumenical Foundation (Knights of Malta). Grand Master, Prince Robert Bassaraba von Brancovan Khimchiachvili, New York, USA. (Brancovan is a fugitive from the law and members of his executive are in prison in the USA since 2001).

11. Grand Sovereign Dynastic Hospitaller Order of St. John, Knights of Malta. Hereditary Prince Grand Master, Prince Henry III de Paleologue. Lt. Grand Master, Prince George King de Santorini, Count de Florina, Cannes, France.

12. The Royal Sovereign Military and Hospitaller Order of St. John of Jerusalem, Knights of Malta, Ecumenical. A Reigning Territorial Sovereignty. Grand Master, Prince John de Mariveles d'Anjou, Virginia Water, UK.

13. The Australian Order of St. John of Jerusalem. Knights Hospitaller Limited. Incorporated in Victoria, Australia. Prior of Victoria, Edwin E. Bonello, Watsonia, Victoria, Australia.

14. Sovereign Military and Hospitaller Order of St. John of Jerusalem, Ecumenical, Knights of Malta. Prince Grand Master, Prince Jorge I (Jorge de Alvarado). Grand Chancery, La Coruna, Spain. Grand Priory of America, Napa, California, USA. Grand Priory for the Netherlands and Great Britain, Rotterdam, Netherlands. Commaderies in Belgium and France.

15. The Swiss Command of the Sovereign Military and Hospitaller Order of St. John of Jerusalem, Ecumenical Knights of Rhodes and Malta. Grand Commander, Bruno Giulio Burzi Lugano, Switzerland.

16. Knights of Malta. Sovereign Order of Reformed Hospitallers of St. John of Jerusalem. Grand Master, Prince Amaldo Petrucci di Vacone e Siena. Grand Chancery, New York, USA. Agency, Knights of Malta OSJ Foundation, Rome, Italy.

17. The Sovereign Order of the Hospital of St. John of Jerusalem of Denmark. Storkansler, Mogens Tvermoes. Chacery, Copenhagen, Denmark. Priories in Norway and Sweden.

18. Den Danske Malteser Orden. Den Autonome Gejstlige Ridderlige Malteserorden i Daci.

19. Sovereign Order of St. John in the Americas. Grand Master F. Flores-Banuet, San José, Costa Rica.

20. Sovereign Military Order of St. John of Jerusalem, Knights of Malta, Independent and Ecumenical Priorate of the Holy Trinity of Villedieu. Patron, Prince Pierre Phillippe de la Chastre. Grand Master and Grand Prior, Marquis Carlo Stivala do Flavigny, Valetta, Malta. Grand Priory of Australia, Priory of Quebec, Canada.

21. Sovereign Order of the Orthodox Knights Hospitaller of St. John of Jerusalem. Claimed High Spiritual Protector, Patriarch Aleksey II of Moscow (Patriarch Aleksey II issued a statement disassociating himself from the High Spiritual Protectorship of this organization. In fact, he has issued a letter in which he asserts that the only valid order of St. John he recognizes is the SMOM). Grand Prior, Count Nicholas Bobrinskov, Mt. Vernon, Virginia, USA. Dependent,

The Order of Orthodox Knights Hospitaller of St. John of Jerusalem. Priory in
Malta and Priory of the British Isles.[84]

The Federal Association of the Order in the USA has also published a list of
spurious American and Canadian orders that have no affiliation with SMOM
and are not recognized by the Vatican. They include some of the American orders listed above, plus others such as the "Illustrious Order of the Knights of
Malta" from Reading, Pennsylvania, "Knights of Malta, The Grand Chancel-
lery" of Great Neck, New York, and the "Knights of Malta, Sovereign Order of
the Hospitallers of St. John of Jerusalem" of Bellevue, Washington among many
others.[85]

James J. Algrant lists twenty-four false orders, including such confections
as the "Byzantine Protectorate of the Military and Hospitaller Order of St. John
of Jerusalem," "the Autonomous Priory of Dacia of the Order of Malta," and
"Royal Archconfraternity of the Saints John the Baptist and John the Evangelist
of the Knights of Malta, *ad honorem* of Catanzaro."[86]

Perhaps more serious challenges to the legitimacy of SMOM have been
hatched by the alleged descendents of the knights exiled from Malta to Russia
by Napoleon, and "The Ancient and Illustrious Order Knights of Malta/The
Royal Black Institution." The latter owed its existence to Freemasonry, which
in many circles is a nemesis to the Church. The Jacobite Andrew Michael Ram-
sey (1686-1743) provided a mediaeval antecedent to the Masons with the examples of the Order of St. John (and by implication the Knights Templar). He
claimed that Freemasons were the inheritors of this organization, with attendant
rights and responsibilities.[87] These sentiments were given broad acceptance for
nearly 200 years, although today are generally rejected by most Masons.

During this long period, however, some "Orders of St John" claimed direct
connection to the true Order (as well as the Templars). In one tale, during the
time of Grand Master De Rohan, a Masonic Lodge apparently existed on Malta
whose members included knights of the Order.[88] An account of the history of
the Scots order is interesting as it is typical of the historiographic pattern of conventional historic fact and fanciful reconstruction, in this case in a document
written by the head of a Masonic order of "Knights of Malta": The original Order and hospital in Jerusalem are presented in the account, replete with the
Blessed Gerard and the general facts of the Latin Kingdom and the various Crusades. The Order was first established in Scotland by King David I (1124-1153),
and a grand priory was maintained at Torphichen.[89] King Robert the Bruce, on
his deathbed, gave his heart to a knight to be deposited in the Holy Sepulchre. A
member of the Sixth Langue, the Scottish branch, like England, "outgrew" its
parent, the SMOM at the Protestant Reformation. The Scotsman James Sandiland, the last Grand Prior of the Order of St. John, gave over the property of the
Order, upon becoming a Protestant, to Mary, Queen of Scots. The queen, apparently touched by his chivalrous behavior, returned to him personally the lands of
Torphichen and made him a peer. These separated the knights from the State in
Scotland, and, as many argue, from the legitimacy created by recognition by

Catholic sovereigns and the pope. This makes it a self-styled order, one that was adopted as a Masonic group. Subsequent years dipped Sandiland's organization into Freemasonry, the clouds of smoke clearly conjured forth by their current master:

> From this time forward the Order has been separate from the State, and therefore from under the eye of the historian, a circumstance which forces us to be content with side-lights being shed across our path, while other matters are under review, until we again come into the full light of documentary evidence.[90]

This pattern has been seen countless times in a revisionism that could be called "grey historiography."[91] This method is most evident following the dispersal of the Knights Templar and their "miraculous re-appearance" several centuries later in the guise of Free Masons, blaming, like the false Anastasias, the lack of documentation of such inheritance on their circumstances of disenfranchisement, e.g. amnesia, penury, or conspiracy.

A Masonic group known as the Orange Order was founded in 1795 to support Protestant ascendancy in Ireland (Orange being the Royal House of William III who defeated Catholic King James II in 1690). It allegedly had its origins in the Scots knights of St. John founded by Sandilands, who were introduced to Ireland in 1643 to protect Irish Protestants. It was organized into a grand priory of Ireland in a manner similar to the original SMOM branch of the English langue. A brother order, the Royal Black Institution, emerged in 1797, again intimately associated with the Masons. In 1807 Ernest Augustus of Cumberland became the Grand Master of the Orange Order until 1836, when he dissolved it. A year later due to the Salic Law, he became king of Hanover while his cousin Victoria became queen of the United Kingdom. Members of the Orange Order revived their association in 1845, eventually forming branches throughout the British Empire. The Black Association had spread to New York by 1868, styling themselves "Knights of Malta." In 1874, Robert Land was elected as Grand Commander of the Order of the Knights of Malta in 1874, in their "Supreme Grand Black Encampment." In America, the order moved away from its fraternal aspect to assume a more chivalric character, and began to call itself the "Ancient and Illustrious Order of the Knights of Malta."[92] Late nineteenth-century ceremonial swords, hats, and badges can still be found from this organization in on-line auction houses.

Robert Land continued to lead the "Ancient and Illustrious Order" based out of Toronto, Canada. The organization eventually began to lose its fraternal nature, becoming an insurance club in 1882. This became somewhat unpopular to members, and a faction split off in 1906 headed by Charles Hayward, becoming the "Order of Knights Hospitaller." That group lasted until 1921. In 1910, the Ancient and Illustrious Order of insurance men suffered ten member deaths within a short period and could not meet its obligations. The Superintendent of Insurance of the State of New York then issued an order of liquidation. The group's Grand Chancellor committed suicide. At this disarray, the Grand Priory of Canada declared independence. The USA knights struggled onwards, though. In 1928 it reconciled with the Canadian Priory, and brought in knights claimed to be of the Spanish orders. It now called itself "The Sovereign Order of St. John and Malta." By the 1950s it had split into two commanderies, one in Pennsylvania led by Franklin West, and California (Priory of the Pacific) led by Robert Formhals.[93]

Perhaps the most colorful of the spurious orders were the Knights of Malta, a leather gay club located on the West Coast of the United States and Canada. They originated in Seattle in 1973 and have had chapters in Reno, Denver, Portland, Fresno, Modesto, Salt Lake City, Vancouver, and San Francisco. Every Labor Day weekend these leather "knights" held a conclave at one of the member chapters. The Seattle chapter called itself the "Jet Chapter" and affiliated itself with the "900 year history of the Order in more than sixty countries."[94]

However, "like the Legendary Order of St. John, the modern Knights of Malta is an adult social club that is dedicated to community service and in having a good time while doing it."[95] The problem is that the real Order of Malta is real, not legendary, and they take their charisma seriously. The Website of the leather knights presented photographs of burley men wearing little more than leather harnesses. Their emblem was not the eight-pointed Maltese Cross, but a knock-off of the German Iron Cross known as a cross *formée pattée*. The San Francisco Chapter of the Knights of Malta participated in a yearly Folsom Street Fair for the leather/levis set, which usually involves manning a booth selling beverages and souvenirs. The Dogwood Chapter was formed in 1980 in Vancouver, British Columbia, Canada to "foster fraternal relations and to meet our brother and sister (*sic*) Knights." This chapter raises money for charitable causes, such as the work of the Vancouver Gay & Lesbian Food Bank as well as the Vancouver Food Bank, and serves as an honor guard for Vancouver's gay community. The band seems to have little knowledge of the reality of SMOM, despite their apparent service to the poor. Recently, the genuine Order and the leather knights reached an agreement, and the latter has changed its name to the "Knights of Mantra."[96]

In an attempt to banish all these spurious orders and relegate them to the dustbin of history, SMOM established a commission, headed by Frà John MacPherson of the Sovereign Council, and intellectual property attorneys such as Michael Grace of the Western Association-USA, have registered SMOM's distinctive shield and various service marks and names with international and national trademark registries to help prevent future poaching of the Order's name and reputation. This is a job once done by heralds, hereditary or hired officers of the Crown, which registered pedigree and policed sumptuary laws related to heraldry and the use of patented symbols. With fewer monarchs in Europe, there are fewer heralds to regulate matters, leaving much of the burden to the Order itself. To a great extent, SMOM expresses its sovereign through this regulation of symbols. It is an expression parallel to the defense of borders.

The Modern Era

The two extraterritorial properties of the Order are located in Rome. Other than the consular extraterritoriality of its offices around the world, all other properties of SMOM fall under the jurisdiction of their respective countries, most notably Italy. However, the Order is the largest private landowner in Italy.

The more spectacular of the two Roman sovereign territories is the Villa del Priorato di Malta constructed on the Aventine Hill overlooking the Tiber and the Dome of St. Peter's. Like the great Christian church built on the apex of the Mons Vaticanus displacing Roman pagan temples, the Aventine also became ornamented with important Christian architecture. The villa is the site of the *Aedes Junonis Regina,* the ancient temple of Juno, Queen, wife of Jupiter and thus a very important civic temple. With the ban on paganism in the A.D. 390s, the temple's Corinthian columns were removed to a property next door, which became one of the first Christian churches in Rome, Santa Sabina, finished in 422. The future knights' property then became a palace for the papal nobleman Alberic III. He gave his estate to St. Odo of Cluny, who established a reformed Benedictine monastery there in 939, the Chiesa dei SS. Bonifacio e Alessio.[97] It then became property of the ill-fated Knights Templar, and when that order was disbanded, the monastery was given to the Knights of St. John. When SMOM was on Malta, the grounds became the headquarters of the Grand Priory of Rome.

In 1765 the Grand Prior, Giovan Battista Rezzonico, reconstructed the ancient church at the Aventine property. It was given the name Santa Maria del Priorato. The famous Venetian architect G. B. Piranesi rebuilt the adjoining villa and gardens. Fruit trees surround a fountain and well that are features of the medieval monastery. Grand Prior Benedetto Cardinal Pamphili built a coffeehouse. King Ludwig I of Bavaria resided here for a time and planted the rows of palm trees seen today. The interior of the Villa del Priorato di Malta houses portraits of the grand masters and scenes of the great maritime victories of the knights. Much of the upper floor of the villa is occupied by the great meeting chamber of the Chapter General, the Order's legislature in constitutional matters. Its glass windows look out upon the Priory's gardens, St. Peter's Basilica, and out across all of Rome. The Villa del Priorato di Malta houses the Order's embassies to Italy and Vatican City. The keyhole in the great doorway of the villa grounds reveals a remarkable scene of a tree-lined path with the Dome of St. Peter's at the end—a famous Roman tourist must-see of three countries simultaneously.

While the villa is extraterritorial primarily because of its ambassadorial role, the Grand Magistral Palace at 68 via Condotti is independent because of its position as the seat of the grand master. Although small, these territories do exist and are independent from any other polity. As such, they help define SMOM as a state rather than merely an international organization.

The government bodies of the Order also define its true status as a state-level organization. The Council Complete of State elects the grand master or his Lieutenant. It consists of the Lieutenant, members of the Sovereign Council, the prelate, the priors, professed bailiffs, two professed knights of each priory, and fifteen representatives of the National Associations. The Chapter General represents the knights-assembled, and meets every five years to elect the Sovereign Council and is composed of members of the priories and national associations around the world. The Sovereign Council is the government of the Order, and consists of the grand master, the four great officers and six others. The Sovereign Council meets in special chambers at the Grand Magistry at 68 Via Condotti. The Government Council advises the Sovereign Council on matters of political, religious, and humanitarian assistance. Chaired by the grand master, it consists of six chancellors elected by the Chapter General. The Board of Auditors oversees income and expenditures of the Order, and consists of a president, four chancellors, and two alternates. Also elected by the Chapter General, it advises the Receiver of the Common Treasure. The Communications Board supervises internal and external communications and assists the grand chancellor. The Juridical Council is an advisory board that may council the grand master on legal matters: Canon, international, and Magristral. The judiciary of the sovereign state is exercised through the Magistral Courts, the courts of first resort and appeal. It is appointed by the grand master and the Sovereign Council. The courts follow procedures established by the State of Vatican City, and may, under petition by the states involved, serve as a court for international disputes. The Office of the Advocate General provides legal assistance to the Order, and is composed of one advocate general and two alternates appointed by the grand master and Sovereign Council.

Great expansion of the diplomatic outreach of the Order was achieved during the reign of Grand Master Prince Andrew Bertie. This was especially seen in representations from countries beyond Western Europe, and the Order saw much activity in the New World. The Order presently has diplomatic relations with 104 countries. Of particular rising importance in the last twenty years has been the growth of the three associations of the United States. Combined membership represents nearly a third of the Order, and their relative wealth and business acumen is highly important to the Grand Magistry. Richard Dunn, prior president of the Western Association-USA, served two terms in the Sovereign Council, and was succeeded by another Western Association officer, Antonio Sanchez-Corea II. This was the first time Americans have served on the council. In 2010-11, no less than four knights, enrolled in the Western Association and the Sub-priory of Our Lady of Philermo, began their vocations as professed knights. Upon retirement from the Sovereign Council, Dunn was made Bailiff Grand Cross of Honor and Devotion in Obedience.

Frà Andrew Bertie also led an effort to improve relationships with the Republic of Malta. In 1998 the knights were invited to return to their former headquarters on the island, Fort Sant' Angelo, under a ninety-nine year lease, with extraterritoriality. After two centuries, the flag of the Order again flies high above the fortress that changed the course of world history. In fact, the Republic of Malta considered completely ceding the sovereignty of the fortress and the land under it in perpetuity,[98] adding a further territorial qualification in SMOM's position as the smallest state.

The Holy Relics of the Order

The arm and hand of St. John the Baptist and the precious icon of Our Lady of Philermo helped symbolize the continuity of the Order through their various travels and changes of fortune. The arm of the Order's patron saint once wore a ring—Napoleon had apparently wrenched the jewel off with the comment, "What good is it on him?" He allowed the defeated knights to keep the remainder of the arm, which was taken with them into exile.

The icon of Our Lady of Philermo, found on the highest mountain of Rhodes, is alleged to have been painted by the apostle St. Luke himself, thus being a life-portrait of the Virgin and subject of great veneration. It was brought out at all the great battles of the Order, and figured prominently during the Great Siege. At Valetta the icon was placed in a crystal panel dressed with silver, pearls, and precious stones in the chapel of the conventual church. Hompesch was allowed to remove the relics, which made their way to Russia under the sponsorship of Emperor Paul. They were presented to him at the country palace of Gatchina. Spending most of their time at the Winter Palace in St. Petersburg, they probably were at the remote Gatchina Palace during the beginning of the October 1917 Revolution (12 October was traditionally the date of veneration of the relics at Gachina). It seems logical that they were removed from there to be given to the Dowager Empress Marie Feodorovna, widow of Emperor Alexander III, herself heading for exile in native Denmark.[99]

According to the "Peter Order" legend, the head of the Imperial House of Romanov became the protector of the Order's Holy relics during the period of the Russian exile. During the Russian revolution the precious relics of the Order (the arm of St. John the icon of Our Lady of Philermo, and a splinter of the True Cross), were transferred to the protection of the Royal House of Yugoslavia (Karageorgevitch) under the command of Emperor Nicholas II. This is the basis of the hereditary basis of protectorship of the relics as promoted by the Peter Order, extending to a notion of the protectorship and rule of the Order itself. A myth emerged within the OSJ, that the monastery where they were kept gave the relics to the Nazis who removed them, never to be seen again.[100]

The Reverend Dr Michael Foster, SSC MIWO, has concluded that the "relic theory" cannot be upheld as a claim of legitimacy for the "Peter Order" (OSJ): 1) the order that King Peter led was not a continuation of the Russian Grand Priory, the legitimate subordinate to SMOM, 2) King Peter was not a successor to the Russian throne, and the Romanovs are still in existence. Thus it is the successor to the Russian throne who is protector to the Russian Grand Priory;

and 3) even if the trusteeship of the relics defied logic and mere possession could represent the legitimacy of the true Order, it would devolve to the Head of the Royal House, as decreed by King Peter. This would have been his son, Alexander or in default to the direct descendants of Princess Yelena. The protectorship was eventually repudiated by Crown Prince Alexander, a Bailiff Grand Cross of Honor and Devotion in the SMOM of Rome.

King Peter II, by his leadership of an order within the tradition of the Hospitallers of St. John (Knights of St. John of Jerusalem, Knights Hospitaller, i.e. OSJ), provided his own *fons honorum* as a sovereign. Thus, the order as such was legitimate in its own right—but it was not the SMOM traced back to the Crusades. The king's constitution provided for hereditary succession of this assumed protectorship to the Head of the Royal House of Karageorgevitch. This was not to be. With the gradual realization that the history of the years 1908 to the 1950s could not be verified, and at worst, was a fable, the groups operating under King Peter's constitution placed a greater reliance upon King Alexander of Serbia's subsequent passing on of the relics of the order to his keeping. The relics were seen as symbolizing the Order's "moral contents." Their transfer to the Karageorgevitch Royal House was a circumvention of the rights of Grand Duke Kyril Mikhailovitch, successor to the Russian throne, in favor of King Alexander. The latter line continues through his son Grand Duke Vladimir, to his daughter Maria, and will pass eventually to her son George. Like Crown Prince Alexander, the Grand Duchess Maria Vladimirovna, titular Empress of All the Russias, has disavowed recognition of the Order of St. John of Jerusalem, Knights Hospitaller, and all other organizations save SMOM in Rome. Thus this order begins with King Peter II, and does not rely upon any arguments about the re-establishment of the Russian Priory. The current patron is H.R.H. Prince Karl-Vladimir Karageorgevitch, nephew of Crown Prince Alexander.[101]

The claim of the Peter Order, when examined against the facts fails to be convincing. To save the relics of the Order of St. John in Russia from desecration and destruction by the Communists, they were taken by Father Bogoyavlenski in 1919 to Reval in Estonia. Later they were handed over to General Count Alexei Ignatiev for delivery to Copenhagen, Denmark, to be given to the mother of Emperor Nicholas II, the Dowager Empress Marie. They were kept at her villa in Hvidore. Shortly before her death in 1928, the old empress bequeathed the relics to her "cousin-niece" Yelena Karageorgevitch, daughter of Peter I of Yugoslavia and sister to King Alexander I. The South African Association of SMOM suggests, however, that the empress' daughters, Olga and Xenia, passed the icon on to the President of the Russian Orthodox Bishops in Exile, Archbishop Antoniye of Kiev and Galizia, and from there to an Orthodox church in Berlin until 1929, when it was given to Alexander of Yugoslavia.[102] A variant account states that the relics were given to King Alexander by a special deed of trust.[103] However, the relics were never publically mentioned by the dowager empress' daughter, Grand Duchess Olga Aleksandrovna, who lived with her mother in her last years and wrote a candid autobiography.[104] Olga only mentioned that her family was particularly close to the king's sister Yelena, a

Montenegrin princess. The Romanovs were intimate with many members of the royal family of Montenegro, including Queen Zorka, Alexander and Yelena's mother, and Zorka's sisters Elena, who married Victor Emmanuel III of Italy, and Militsa and Anastasia who had married, respectively, Alexander III's favorite cousins Nicholas and Peter Nicholaievitch.

What is certain is that the relics did end up in the care of the Yugoslavian royal family and were kept in the private Chapel of the Royal Palace in Belgrade. King Alexander, godson of Emperor Nicholas II, had trained at the Military Academy in St. Petersburg at the Corps de Pages[105] and was acquainted with the "Orthodox tradition" of the Order of St. John. Alexander was assassinated in 1934, and his cousin Prince Paul took his place as regent. On 27 March 1941, through a military coup d'etat, Alexander's son Peter II became king. In April 1941, with the advance of the Germans, the relics were placed in Ostrog Monastery near Niksic in Montenegro, perhaps having been arranged by two Montenegrin princesses, Queen Elena of Italy and her niece Princess Yelena of Yugoslavia.

After the end of the War, the Government relocated the icon to the national museum in the former Montenegrin capital of Cetinje where it was kept in the reserve collection and never exhibited.[106] From 1941 to 1997 the Holy Relic had disappeared from public sight. The icon was feared lost during the bombing raids of Belgrade. Others suggested it was placed on a submarine that was destroyed. Another version claimed it was placed in a Swiss bank and forgotten. Finally in 1997, an Australian knight, Richard Divali, found the painting at a museum in Cetinje, not far from Medjugorje, where previously Marygrace Dunn, Dame of Malta, had handed out hundreds of prayer cards with the image of the Lady. It is possible that one of the pilgrim's cards led Divali to the rediscovery.[107] The rediscovery of the icon in 1997 was a triumph, and was announced by the SMOM Grand Chancellor, Prince Carlo Marullo.

Both the Grand Magistry in Rome and the Serbian Orthodox Monastery in Cetinje, as well as the Topkapi Museum in Istanbul and Mt. Athos in Greece, claim the right arm of St. John. There are numerous heads as well.

The icon of Our Lady of Philermo is still in the National Museum in Cetinje, Montenegro, where it is displayed in a blue painted room all to itself. The icon was also conserved there. There was some thought of bringing the icon back to Fort Sant' Angelo in Malta, but it has stayed at the Museum.[108]

Sovereign Symbols

SMOM's greatest identifiable symbol on the world stage is the Maltese Cross. Although Raymond de Puy is credited with introducing the eight-pointed cross to the Order by the chronicler Canon Giraud in the twelfth century, Foster brings to light an interesting observation:[109] There is no painting or other document that depicts the Maltese cross before the late sixteenth century. In examining seals and coins of an earlier era, crosses depicted include the True Cross, the Patriarchal Cross, and the Cross Moline. According to Foster, the modern eight-pointed cross was fixed during the three-hundred-year occupation of Rhodes. First evidence appears on two and four *tari* copper coins of Grand Master Jean de la Vallette, dated 1567. The design was quickly standardized with the building of the city of Valletta on Malta between 1573 and 1577, and has remained consistent to this time.

Being a sovereign state, SMOM has a national anthem, a processional march, with Latin lyrics:

> *Ave Crux alba, summae pietatis signum,*
> *Ave Crux alba, salutis nostra sola spes,*
> *Corda fidelium inflamma aduage gratiam, adauge gratiam.*
> *Ut omnia vincat tuorum ardens caritas,*
> *Ut omnia vincat tuorum ardens caritas.*[110]

The Red Cross and the White Cross

At first glance, it would seem that the SMOM headquartered in Rome has much in common with the International Committee of the Red Cross located in Geneva. After all, both are first-responders to humanitarian crises around the world, both have significant historical foundations, and both are inspired by the charisma of Christian charity to the poor and sick. Both use the Cross of Our Lord with red and white colors. While SMOM and the Red Cross now have similar missions, they derive from substantially different historical trajectories. This may be seen most clearly in an examination of the current international status of each organization.

The International Committee of the Red Cross (ICRC) describes itself primarily as a private humanitarian organization, not a sovereign state. In 1859 a Swiss businessman, Henry Dunant, sickened by the loss of life he witnessed in the Battle of Solferino in Italy, instinctively started treating the sick and wounded of the battlefield. So moved by that experience, Dunant continued to work tirelessly for the rest of his life to establish non-partisan, volunteer hospital facilities on the fields of battle. In 1863, thirty-six European states met to establish a politically neutral humanitarian organization to care for the wounded on the battlefield. A year later the Geneva Convention was established. A treaty between the United States and many of the European states was signed, creating the International Committee of the Red Cross to be housed in Switzerland, to see to the aid of the wounded in war. Parallel to this was the development of numerous national Red Cross organizations.[111]

An agreement with the Swiss government signed on 19 March 1993, affirmed the already long-standing policy of full independence of the International Committee from any possible interference by Switzerland. A current agreement with Switzerland protects the full sanctity of all ICRC property in Switzerland including its headquarters and archives. It grants members and staff legal immunity, exempts the ICRC from all taxes and fees, guarantees a protected and duty-free transfer of goods, services, and money, provides the ICRC with secure communication privileges at the same level as foreign embassies, and simplifies commissioner travel in and out of Switzerland.[112] While the ICRC property may be beyond the jurisdiction of Swiss authorities, it nevertheless remains within Switzerland sovereignty. The ICRC was given observer status at the UN, becoming the first private organization to be granted that status. This status was followed by the Holy See and the Order of Malta. However, because the ICRC requires its commissioners to be Swiss citizens, and is defined as a private association under (and thus subject to) Swiss law, it is technically considered a dependency of Switzerland.

The Order of Malta, on the other hand, is a sovereign entity subject only to international law in its secular activities. The head of the International Committee of the Red Cross, for all the respect it receives by the international community, does not sit with heads of state at great events of the world—the grand master of the Order of Malta does.

The Lourdes Pilgrimage

During her apparitions to Bernardette Soubirous in 1858, the Virgin Mary told the young Gascon girl to build a church and to send the people in procession to the grotto at Lourdes. Bernardette's sincerity and honesty eventually won over civil and ecclesiastic authorities, and even before St. Bernardette's death at the young age of 34, Lourdes had become a major Christian pilgrimage site.

The Lourdes pilgrimage became immensely popular, for it had elements of French piety that seemed untouched by the modern age, with its republicanism and its seemingly heartless industrialization. The great processions of nobility with their *malades* harkened back to the solidarity of the *Ancien Régime*. It also provided a visible opportunity for the largely disenfranchised Catholic nobility of Europe to publically redeem themselves through service to the poor.[113] It was an Ultramontane, monarchical vision of France and indeed all of Catholic Europe that seemed to have been lost. Through the extraordinary circumstances of the national pilgrimage at Lourdes in the latter half of the nineteenth century, it seemed to many that the Sacred Ampoule of Clovis, so viscously destroyed during the Revolution, had miraculously refilled itself. In fact, by 1871, the Comte of Chambord seemed ready to receive the Crown of Charlemagne as Henri V and rule over a rechristened France.

The rituals enacted at Lourdes recreate a solidarity between the rich and poor, the aristocrat and the peasant, the strong and the weak, reviving the ideals of faith, hope, and charity in a universalistic Christian experience harking back to the Middle Ages and the Crusades. The Lourdes pilgrimage became a *sine qua non* for the resurrected Knights Hospitallers, simultaneously allowing the Order to Defend the Faith by organizing and escorting the pilgrims to Lourdes, and to attend to the sick and poor throughout.

Today, the priories and national associations of the Order around the world work with the highly organized Hospitalités and the local Domain officials to bring hundreds of specially chosen sick and poor people to the Grotto each spring. Upwards of 3-4,000 knights and dames serve the pilgrimage, working in the hospitals, pushing and pulling special *malade* carts, or *voitures*, through the streets of Lourdes to the Sanctuary and sites of St. Bernardette's life, helping the priests at the numerous masses through the week, and organizing outings and receptions for the Order and their charges. Many of the knights serve as *brancardiers*, formerly stretcher bearers whose job has evolved to traffic cops monitoring the longer processions through the bus infested streets of the town.

The Lourdes pilgrimage *communitas* is facilitated not just with the overwhelming spirituality of the encounter with the sacred, but with the physically of the experience. Blueblooded archduchesses scrub toilets in the *accueiles* while the Pretender to the throne of France helps an elderly gentleman disrobe at the baths. Rain or shine, the *malades* are pushed and pulled in their hooded carts, cocooned with pillows and blankets, swaddled in red dust jackets, everything emblazoned with the eight-pointed white Cross of Malta. The relationship between *malade* and caregiver is one of touch and active involvement. The annual gathering of the mass of knights and dame Hospitallers is a chance to bear witness to the world the continued existence of the Order and their noble twin vocations.

For most of the participants of the Order's yearly pilgrimage, the events at Lourdes are highly structured both ritually and managerially. Both *malade* and caregiver have their own responsibilities. The *malade*, for one, has to let others serve them. For the caregiver, the *malade* is their lord, in fact a reflection of Christ himself. From dawn to the late hours of the evening, the knights and dames see to the needs of their charges, washing and dressing the *malades,* assisting them at mealtimes, and transporting them to the many highly organized masses and receptions throughout the week. Confessions, washing of the feet of *malades,* the veneration of the Blessed Sacrament (the Body of Christ), walking the Stations of the Cross, participating in the torchlight Marian procession, and anointing of the sick are some of the many religious activities that occupy the days and nights of pilgrims and their aides. The high point for many of course are the trips to the Grotto where Bernadette received her visions. For others it is the giant International Mass held at the underground basilica of St. Pius X, celebrated by the *cardinal patronis*, with the Grand Master, his Knights of Justice, the Sovereign Council, and the entire assembly of the Order, their *malades*, guests, and curious visitors from both sides of the Pyrenees. The grand master himself awards the Pilgrim Cross of Malta to the *malades* and first-time caregivers.

While at Lourdes, one can hear Catalán spoken everywhere, a reminder that Andorra is but a few dozen kilometers away. Triumphantly Catholic Lourdes itself is a vibrant reminder that Catalonia and Languedoc, the Cathars' "prom-ised land of error" (Ladurie), as well as the secular Republic of France itself are well distanced. The pilgrimage presents, as it were, double reversal. Through its adoption of Lourdes, the Order has been instrumental in maintaining not only their own establishment and the ideals of a personalized Christianity, but has become major agent for the re-establishment of the ancient hierarchical relation-ships between the commons and ancient nobility.

State or Not a State

During the Order's long history in Europe, it acquired numerous properties, many from professed knights who transferred their estates to the Order. It is now, for example, the largest private land owner in Italy. Furthermore, a few of these properties enjoy extraterritoriality. The Order's palaces in Vienna and Prague also have won back their extraterritorial status following World War II.[114] The relationship with Italy has been further defined in treaties in 1884, 1915, 1938, and 1956. Consistently, the language of the agreements use the words *due stati*, "two states."[115]

While the professed knights are under obedience to the Church under Canon Law, the Constitution of the Order makes clear that this does not compromise the exercise of its sovereignty.[116] Sainty has summarized the precise privileges that the Order enjoys with Italy, as defined in a Note exchanged between the two governments in 1969. The Order is given 1) the same concessions as any other charitable organization in Italy, 2) the grand master is recognized as a foreign head of state, 3) diplomatic immunity, exception for taxation and other con-straints on "those of its properties in which it presently exercises the prerogative of sovereignty,"[117] 4) exception from customs duty for the grand master and the grand chancellor, 5) recognition of the organizational structure of the Order's government, 6) supporting the enforcement of the Order's judgments on foreign states, 7) equivalence of the decorations and insignia with those of the Italian State. It seems, under this language, that SMOM is indeed a state—the smallest in the world.

Whether SMOM is currently a state or not has never been an issue for the Order, but its sovereignty has. Frà Andrew Bertie remarked that sovereignty allows the Order to follow its hospitaller mission with minimal interference.[118] Vital medicines and supplies could be transported where needed, practically anywhere in the world, without having to pause for customs inspection or be dependent upon political machinations. The same could be said for medical personnel, who travel on behalf of this international humanitarian organization. This arrangement was established just as soon as the Hospital in Jerusalem be-came independent of the Syrian Orthodox and Latin patriarchates, and has held strong for over nine hundred years.

The *esprit de corps* that the Order has built up over the centuries, its sense of profound belonging, a shared vision of uniqueness of culture, code of ethics, and its deep, affective historical consciousness, is exactly parallel to the patterns of ethnogenesis found throughout the world. However, the Order's solidarity is based on transnational rather than national sentiment. Among the hundreds of knights and dames of the Order that I have communicated with over the year, not one has ever expressed a patriotic sentiment for SMOM as a state. Passports are only issued for the most unusual of conditions, i.e. when a former monarch becomes a stateless person. Except for diplomatic reasons, knights and dames are expected to maintain their primary identification through their own country or origin. The primary nexus of *communitas* within the Order is with the universal ideal of *nobless oblige* in defense of the Faith and to the succor of sick and poor, rather than towards the state. In the continuum of statehood, SMOM is precisely on the line between what constitutes a state and what does not, and in defense of its universal ideals that have successfully been reproduced for a millennium, it does not matter.

Notes

1. H.J.A. Sire. *The Knights of Malta* (New Haven: Yale University Press,1994), 212.

2. At the funeral of Archduke Otto von Hapsburg in July 2011, the Prince Grand Master Matthew Festing was accorded precedence just after Prince Hans-Adam II of Liechtenstein, another sovereign prince created by the Holy Roman Empire. Otto, of course, was the last crown prince of Austria-Hungary, heir to the Holy Roman Empire.

3. John Sack, *Nowhere.*

4. Giovanni Morello, "The Origins of the Knights of Malta," *Rivista*, 31 (1999). 24.

5. Morello. "Origins," 24.

6. Helen Nicholson, *The Knights Hospitaller* (Woodbridge, Boydell Press. 2001), 5-6.

7. Norbert Elias, *History of Manners*, Volume 1, The Civilizing Process (New York: Pantheon Books 1982 [1934]). Norbert Elias also points out "The Crusades are a specific form of the first great movement of expansion and colonization by the Christian West. During the migrations of peoples, in which for centuries tribes from the east and northeast had been driven in a western and south-western direction, the utilizable areas of Europe had been filled up with people to the furthest frontiers, the British Isles. Now the migration had stopped, The mild climate, fertile soil and unfettered drives favoured rapid multiplication. The land grew too small. The human wave had trapped itself in a cul-de-sac, and from this confinement it strained back towards the east, both in the Crusades and within Europe itself, where the German-populated area slowly spread." *Power and Civility*, Volume 2, The Civilizing Process (New York: Pantheon Books, 1982 [1939]), 39-40.

8. Nicholson, *Hospitaller*, 6

9. Joseph Attard, *The Knights of Malta* (San Gwann, Malta: Publishers Enterprises Group, 1992), 4.

10. Sire, *Knights*, 7.

11. From an Anglo-Norman text cited by Nicholson, *Hospitaller,* 3-4.

12. Sire, *Knights*, 29.
13. Sire, *Knights*, 29.
14. Sire, *Knights*, 28.
15. Sire, *Knights*, 28.
16. Sire, *Knights*, 32.
17. Sire. *Knights*, 36.
18. Sire, *Knights*, 41.
19. Sire, *Knights*, 42
20. Sire, *Knights*, 42.
21. Sire. *Knights*, 47.
22. Sire, *Knights*, 48.
23. Sire, *Knights*, 49.
24. Sire, *Knights*, 49.
25. A professed knight is technically a monk, but that is a long way from the paramount of the ecclesiastical hierarchy represented in a cardinal electorate.
26. Peter De Rosa, *Vicars of Christ* (New York: Crown, 1988), 92-93.
27. In 1958, another John was elected pope and the first John XXIII was removed from the list.
28. De Rosa, *Vicars*, 94.
29. Sire, *Knights*, 50.
30. Sire. *Knights*, 50.
31. Sire. *Knights*, 51.
32. Sire. Knights,59.
33. Sire. *Knights* , 228.
34. Sire. *Knights* , 61.
35. Sire. *Knights* , 70.
36. Sire. *Knights* , 73.
37. Sire. *Knights*, 221.
38. Sire. *Knights*, 82.
39. Indeed, the Teutonic Order became an appanage of the Habsburg and Wittelsbach families, then was forced to become a strictly religious order after the fall of the Austrian Empire in 1918.
40. Sire. *Knights,* 83.
41. Nicholson, *Hospitaller*, 4.
42. Attard. *Malta*, 88.
43. Attard, *Malta*, 73.
44. Attard. *Malta*, 73.
45. Attard. *Malta*, 98.
46. Attard. *Malta*, 86-7
47. Attard. *Malta*, 88.
48. Attard. *Malta*, 97
49. Subhuti Dharmananda, *Cynomorium: Parasitic Plant Widely Used in Traditional Medicine* (Portland, OR: Institute for Traditional Medicine, 2004), 1-6.
50. Dharmananda, *Cynomorium*.
51. Dharmananda, *Cynomorium*.
52. Dharmananda, *Cynomorium*.
53 Dharmananda, *Cynomorium*.
54. "Cynomonium."
55. Attard, *Malta,* 102

56. Attard. *Malta,* 106.

57. Attard, *Malta,* 115

58. Attard. *Malta,* 119.

59. Attard, *Malta,* 122

60. Attard. *Malta,* 124.

61. Years later one historian suggested that Cagliostro had actually been Pinto's son.

62. Attard. *Malta,* 138.

63. Norbert Elias. *Power and Civility.*

64. Sire. *Knights,* 136

65. Sire. *Knights,* 235

66. Sire. *Knights,* 236.

67. Sire. *Knights,* 239.

68. Sire. *Knights,* 242.

69. Sire. *Knights,* 242.

70. Sire. *Knights,* 243

71. Sire. *Knights,* 246.

72. In Silesia, the House of Liechtenstein firmly upheld and protected the Habsburg interests and those of the Catholic Church, having been leaders against Protestant Germany in the 30 Years War. The family remains prominent in SMOM to this day.

73. Sire. *Knights,* 248.

74. Sire. *Knights,* 249.

75. Sire. *Knights,* 251.

76. Sire. *Knights,* 253.

77. Sire. *Knights,* 255.

78. Sire. *Knights,* 256-7.

79. Sire. *Knights,* 258.

80. This fee once literally represented the passage costs from Europe to the Holy Land.

81. Sire. *Knights,* 263-264.

82. This activity was never an official mission of the Order of St. John—it was, by definition, privately financed and supported, yet ultimately contributed significantly to the economy of the island state.

83. It seems that the white cross on red is really the flag of Christendom, being associated with the shield of Emperor Constantine and later of the Holy Roman Empire battle flag. See Whitney Smith, *Flags* (New York: McGraw-Hill, 1976), 64-65.

84. "Self-styled Orders which illegitimately claim to be an offspring of the genuine Order of St. John/Order of Malta." www.smom-za.org/smom/selfstyled.htm (accessed 3/15/09)

85. "Self-styled Orders."

86. "Self-styled Orders."

87. George David Henderson, *Chevalier Ramsay* (London: Thomas Nelson and Sons, 1952).

88. "The Ancient and Illustrious Order Knights of Malta." The Royal Black Institution. 1880s. www2.prestel.co.uk/church/sjcross/ancient.htm (accessed 2/19/08).

89. "Sixth Language-Scottish Branch." Chapter 3. http://members.tripod.com/~ Blesed_Gerard/PA-3.htm (accessed 4/23/08).

90. "Sixth Language."

Oath of the Horatii—Jacques-Louis David, ca. 1784, Louvre, Paris.
Permission courtesy of Réunion des Musées Nationaux / Art Resource, NY.

Center of Andorra La Vella.
Source: Photograph taken by the author.

Prince Hans-Adam II of Liechtenstein.
Courtesy of the Secretariat, Princely House of Liechtenstein.

Foundations of Schellenberg Castle, Liechtenstein.
Source: Photograph taken by the author.

Country house in the Liechtensteiner uplands.
Source: Photograph taken by the author.

The Library, Schloss Vaduz, Liechtenstein.
Permission courtesy of Walter Wachter. Information and Communication Office of the Government of Liechtenstein. Globetrotter. (Copyright by Press Office of the Government of Liechtenstein.)

Sovereign Council Grand Salon, Villa di Malta, Aventine, Rome.
Source: Photograph taken by the author.

Grand Master's breakfast room, Magistral Palace, Rome.
Source: Photograph taken by the author.

Frà Matthew Festing, the Grand Master of the Sovereign Military Order of Malta.
Courtesy of Flickr, and author James Bradley. http://www.flickr.com/photos/jamesbradley/
4508141068/IMG_6583.

Our Ladies of Lourdes—an overstocked gift shop at Lourdes, France.
Source: Photograph taken by the author.

A Knight of Malta on Lourdes duty.
Source: Photograph taken by the author.

The Grand Harbor, Valetta, Malta.
Courtesy of Thinkstock (#114328702).

Rooftops of San Marino.
Source: Photograph taken by the author.

A Guard of the Rock, San Marino.
Source: Photograph taken by the author.

San Marino Postage stamps—still popular souvenirs.
Source: Photograph taken by the author.

The Source of Divine Right: The Sacred Ampoule of Clovis, Palace of Tau, Reims, France.
Permission courtesy of Centre des Monuments Nationaux.

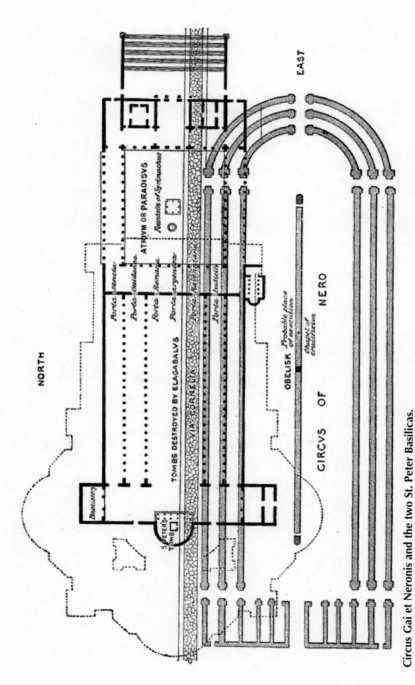

Circus Gai et Neronis and the two St. Peter Basilicas.
Source: Rodolfo Lanciani, Pagan and Christian Rome (Boston and New York, Houghton, Mifflin and Co., 1892). (Public domain.)

North side, Apostolic Palace, Vatican.
Source: Photograph taken by the author.

The Grimaldis of Monaco, 1949. Left to right: Antoinette, Charlotte, Rainier III, Pierre.
Source: Archives du Palais Princier de Monaco.

Château de Bidache.
Courtesy of Jibi 44.

Goust, 1853.
Courtesy of Joseph-Bernand Abadie (Cascade du pont d'Enfer et hameau de Goust près les Eaux-Chaudes). Source: http://numerique.bibliotheque.toulouse.fr/cgi-bin/superlibrary ?a=d&d=/ark:/74899/B315556101_A_ABADIE_4_060.

Archduke Eugen von Habsburg, last lay Hochmeister of the Teutonic Order, ca. 1894.
Courtesy of Bain News Service.
Library of Congress. (Public domain.)

Island of Tavolara from South.
Courtesy of Mikołaj Kirschke.

91. This differs from the "invention of tradition" introduced by Handler and Linnekin in that the agency of origin is less important than its impact. In this example, while both the Templars and Freemasons were real, the links between the two have been disregarded by the latter. See Richard Handler and Jocelyn Linnekin. "Tradition, Genuine or Spurious," *Journal of American Folklore*. 97 (385). 1984.

92. "Sixth Language."

93. "Sixth Language."

94. "Knights of Malta. Seattle Chapter." http://www.jetchapterkofm.com (accessed 12/1/02).

95. "Knights of Malta." Seattle Chapter.

96. Shaun Knittel, "Jet Chapter K of M changes name after 38 years," *Seattle Gay News*. Volume 38, Number 09 (26 February 2010). http://www.sgn.org/sgnnews 38_09/mobile/page11.cfm (accessed 4/21/12).

97. http://www.italycyberguide.com/Geography/cities/rome2000/J43.htm (accessed 4/ 23/09).

98. Stephen Klimczuk and Gerald Warner, *Secret Places, Hidden Sanctuaries* (New York: Sterling, 2009), 88.

99. Russian Ambassador Sergey S. Zotov suggests in an interview by Maltese historian Francis Cachia, that all Imperial church property was taken to Moscow for safekeeping. The relics, considered Romanov property, were returned to the Dowager Empress in exile in 1919. This is considered unlikely, considering the Bolshevik hostility towards the Tsar's family. "Dr. Francis Cachia interviews Russian Ambassador Dr Sergey S. Zotov," *The Times*, Malta. In http://smom-za.org/smom/saints/philerme.htm (accessed 4/30/2007).

100. Michael Foster, "The Patronage of the Order of St. John, Knights Hospitaller (OSJ) by the Karageorgevitch House and the Claims Concerning the Sacred Relics," 5. www.homeusers.prestel.co.uk/church/kposj/relics.htm (accessed 4/17/00).

101. Relics of the House of Karageorgevitch. http://www2.prestel.co.uk/ church/ kposj/relics.htm (accessed 7/31/05).

102. "Our Lady of Philermo," 2. http://www.smom-za.org/smom/saints/philerme. htm (accessed 2/3/06).

103. *The Times of Malta* 28 May 97, 60, provides information that the relics were bequeathed to Princess Yelena. *The Sunday Times of Malta* 26 April 1998, 42 ART, provides that they were entrusted to King Alexander I. See also Edwin J. King (revised by Harry Luke). *The Knights of St. John in the British Realm: Being the Official History of the Most Venerable Order of the Hospital of St. John of Jerusalem. Order of St. John* (St. John's Gate, London, 1967), 136 (n).

104. As told to Ian Vorres in his *The Last Grand Duchess* (Charles Scribner's Sons: New York, 1964). Olga was the main member of the Imperial family to meet and interview Anna Anderson, who infamously claimed to be her niece, the Grand Duchess Anastasia.

105. King Peter of Yugoslavia, *A King's Heritage* (London: Cassell, 1955), 14

106. "Our Lady of Philermo," *The Sunday Times of Malta*, 42.

107. Personal communication, HE Richard Dunn.

108. Personal communication, HMEH The Prince and Grand Master Frà Andrew Bertie, 5 April 2005.

109. Michael Foster, "History of the Maltese Cross, as used by the Order of St. John of Jerusalem." 2004 .http://www2.prestel.co.uk/church/oosj/cross.htm. (accessed 4/5/ 05).

110. "Hail, thou White Cross, the highest sign of piety, Hail, thou White Cross, our only source of health and hope, Inflame the hearts of the faithful with abundant graces, abundant graces. With your ardent charity, all things shall be overcome. With your ardent charity, all things shall be overcome." Courtesy of the Grand Magistry, SMOM, Rome.

111. Caroline Moorehead. *Dunant's dream: War, Switzerland and the history of the Red Cross* (London: HarperCollins,1998).

112. David P. Forsythe. *The Humanitarians. The International Committee of the Red Cross* (Cambridge: Cambridge University Press, 2005).

113. Ruth Harris, *Lourdes: Body and Spirit in the Secular Age* (Penguin: London, 1999), 147.

114. Guy Stair Sainty. "The Order of Malta, Sovereignty, and International Law." 1998. www.chivalricorders.org/chivalric/smom/maltasov.htm (accessed 7/15/02). 2

115. Sainty, "Order," 3.

116. "Constitutional Charter, Order of Malta," Title I, Article 3 (Rome: SMOM, 1961). http://www.orderofmalta.int/wp-content/uploads/2010/06/order-of-malta-constitution. pdf (accessed 4/25/12).

117. Sainty, "Order," 14.

118. Personal communication.. HMEH The Prince and Grand Master Frà Andrew Bertie.

Chapter Five
Republic of Malta

For many months I debated whether the section on the Republic of Malta belonged in the chapter on the Sovereign Order of Malta, or that the SMOM belonged on a chapter about Malta. Eventually, though, it became evident that the Order's sovereignty was never based on the territory it ruled. The popes early on established the Order's special prerogative such that it could operate the Hospital at maximum efficiency without interference from the local authorities, diocesan or secular. That leaves the polities of the Kingdom of Jerusalem, Rhodes, Malta, and Rome something entirely different from the phenomenon of SMOM. The islands of Malta had inhabitants, a history, a distinctive culture, a language, and an ancient people before and after its occupation by the knights. Weighing in at only 316 sq. km (122 sq. miles), the Republic of Malta is clearly a European microstate, and very much a something other than what was left when the knights left in 1798.

Lying dead center in the Mediterranean Sea, Malta was forever at the crossroads of history—great empires north and south stopped here on their way to fight for supremacy of the ancient world. Malta's sheltered harbors were convenient hideaways for pirates, too. With the victory of the Knights of St. John over the Ottoman Turks, Europe lavished its riches upon the rocks, transforming little Malta into the baroque confection that is seen today. The British Empire prized Malta as a strategic refueling center for its Mediterranean fleet and ships bound for India. Free at last in 1964, Malta has just begun to fold its many layers cultural history into a national identity. Unlike the other microstates of Europe, the Republic of Malta is a classic example of a modern nation-state emerging from centuries of maritime, imperial colonial domination.

"Malta" is probably derived from Maltese/Phoenician *malat*, meaning "refuge," in the sense of safe harbor. It is also possibly derived from the Greek *melitē*, "honey-sweet," the islands being a popular source of honey. The two terms have probably conflated. Maltese identity has been built up from wave after wave of seagoing merchants, sailors, settlers, pirates, and knights over the last seven thousand years. The earliest settlements are dated to about 5,200 B.C., a Neolithic culture who seem to have arrived from Sicily. Some of these first peoples lived in caves, as was found in the excavations of the site of Ghar-

109

Dalam. The island of Malta itself is the high point of a range of mountains that formed a land bridge from Africa to Europe during the last worldwide glaciation, with a similar bridge existing across the straits of Gibraltar and several large lakes in between. As such, animals from each region could easily cross from continent to continent. As the ice caps melted and the sea levels rose, the Maltese islands were isolated. Malta then exhibited a trend in insular dwarfism among its Pleistocene megafauna, and it seems like the last pygmy hippopotamuses and elephants disappeared soon after the appearance of humans.[1] A megalithic culture is seen developing by 3,600 B.C. Some of their ancient temples are still standing, rectangular block structures of limestone with statues of corpulent women as the apparent cult images. They most likely represented fertility. This culture disappeared about 2,500 B.C. and a Bronze Age people appeared, characterized by their slab altars or dolmens. On the island of Gozo, the Ggantija site is the oldest free standing megalithic temple in the world, and is listed as a World Heritage Site by UNESCO.[2] Malta itself is mostly limestone, and flat. Its highest elevation is Ta'Dmejrek at 253 m.[3]

Being strategically located at the center of the Mediterranean Sea, Malta was an important stop between the empires of the Mediterranean world, both ancient and modern. The Phoenicians arrived about 1,200-1,000 B.C. They were the dominant culture on the Maltese islands between 1,000-300 B.C. At its cultural and linguistic base, Malta is Phoenician, the friendly Semitic people who gave the West its alphabet. They are the biblical Canaanites. As such, the modern Maltese language is closely related to Arabic, Egyptian, Hebrew, Amharic, and Aramaic, the native tongue of Jesus Christ.

The Phoenicians were a maritime people from Tyre and Biblos in Canaan (Phoenicia) who established colonies throughout the Mediterranean. They were noted particularly for the trade of Tyrrean purple dye from the *Myrex* shell of the Levantine coast to the elites of Greece and Rome. The Phoenician Canaanites did not establish an empire, but rather a collection of widely dispersed city-states. The Phoenicians introduced glass making and weaving onto the islands.

The great Phoenician state of Carthage was dominant in North Africa for centuries, a clear rival to Greece and Rome for control of the Mediterranean world. During the time of their ascendency, ca. 400-218 B.C., nearby Malta was a part of the Carthage state, and Punic Phoenician was the language spoken on the islands. Mdina was the capital of Malta. The Roman Empire seized Malta in 218 B.C. during the Punic Wars, Carthage itself being destroyed by Rome in 148 B.C. Carthage, "New Tyre," was the last great Phoenician city.

Malta's history traditionally acknowledges the New Testament *Acts of the Apostles'* account of the shipwreck of the Saint Paul on Malta, whereupon he began teaching to the inhabitants. This was around A.D. 58-60. Christianity has been the official religion ever since, making it among the oldest Christian communities anywhere. The first Christian burials are found on the island dating to the third century. Malta is discussed in a Christian context during the Council of Chalcedon (451).

In A.D. 440 Malta was occupied by the Vandals as part of their North African colony. Its capital was a rebuilt Carthage. Malta remained in their possession until taken back by the Greek Roman Empire in 534 by Byzantine general Belisarius. Malta then became part of the province of Sicily, where it remained for over 300 years. Sicily was to add another primary layer, an Italian one, to Maltese society.

In 870, the Fatimids, an Islamic Arabic group from Tunis (the site of Carthage), succeeded in conquering Sicily and Malta. Their linguistic influence was strong, leaving Malta with another Semitic language which eventually developed into Maltese. Despite the linguist accretions, however, many Maltese resisted the introduction of Islam and remained steadfastly Christian.

At the end of the first millennium, the Norman Vikings took the islands and Sicily. Like the Phoenicians before them, they burst out of their homeland (West Norway) and colonized areas in Europe via their superior maritime prowess. We don't normally associate the Vikings as being a Mediterranean power, but they were highly successful in North Africa, Sicily, and the Levant, where they established the Crusader state of the Kingdom of Jerusalem. This state of course spawned the Order of Malta. So four centuries later, it was not so much of a stretch of the imagination for the knights to consider Malta as their next stronghold. Malta, for over four hundred years, was an appanage of the Kingdom of Sicily.

The Norman king Roger II, who was a tolerant and well-loved ruler, restored Christianity as the dominant religion in Malta. He was also kind to the Muslims, and through the Norman kings, Sicily and Malta developed a unique Norman-Arab-Byzantine style of art and architecture. The Kingdom of Sicily also occupied much of southern Italy and Naples, greatly disturbing the Amalfians in southern Italy. Many Amalfians left their country to participate in the Crusades. While in the Holy Land, they began to participate in maintaining the much needed Hospital of St. John. They also developed a militaristic profile to help with the protection of pilgrims. They became the Knights of St. John of Jerusalem. Their heirs would come back several generations later as the Knights of St. John of Jerusalem, of Rhodes, and now of Malta. During these times, Italian became a prominent language on the islands, although Arabian Maltese continued to flourish.

Malta, now being so politically tied to Southern Italy, developed feudal relationships with several succeeding dynasties. Between the twelfth and fifteenth centuries, Malta was ruled by succeeding dynasties from Norman Genoa, Swabia, Anjou, Aragon, and Aragon/Castile-Leon (Spain).

The pirate Margaritone of Brindisi, became the first Count of Malta in 1191 by a grant of Tancred, then King of Sicily. Margaritone began his career as a local bandit but by 1187 was in charge of the King of Sicily's fleet. When Greek ships tried to take over Cyprus, Margaritone attacked and took the admirals prisoner. He went on to conquer the Ionian Islands. He was an exemplary among pirates, rising as he had to the nobility. But Margaritone's reign was over only two years later, when Emperor Henry VI of Hohenstaufen obtained Sicily in marriage to the Norman heiress Constance. To consolidate his power, Henry deposed many of the Sicilian nobles, including Margaritone, who was blinded as punishment for supporting the Norman Tancred's heir, William III.

With the decline of the Hohenstaufen rulers from Swabia, the succeeding French from Anjou were never popular. An uprising of the people known as the Sicilian Vespers of 1282 removed the Angevins and restored the kingdom to the rightful scion of the Norman Kingdom of Italy, now King Peter III of Aragon. Thus Aragon assumed rule of an empire which included Malta. Two centuries later, Ferdinand II married Isabella I of Castile-Leon, merging the two realms. It was the unified Spanish kingdom that established the aristocracy on the islands, the oldest title being the Barony of Djar-il-Bniet e Buqana. The islands were entrusted to the Counts of Malta, who were usually illegitimate sons of the kings of Aragon, but usually the local nobility were granted a generous amount of autonomy.

The Knights of Malta

Much of the national character of the modern state of Malta derives from the profound experience of rule by the Order of St. John of Jerusalem, a religio-military organization that held little affectation to territorial essentials at any time. The knights, in fact, were among the first transnational organizations any-where. The knights' lack of interest in creating a homeland in fact allowed Mal-tese culture to thrive apart from the rule and occupation of the islands.

In 1530 the Knights of St. John arrived from Rhodes. Charles V of the Holy Roman Empire had inherited the Spanish Empire and saw Malta, as had most clever monarchs, as a vitally strategic fortress guarding the Western world from the Arabic and Turkish expansion. Since the West's best champions, the Knights of Malta, had been booted off Rhodes by the Turks, Charles clearly saw how settling the knights of Malta would be a clear solution to two problems. In 1530 he gave the Order the islands, under technical suzerainty to the Kingdom of Sici-ly, itself under the Crown of Aragon. The yearly feudal duty was one falcon.

Under the knights, the general wealth and population of Malta grew tre-mendously. About 25,000 knights, priests, servants, brothers, nuns, and natives lived on Malta after settling in 1530; when they left in 1798, the population had grown to 114,000. The city of Valletta was founded at this time, with is palaces, gardens, churches, and fortresses abounding. During the time of the knights, the ancient Aragonese nobility flourished, but their society was kept at a distance from the magistral court. Individual knights often were "adopted" by Maltese families, but by no means were the knights and the locals assimilated into a common culture. The knights, always a supranational organization, were always uneasy with the burdens of territorial possession. The rulers and the ruled main-tained separate identities and historical trajectories.

The great new capital of Valletta was built in a manner to show the triumph of Christianity after the Great Siege. It was one of the gems of the Renaissance. Much of the building of Valletta was entrusted to native Gerolamo Cassar. His works include the Grand Master's Palace, the seven *auberges,* St. John's Co-Cathedral in Valletta, and Verdala Castle in Rabat.[4] Caravaggio was commissioned by the Order to paint the masterpieces *St. Jerome* and *The Beheading of St. John.* In 1693, a horrific earthquake destroyed much of these earlier constructions, including most of the city of Mdina. A new cathedral was built there by baroque architect Lorenzo Gafà, as were Gozo Cathedral in Victoria and St. Paul's Church in Rabat.[5] Due to the construction under the rule of the Order of St. John, the city of Valletta has been made a UNESCO World Heritage Site.

The year the knights arrived the Collegium Melitensae was founded, under the auspices of Pope Clemet VIII. The university is one of the oldest continuous colleges in Europe. A School of Anatomy and Surgery was founded by Grand Master Cottoner at the Sacra Infermeria in Valletta in 1676. It was the state-of-the-art at the time, in keeping with the Order's superior knowledge of the medical field and hospital administration.

The departure of the knights from Malta in 1798 was a rather ignominious affair. The French Revolution had hit the Sovereign Order hard, especially when the Republic seized the assets of the French knights. Grand Master Rohan himself helped bankroll Louis XVI's attempted flight. When Napoleon assumed leadership of the Revolution and began his aggressive conquest of Europe, the knights on Malta were in a drastically weakened state. Leadership was feeble, as Rohan had had a stroke, dying in 1797. Ferdinand von Hompesch, the Imperial Ambassador to the Order, was elected Grand Master. A great diplomat, Hompesch seemed to have resigned the Order to its fate with Napoleon, as he did little to arm the fortress that was Malta. Part of the inaction was due to the lack of enthusiasm the Maltese now had developed for the long rule of the occupying Knights of St. John. Perhaps most importantly, Hompesch was acutely aware of the prohibition of any knight of the Order to raise arms against a fellow Christian, which the French certainly were, despite the Revolution. The Maltese themselves did not want their little island to become a slaughterhouse for the great powers of Europe fighting for dominance. The city of Notabile was offered up to Napoleon by the Maltese themselves. Gozo fell next.

Hompesch arranged for pensions for the knights, and surrendered. The Grand Master and his knights left almost immediately, carrying only the relic of the hand/arm of St. John the Baptist and the icon of Our Lady of Philermo. Napoleon's sailors helped themselves to the inestimable treasure of silver plate from the Hospital and the centuries of accumulations of the Sovereign Order. Napoleon, only spending six days in his conquest of Malta, sailed away to Egypt with his booty. Napoleon must have been surprised by the swiftness of the capitulation, for he had given orders to abandon Malta should resistance develop— the Egyptian campaign was far more important to him. The great island fortress was simply abandoned.

Malta Becomes a Part of the British Empire

Napoleon left a French administration to run Malta, but it was short-lived. The British, in hot pursuit of Napoleon, knew the immense strategic value of Malta and its fortified harbors. The Maltese themselves realized the ascendency of the British Empire, and were disappointed with the French attacking Catholic institutions. Nelson blockaded the islands in 1800, leading to a surrender of the French. The islands were then offered to the British Empire by the Maltese themselves. In the Treaty of Amiens with the French Republic of 1802, the British were supposed to quit Malta, but they never did. With the opening of the Suez Canal in 1869, Malta took on an even greater significance. It became headquarters of the Royal Navy's Mediterranean fleet until the eve of World War II, when the operations moved to Alexandria, Egypt.

Malta was run as a military colony from Great Britain without home rule until 1921. The instability of cycles of military build-up and demobilization left Malta's people generally poverty-stricken throughout the nineteenth century. With British influence, Italian was slowly discontinued as an everyday language. English became the second language, with Maltese holding strong to the present.

During World War I, Malta remained important as a strategic naval base for the British fleet. However, it became better known for its many fine hospitals. Malta became known as the "nurse of the Mediterranean" due to the rest, rehabilitation, and skilled hospital care it provided. This medical infrastructure was a legacy of the Knights Hospitallers. From 1915 to the Armistice, Malta's hospitals treated over 135,000 patients from the horrors of Gallipoli and Salonika.[6] The extent of the Maltese hospital service was staggering. Facilities included Valletta Military Hospital, Zammit-Clapp Hospital in St. Julians, Mtarfa Hospital, Spinola Palace, Bighi Hospital, Cottonera Hospital, Hamrun Hospital, St. George's Hospital, St. Paul's Hospital, St. Andrew's Hospital, St. David's Hospital, St. Patrick's Hospital, St. John's School—Sliema, St. Ignatius Hospital, Tignè Hospital, St. Elmo and Baviere Hospitals in Valletta, Manoel Hospital, Ghajn Tuffieha Camp and Fort Chambray on Gozo.[7]

World War II

The greatest event in the history of Malta was the Great Siege in 1565. The second most important was the Siege of Malta during World War II. The two great and prolonged battles were fought essentially for the same reason—to gain mastery over the Mediterranean Sea.

When hostilities broke out between Great Britain and Germany in 1939, it seemed immediately obvious that the old headquarters of the British Navy in the

Mediterranean was vulnerable on Malta. Germany was developing a strong presence in North Africa, so the island was strategic to them as well. Valletta was attacked by the Italian Air Force the day after Mussolini declared war on Britain. The British high command began to make preparations to move their fleet to Alexandria, Egypt, and leave the defense of the western Mediterranean to the French. However in 1940, France was forced to capitulate, leaving most of the Mediterranean potentially in German hands. Great Britain began to heavily fortify Gibraltar in response. Malta had to be reinforced. Air fighters were sent. Malta became a base where Axis supply lines to North Africa could be intercepted, using submarines, aircraft, and surface vessels in addition to aircraft.

In 1941, Malta received severe bombings from the German Luftwaffe. The city of Valletta was particularly hard hit; in fact, it became one of the most completely destroyed cities of the War. Nearly 7,000 tons of bombs were dropped here.[8] But Malta held fast over 154 days of bombing. Winston Churchill, First Lord of the Admiralty, sent a new fleet of cruisers and destroyers into the fray, and in late 1941, completely destroyed a convoy of seven German supply ships and their escort destroyer. One other destroyer was hirt, another sunk by a British submarine. As a result, Italian support backed off, announcing that Tripoli had practically been blockaded.[9] Churchill, delighted that his "Crusader" campaign was so successful, had two more destroyers and two cruisers sent to Malta. The German North African occupation under Rommel was suffocating for lack of supplies.

But soon things fell against the Allies. The Malta attack fleet sailed into a minefield in Tripoli harbor, with two ships sinking and one badly damaged. The German convoy arrived safely and replenished Rommel. Hitler also sent aircraft reinforcements to Sicily to plan another siege of Malta. A British battleship and an aircraft carrier were sunk. Torpedoes in Alexandria disabled the two remaining British battleships of the Mediterranean fleet. Germany was also preventing supplies from reaching Malta. In the spring of 1942, dozens of fighter planes were sent to Malta. Some relief occurred when the German Luftwaffe was diverted to help Rommel. Newly appointed Air Vice Marshal Sir Keith Park decided to pick off bombers as they approached, rather than retreat from Malta—this was the strategy of the successful Battle of Britain. It was also highly successful on Malta. The Siege howled on that summer of 1942.

Malta, however, was running out of fuel. A supply convoy was desperately needed. In response, nearly the entire Royal Navy was put into defending a convoy of seven supply ships coming from the west. This included three carriers, two battleships, twenty-four destroyers, and seven cruisers. The British suffered heavy losses, but three of the merchant ships and an oil tanker did get to port safely in Malta on 15 August 1942. This is known today as the Santa Marija Convoy in Malta due to its arrival on the Feast of the Holy Virgin. The island then entered a long period of attrition of both Allied and Axis resources. Eventually, Allied wins in North Africa ruined Rommel's power, and the siege of Malta was lifted.

In 1943, Malta became the primary base from which Allied raids into Sicily and the Italian mainland were staged. In September of that year, the Italian Navy surrendered.

Because of the valor of its people and the strategic importance of the island fortress to help assure an ultimate Allied victory in World War II, King George VI awarded Malta the George Cross, the highest British decoration for bravery, in 1942. The Cross was given uniquely to the entire people, not individuals. The insignia now graces the Maltese flag. After the war the islands were finally granted home rule. The war left Malta physically and economically in shambles. In 1947, Britain gave Malta £30 million to help rebuild.

Independence and Current Government

In the post-war decolonialization process that Britain was forced to begin due to worldwide economic and political issues, it was suggested at Whitehall that Malta be incorporated directly into the United Kingdom, much as the French territories became departments in the Republic. This was a singular petition that was not offered to any other colony, even to Gibraltar. Although 77 percent of the voters agreed to this initiative, it was not successful due to a poor voter turnout. Instead, Malta was given its independence in 1964, becoming a monarchy under Elizabeth II and a member of the Commonwealth. In 1974, Malta opted to become a republic, and elected the last governor-general, Sir Anthony Mamo, its first president. Nobility was abolished the following year. This is the first time in its long history that Malta had achieved independence. The British naval bases were finally removed in 1979.[10]

The president of the Republic is elected by the House of Representatives for a five-year term. The president appoints a prime minister, who is usually the majority leader of the Representatives. The unicameral House usually consists of sixty-five representatives elected for five-year terms by the electorate, citizens eighteen years and older. The judiciary consists of a Court of First-instance, Appeal, and a Constitutional Court. Judges are appointed by the president on the advice of the House.[11]

The knights were allowed back to Malta in 1998 and given back their Fort Sant' Angelo. President De Marco stressed the close ties of tradition and action that link the Republic of Malta with the Order, the former who owe much to the assignment of the island to the knights. The Order is currently represented at Fort Sant' Angelo by Frà John Critien, Knight Grand Cross of Justice, who is the Keeper and Resident knight of the fort. De Marco stated that Malta's own current independence is due precisely to the presence of the knights, which led it to develop a different political entity from that of the other islands of the Kingdom of Sicily.[12]

The county was divided on the issue of EU membership, with the Nationalist Party in favor and the Labor party opposed. Finally, a referendum settled the issue, and Malta joined the EU in 2004. In 2008, the Republic of Malta became part of the Eurozone.

Malta has the highest population of the European microstates, with 409,000 inhabitants (2012 est.).[13] Malta has a combined navy, air force, and army, which since 2010, has been all-volunteer.

Being at the crossroads between Africa and Europe, and between the Levant and the West, the island republic always has been in the center of movement of people, whether licit or otherwise. Piracy has always added color to the history of Malta. According to the CIA:

> Malta is a source and destination country for European women and children subjected to sex trafficking; Malta is likely a destination country for men and women subjected to forced labor, including in restaurants, private households, and in unskilled or semi-skilled labor; Malta may be a transit country for African women subjected to sex trafficking in continental Europe.[14]

Malta has recently appointed anti-trafficking officials, and has stepped up investigations and deportation of traffickers in response to international criticism.

Malta was also implicated as a staging area for terrorists involved in the bombing of Pan Am flight 103 over Lockerbie, Scotland in 1988. The courts concluded that the bomb had been initially loaded onto a connecting aircraft at Malta. This allegation has been refuted by Malta, however.[15]

Economy

Malta has limited agricultural capacity, and increasingly relies on desalinization, having few fresh water resources. It only produces about twenty percent of its food needs.[16] Its GDP per capita per year is about $26,000, being the lowest of the microstates. Its unemployment rate is about seven percent (2011), which is higher than most microstates of Europe, but below most of the microstates. The country also has significant national debt, prompting a lowering of credit ratings in 2011. When Malta entered the Eurozone, it replaced the Maltese *lira* with the euro. Malta is 100 percent dependent on the import of oil for its energy needs.

Malta does have splendid tourist attractions, and currently receives 1.2 million visitors per year. The tourist section represents 35 percent of current GDP. Cashing in on its dry, warm climate and its history as a hospitaller state from the knights, Malta is a strong destination for medical tourism. And Malta maintains a good export of goods and services. Malta also has a huge merchant marine fleet with over fifteen hundred ships.[17] Its home port is Marsaxlokk.

Due in part to its sunny, warm climate, and also the great ruins and fortifications, Malta is sometimes called the "Hollywood of the Mediterranean" for its utility in the movie industry.

In many ways, Malta is an exception to the microstates of Europe. It has been a colony of outside powers for most of its existence, and its ethnogenesis as a modern nation-state has been represented only recently. Its development as an ethnic community, however, has been proceeding for centuries, despite or even because of its occupation by various powers. Although it shares with many of the continental microstates some characteristics of post-modernism, Malta has nevertheless joined the Eurozone. In its process of ethnogenesis, Malta has appropriated much symbolic content from the Knights Hospitallers. Today this is evident in the symbiotic relationship and sharing of cultural heritage between the SMOM and the Republic.

Malta Cuisine

The national dish of Malta is *fenkata,* a ceremonial meal with stewed rabbit. It is said it developed as such because the Knights of Malta put a hunting restriction on the locals and would not let them consume rabbit. Therefore, in defiance of the Order, eating rabbit became a symbol of self-determination. Fenkata became the patriotic meal *sine qua non.* Here is a recipe from Lala's Kitchen:[18]

> 2 whole rabbits, cut into large-ish portions.
> Red wine vinegar
> 2 heads garlic
> 2 large onions, slice lengthwise
> 4-5 bay leaves
> 1 teaspoon *hwawar tal fenek* (rabbit seasoning)
> 3 heaped tablespoons *kunserva* (tomato paste is an acceptable substitute)
> 2 bottles dry dark red wine (Nero d'avola or a Shiraz is ideal)
> Mediterranean seasalt
> Good olive oil
> A heap of nice waxy potatoes
> Pepper, a few sprigs of rosemary
> 750g-1kg spaghetti or spaghettoni
> 2 tins of marrowfat peas
> Grated cheese to serve, e.g. parmiggiano, kefalotiri, or pecorino
> One large *hobza Maltija* (or a large fresh white sourdough loaf if not in Malta) to serve

Preparation

The day before, invite two rabbits to your house. Dispatch while they are distracted; clean, skin, and cut into serving pieces. Write condolence letters to rabbits' families. In the morning, wash the rabbit pieces in vinegar. Separate the boney pieces from the meaty ones.

Malta Cuisine (cont.)

Sauté the onions in olive oil until brown. Heat a generous quantity of olive oil in a frying pan and add the garlic. Remove when softened. Put a quarter of the oil in the pan with the onions; place the remainder of the oil in a casserole for frying the rabbit. Fry the meaty chunks of rabbit on high heat, sprinkle liberally with sea salt, until golden brown. Remove. Then brown the boney bits and remove to the smaller pan.

To the large pot add the meaty chunks, 2-3 bay leaves, a bottle and a half of red wine, and additional sprinkle of salt and cover, leaving on a medium flame until the wine starts bubbling. Turn down to low.

To the small pot with the boney pieces add a couple of bay leaves, half a bottle of wine, the rabbit seasoning, and the *kunserva*, stirring until well blended Cover and simmer. Every 15-20 minutes, check on the pots, rearrange the chunks of meat to insure adequate cooking.

The wine and garlic rabbit in the large pot will be ready after about 1.5-2 hours of cooking, as indicated by the meat falling off the bone. It is best to cool and reheat at serving time.

The meat in the smaller pan will also be done when it falls off the bone. Remove the meat and bones with a slotted spoon, cool slightly, and debone, reserving the meat for the sauce in the small pan.

Boil the potatoes in plenty of salted boiling water until just tender. Quarter (and peel if you like) and toss them with some olive oil, rosemary, heaps of salt and pepper. Place in a roasting dish and leave until the guests arrive.

Prepare a large pot of well salted water for pasta. Cook spaghetti according to instructions. Reheat large casserole. Reheat pasta sauce, adding the drained marrowfat peas. Toss potatoes, ensuring they are covered in oil, and bake briefly in a hot oven. Serve the pasta and pasta sauce with the grated cheese. Serve the stewed rabbit with the golden potatoes and Maltese bread broken into chunks. Serves ten.

Notes

1. C. Savona-Ventura and A. Mifsud, "Palaeolithic Man and his Environment in the Maltese Islands," 2009. http://pmhem.org/old/palaeol.html (accessed 4/22/12).

2. "World Heritage Sites." http://www.visitmalta.com/ (accessed 2/20/12). A parallel example of island dwarfism followed by extinction soon after the arrival of the first human settlers can also be seen among the Channel Island pygmy mammoths in California.

3. "CIA World Facts—Malta." https://www.cia.gov/library/publications/the-world-factbook/geos/mt.html (3/15/12).

4. Eccardt, *Secrets,* 235.

5. Eccardt. *Secrets.*

6."Malta in World War I." http://www.killifish.f9.co.uk/ Malta%20WWII/WW1/ Malta_WWI.htm (accessed 6/21/12).

7. "Malta World War I."

8. "Malta in World War II". http://www.visitmalta.com (accessed 2/19/12).

9. "Siege of Malta in World War II." http://www.bbc.co.uk/history/worldwars/ wwtwo /siege_malta_01.shtml.

10. "Siege of Malta."

11. "CIA World Facts—Malta."

12. "Order of Malta," *News Archives,* 2002. www.orderofmalta.int. (accessed 3/12/12).

13. "CIA World Facts—Malta."

14. "CIA World Facts—Malta."

15. "Pan Am 103 Lockerbie Appeal Judgment." www.Terrorismcentral.com. (accessed 3/2/12)

16. "CIA World Facts—Malta."

17. "CIA World Facts—Malta."

18. Adapted from Lala's Kitchen blog. "Fenkata." http://oliveoilandheart.Blog-spot.com/2010/07/fenkata.html (accessed 3/29/12).

Chapter Six
Republic of San Marino

The Serene Republic of San Marino is all about Mount Titano—an isolated peak rising 749 m (2,457 feet) from a spur of the Apennines in North Central Italy. The country is the mountain and foothills, all sixty-one square kilometers of it (twenty-four square miles). It is an enclave within Italy, only about ten kilometers from the Adriatic Coast and the ancient town of Rimini. With the possible exception of Vatican City, San Marino is the only Italian fortress city that has retained its independence since it the days of the Lombards (newer Monaco was a former Genoan principality). The former principality of Seborga (see Chapter Nine) is structurally similar to San Marino, having both been founded by religious orders and maintained by the Empire as sovereign principalities. Then, sovereign city states were the norm, not the exception, built with walls and fortifications and nearly completely self-sufficient. The so-called Lombardic pattern of settlement reminds one of the medieval German towns (Rothenburg in Bavaria is a notable survival) most plausibly because the Lombards were a Germanic tribe. Lucky and wily San Marino—it survived everything the current of history has thrown at it for seventeen hundred years. It is a most notable example of the persistence of a state-level community, which despite nearly continual pressure from the powerful Roman Church, has retained its independence. In fact, the Christian community on Mount Titano predates the rise of the Papacy itself.

Prehistory

Like many of the other microstates of Europe, the evidence of human occupation dates back only to around 5,000-4,000 B.C., during the European Neolithic. In the township of San Giovanni, a Stone Age hammer was found. The Bronze Age is evident in an axe found near the Castle of Casole, which dates to around 2,000 B.C.

The Villanovan culture is also represented in the San Marino area, dating back to around 900 B.C. Villanova is a nearby town just a few kilometers southeast of Bologna. This was an Iron Age culture of small settlements. Nearby Verucchio is also one of the most important centers of Villanovan culture. The excavations at Castellaro record Villanovan burial practices, which are characterized by cremation followed by burial of remains in pottery urns. These ceramics show a distinctive double-cone shape with engraved ornamentation. It appears that the site itself was disturbed by the construction of the castle itself.

This leads into the traces left by the Etruscans (Tuscany), one of Italy's greatest protohistoric cultures. The site of Casole shows clear traces of Etruscan culture, through the discovery of its distinctive red and black painted plates and vases. Traces of human habitation were also found at Santa Mustiola, Fiorentino and on the ridge of Mount Titano itself, and include burials and the remains of dwellings.

The early Roman Republic expanded to the east coast of Italy and founded the colony of Ariminum (Rimini) in 268 B.C. The region including modern San Marino was incorporated in one of the eight Roman regions known as Aemillia. In the Fiorentio tombs in Castellaro and Chiusa on Mount Titano, Roman clay objects and amulets were discovered. Many coins from the Roman Republic were found at Domagnano. At Mustiola, numerous Roman clay objects have been unearthed, as well as a bronze statue of Mercury (A.D. first to second century).[1]

Foundation of the Republic

Unlike the other microstates of Europe, San Marino has always been a republic—in fact, an ancient Roman style republic. As with many hagiographies, early stories of the historic founder of San Marino are full of rather fanciful accounts and revisionisms. What does seem to be solid is the following account: In the late third century, a stonemason named Marinus from Arbe (Rab) on the Dalmatian coast and his friend Leon sailed to the town of Rimini on the other side of the Adriatic. The walls of the city of Rimini had been destroyed by marauders and the Emperor Diocletian sent out an order to rebuild them. Stonemasons throughout the empire, in fact, were called to task. Attempting to ply his trade and practice his religion, however, the Christian Marinus ran headlong into the persecutions which soon reached epic proportions under the Emperor Diocletian.

Marinus used to quarry stone from the region of Monte Titano, a few kilometers west of Rimini. During the persecution, he realized that Titano would make a secure place to escape. Here, Marino found peace and set about establishing a small Christian community with the blessings of the Bishop of Rimini. Some dates give this event at A.D. 301, although the formal persecution started in Rome in 303. Marinus was first made a deacon, then ordained a priest by the bishop, who would be latter known at St. Gaudentius of Rimini. The bishop was martyred by the Arian heretics in 359.

The little community came under the patronage of Donna Felicissima of Rimini, who bequeathed Mount Titano to the community. In her will she reminded the Christians to stay united. Marino died remembering her words, "*Relinquo vos liberos ab utroque homine.*"[2] When Marino passed away in 366,

Rome was transitioning into a Christian empire. Marino was eventually recognized as a saint, his community became known as the lands of San Marino.

The community perhaps adopted another patron saint during Marino's time, since Marino was not recognized as a saint until long after he died, and St. Agatha was among the earliest and most celebrated Christian martyrs. Agatha of Catania, Sicily, was a pious and beautiful Christian virgin who suffered under the persecution of Emperor Gaius Decius around A.D. 251. This persecution was launched while Rome was under severe crisis due to the plague, an economic downturn, and attacks by barbarians. Hostility to the Christians was used to help unify the Roman people. In Catania, Agatha spurned the attentions of a patrician would-be suitor, Senator Quintianus. The unfortunate young woman was arrested and tortured. At one such session, her breasts were amputated. This action became the symbol of her martyrdom, although she recovered apparently through the intercession of St. Peter. She died still imprisoned. Clearly the pattern of persecutions continued to St. Marino's day. St. Agatha is remembered in numerous paintings of the saint, where she usually is depicted carrying her severed breasts on a silver platter. She is also the patron saint of Malta. A knightly order, the Order of St. Agatha, is the chief honor of the Republic of San Marino today.

Another archaeological discovery in the nineteenth century found evidence of the existence of Goths in the Domagnano areas. The "Domagnano Treasure" consists of various gold funerary objects, most like from an Ostrogothic noblewoman who lived in the fourth or fifth century.[3]

The Middle Ages

A few documents refer to a monastic community upon Mt. Titano in the sixth century, including a report of the life of a monk named Basilicio; the ninth century Feretrano Decree reported a well organized, open community under the rule of the local bishop. The document, still preserved in the State Archives, demonstrates an organized commune that forbids anyone from claiming rulership over Mt. Titano, even the Church.

Under Lombard lords, San Marino was a fief of the Duchy of Spoleto, founded in A.D. 570 by Faroald. Spoleto was one of four Lombard duchies, whose capital was at Pavia and the land was governed under civil law. The successor of Lombard king Liutprand, Ratchis, proclaimed the duchies of Spoleto and Benevento (south of Rome) foreign countries. The Lombard kingdom lasted until 773. Spoleto was conquered by Charlemagne in 776 and remained a fief of the Holy Roman Empire until given to Pope Gregory VII Hildebrand by the Countess Matilda of Tuscany in the mid-eleventh century. Spoleto still struggled to maintain its independence. By 1213, it was occupied by Papal forces. San Marino, as well as the surrounding Spoleto, was to become deeply embroiled in the battle between the emperors and the popes. The struggle with the Papacy is the singular defining structural feature that characterizes San Marino's long history.

From the start, the government of the Republic was based on an assembly known as the *Arengo*, composed of the heads of each resident family. In this sense it was a direct descendent of the Roman Senate, which was established by the *patres familia* of Rome. Similarly, like the Roman Republic, San Marino has a distaste for concentrating executive power. In 1242 the community on Mt. Titano appointed two captains regent to become joint heads of state. These positions would be of short duration (six months each), preventing any one individual from consolidating exclusive power. This has continued to the present day. In keeping with this de-emphasis of any sort of cult of leadership, San Marino has very few historical figures who remain prominent in European history. While the stories of Liechtenstein, Andorra, and the other microstates are told primarily through the lives of its rulers, San Marino history is best told through its institutions. In this sense it is a true *res publica*, a regency of the people.

In the ninth century, San Marino officially became a commune, a city-state, with its own permanent consuls and statutes. Expanding in its own way, San Marino purchased the adjacent Pennarossa region and the Castles of Casole. San Marino is a classic example of the "field and fort" system brought to Italy by the Germanic Lombards, with its garrisoned, defensive centers surrounded by agrarian plots. The castle on the hill, the peasants toiling in the lowlands, the stuff from which fairy tales are made, are essentially Germanic.

By the tenth century fortifications and walls were built around the little community at the top of Titano. Cisterns were carved into the earth to create fresh water reserves. The first of three towers was built—La Rocca Guaita. Its style is typically early Romanesque, and consists of two encircling walls. A drawbridge once allowed passage into the inner courtyards.[4] The "Diploma of Berengario" of 951 and "Onorio II's Bull" of 1126 indicate that the town was fortified.[5] By the fourteenth century, the three towers and their walls stood guard at the highest peak of Mt. Titano: La Rocca Guaita, La Cesta o Fratta, and Montale. La Cesta was built in the first half of the twelfth century, and is a bit more classical Romanesque that Guaita, as noted in its rounded features. La Cesta and its eastern walls are built directly up from the sheer cliff face of Mt. Titano. A path, called Passo delle Streghe (Witches' Pass), extends between Guaita and Cesta. The third tower, Montale, was probably built before 1370, as a writer of that time noted the three fortifications. Its style is also Romanesque, but it is a lone tower without additional walls. It was perhaps a project that was never completed.

During the great battles between the Ghibellines and the Guelphs that began under Hildebrand with the Investiture Controversy, the San Marino residents generally supported the emperor as *Ghibellini*. This is unlike Monaco at the time, where the Grimaldi ruling family supported the pope as Guelphs. In general Guelph cities tended to be in areas where the emperor was more of a threat to local interests than the pope, and the Ghibellines clustered in regions where the expanding Papal States were more of a threat. Monaco and San Marino clearly follow this pattern, albeit on opposite sides of the conflict.

Although the Empire under Charlemagne now controlled the Duchy of Spoleto, the bishops of Rimini still claimed control over the region and San Marino. Rimini was strongly Guelph under the bishop and the dictatorial Malatesta family. The Bishop of Feretran, Ugolino Feltria, however, was a strong supporter of the rights of the little republic. For this, both San Marino and the bishop were excommunicated by the pope. In 1249 they were absolved, but it did not stop the fighting. Finally in 1291, the Canon Teodorico attempted to force the San Marino people to pay taxes to the pope. The populace refused. The case wound up in a court at Rimini. Judge Palamede ruled in favor of San Marino. The first laws of San Marino that have survived are dated to 1263. In 1296, another case from the Feretrani family that claimed Titano was brought before Pope Boniface VIII. His legate affirmed the previous ruling of Palamede. With this judgment, the Holy See confirmed the independence of San Marino as an enclave within the Papal States.

All was not settled locally, however. The long-smoldering feud between San Marino and the Malatesta family erupted into outright war. From 1322 to 1463 the Republic fought the Malatesti, the former having aligned with the Church. Victory came against Sigismondo Pandolfo Malatesta, Lord of Rimini, and the family was forced, under papal decree, to cede the castles of Fiorentino, Montegiardino, and Serravalle to San Marino. The castle of Faetano joined the Republic voluntarily. This increased the land of the Republic by about a third, and it has remained the same ever since. Serraville now has a population of about 10,000, making it the largest *castile* in the country. Its main town is Dogona, a shopping region at the border. San Marino has been invaded and occupied three times since Malatesta times.

The Renaissance

The infamous Cesare Borgia, former cardinal, son of Pope Alexander VI and his mistress Vannozza de' Cattanei, was an intensely ambitious man. As tall and handsome as he was cruel and crafty, he befriended men like Niccolo Machiavelli and Leonardo da Vinci. He was allied with the king of France, Louis XII, who made Cesare the Duke of Valentinois the day Cesare resigned his cardinalate. Cesare had also been made *gonfaloniere*, or standard bearer, of the Church. The French king invaded Italy in 1499 but was defeated by the Papal States. Cashing in on his victory, the pope wished to carve out a state for his son in northern Italy, and subsequently declared his legates in Romagna and Marche deposed. In 1502 Cesare captured Urbino and Camerino. In 1503 he occupied San Marino, but his father died. Alexander VI's prestige had sunk to the lowest in the history of the Papacy. His successor Pius III even forbade the celebration of Mass at Alexander's funeral, "it is blasphemous to pray for the damned."[6]

While awaiting entombment, Alexander's coffin exploded due to his rapid de-composition—an antithesis of the "odor of sanctity" and an ill-omen for one of the most despised families in history.

With the death of his father in 1503, Cesare immediately lost vital papal pa-tronage. An uprising brewed in the Duchy of Urbino, which was supported by the resources and men of San Marino. Cesare was captured in Romagna and imprisoned near Perugia. His lands were confiscated by the Papal States and San Marino independence returned. The ruthless Duke of Valentinois,[7] Cesare Borgia, died in exile in Spain in 1507.

In 1542, during the reign of Pope Paul III, Fabiano da Monte Sansavino at-tempted an invasion of San Marino with an army of 500 men. But a thick morn-ing fog prevented the army from scaling the walls and leading a surprise attack upon the Sammarinese. The tiny community held on to its independence. Dur-ing this era, the Emperor Charles V lavished imperial privileges upon the repub-lic, remembering the Sammarinese's pro-imperial Ghibelline leanings. He cau-tioned them to be leery of the papal legates of Romagna, as if the residents were not already sensitive to the nearly thousand-year struggle with the bishops of Rimini. The last Duke of Urbino died in 1637, and the administration of the duchy was transferred directly to the Papacy in Rome. The little Republic and the Holy See signed a treaty of protection in 1602. San Marino was to remain a tiny enclave among the Papal States until the very end of the latter.

For the next 150 years, San Marino was largely marginalized by the powers, and the great events of Italy and the Papal States happened elsewhere. In Rome and Florence the High Renaissance came and went; the popes consecrated their masterpiece, St. Peter's Basilica; the great Baroque palaces of the Orsini and Colonna cropped up everywhere. Not so in little San Marino. Many of the edu-cated and skilled laborers left the community to find work elsewhere, leaving the towns on Monte Titano all but abandoned. The Republic reached a low point in 1739 when it was invaded by the troops of Papal Legate Cardinal Albe-roni of nearby Romagna.

The Napoleonic Era and Italian Unification

The army of Napoleon rolled past San Marino on its Italian campaign in 1797. To escape the incursion into the Papal States, the bishop of Rimini, Monsignor Vincenzo Ferretti fled to San Marino with all his possessions. Napoleon ordered his arrest. Not willing to turn over the bishop and offend the Church, nor to making an entangling alignment with France, the skillfully diplomatic regent Antonio Onofri befriended the dictator and presented his case of San Marino being a "pure republic," in the style of ancient Rome. This struck a chord with Napoleon, a student of the Enlightenment—he was enchanted with the "pristine" Roman republic (He also ignored the possible conquest of Andorra for the same reasons). For all his imperial lusts, Napoleon fancied himself a simple republican at heart. Rather than invade San Marino, the French leader sent orders to respect Sammarinese independence, and further granted that one kiloton of grain and four cannon be sent to the people.[8] Napoleon even offered to expand the territory of the Republic, an offer that was wisely declined. Regent Onofri, for his adroitness in dealing with Napoleon, is often called the "father of the nation."[9]

With the fall of Napoleon in 1815, the Congress of Vienna recognized that San Marino had not been allied with the defeated French, and it reaffirmed its independence. The decision not to accept more territory from Napoleon had worked to its benefit. In 1825 the Papal States again attempted to annex San Marino. The effort failed.

The Italian *Risorgimento* posed a more serious challenge for the tiny republic, being an enclave of the Papal States that were a primary target for dissolution by the liberal unificationists of mid-nineteenth century Italy. The revolutions of 1848 resulted in a tenuous republic in Rome. With its fall in 1849, leader Garibaldi led a retreat across the Papal States in the attempt to reach the allied Republic of Venice. Finding himself surrounded by the combined Austrian and Papal armies, he requested refuge in San Marino and sent messengers to one of the regents, Domineco Maria Belzoppi. The regent accepted the request, on the condition that San Marino would never again be troubled by these wars of unification. The stipulation was agreed upon, and Garibaldi and his fifteen hundred men entered the city-state. They first were housed at the Capuchin Monastery, but later disbanded and spread out through the families of the countryside. A few days later Garibaldi left, evading the twelve thousand-strong Papal-Austrian Army camped in the lowlands surrounding San Marino. He took only 150-250 men with him, and headed for Venice.[10]

The last Papal intrigue occurred in 1854, when Pius IX requested the Duke of Tuscany to invade San Marino due to its harboring of Italian patriots and "liberals." The strongest supporter of the Papal States, Louis Napoleon (III), however, warned the pope not to covet San Marino, echoing the sentiments his uncle had for the "archaic" republic. Needing the support of the French army to resist his own amalgamation into Italy, the pope backed off.[11]

The new Kingdom of Italy, under King Victor Emmanuel II of the House of Savoy, recognized San Marino as an independent state in 1862. This treaty was revised in 1872. In one of history's ironies, the little enclave of San Marino survived while the expansive Papal States were incorporated into Italy. Only in 1929, with the signing of the Lateran Pact, was the sovereign State of Vatican City created for the pope.

Abraham Lincoln was made an honorary citizen of the Republic, to which the U.S. president replied that a "government founded on republican principles is capable of being so administered as to be secure and enduring," a phrase that was echoed soon after in his Gettysburg Address.[12]

The Twentieth and Twenty-First Centuries

The most characteristic feature of the Sammarinese government is the representative council, the *Arengo*. It is composed of the heads of household throughout
the city-state, exactly like the Roman Senate of which it is a direct descendent.
Later, as the population increased, the Arengo appointed a grand council to handle legislative matters. The Arengo still retains the right to amend the country's
statutes and to petition the heads of government. In 1906 the Arengo removed
the lifetime tenure of the council members and made their positions dependent
on election by the populace.

The council, known as the "Council Great and General," is composed of
sixty members with five year terms based on proportions. Unlike most other
European countries, all legislative, judicial, and executive power is held by the
council. It appoints two captains regent every six months, who serve as heads of
state, plus the Council of Twelve, Government Syndics, and Regency Inspec-
tors.[13] Since 1945 there has also been a State Congress, which serves as the operating government of the republic.   Ministries of foreign affairs, interior,
finance, commerce, environment, tourism, health, education, labor, and justice
are seated secretariats.

San Marino faced great outmigration and an economic depression in the late
nineteenth century, as thousands of Sammarinese left to find employment in
more industrialized regions. Many citizens of San Marino left for the cities of
Italy, others went to Greece, Germany, Austria, United States, Argentina, and
Uruguay. This continued into the 1970s. About one-third of San Marino descended people live outside of the country now.

San Marino was fortunate to remain neutral during World War I, while Italy
itself declared war on the Axis powers. As in Italy, fascism dominated the government of San Marino in the 1920s.

During the worldwide depression of the 1930s, San Marino took the opportunity to begin to transform its agrarian society. Much energy was focused on
infrastructure—a new railroad line was constructed, linking the country to the
Italian network; highways were similarly built. San Marino's isolation had
ended.

In June 1944, thinking the Germans had occupied the republic, the British
air force bombed San Marino. Sixty-three people died and the railroad to Rimini
was destroyed. The next month, however, German forces did arrive. An officer
appeared, demanding the requisition of two buildings to be converted into field
hospitals for wounded soldiers. The government immediately sent letters of
protest to Hitler, German foreign minister von Ribbentrop, and Mussolini. San
Marino's sovereignty was respected.[14] During the Battle of Rimini, San Marino
became a refuge for 100,000 people caught up in the conflict. The tiny population of fifteen thousand took care of the destitute.

The post-War world was a time of transition for San Marino. The republic became the first county in Western Europe to elect the Communist Party into power. They remained in control between 1945-1957, in a coalition with the Socialists. Soon after, the town of Rovereta, on the slopes of Monte Titano, was the scene of a civil war. The Rovereta Affair *(fatti di Rovereta)* began on 30 September 1957 when a right-wing syndicate began to occupy an abandoned industrial building there and set up a ruling cabinet to take over the government. They were supported by the Italian and American governments who were at odds with the governing fascists. The Italian *carabinieri* were sent in to protect the building. The ruling co-regents drafted an army in response. Ettori Sozzi, Commander of the Gendarmerie, was given full powers and ended the conflict between 8-10 October 1957. The provisional government triumphed over the fascists, and assumed leadership of the republic.

Women received the right to vote in San Marino in 1960. During the next decade women could stand for elective position. And in 1981, Maria Lea Pedini-Angelini became the first woman elected co-regent. Since this time there have been several women co-heads of state. To prevent young foreign women from acquiring San Marino citizenship by wedding elderly men, an anti-gold digger law was passed in 1999 that restricted the hiring of female domestic staff to women over fifty.[15]

Having been founded by monks, and fought over by bishops and popes for centuries, it is no great surprise that most residents are Roman Catholic. Like Andorra, there is no national see—the parishes of San Marino now fall within the neighboring Italian Diocese of Montefeltro, an ancient see first mentioned in the Donation of Constantine that conferred the Papal States upon the popes.[16] Like Andorra and Southern France, San Marino also has a Waldensian church. Jewish traditions are also continuing in the republic, having been a part of San Marino life for centuries.

San Marino's military is largely ceremonial, much like the Vatican's and Andorra's guard. The Crossbow Corps is an example. There are also the Noble Guard (Guard of the Council Great and General), the Guard of the Rock who patrol the Palazza Pubblico in their red and green uniforms, and the Company of Uniform Militia (which is the closest thing to an active and army defensive unit). A gendarmerie and a volunteer force round out the country's defenses.

Federico Fellini International Airport, shared with Rimini, is the major port of entry for the republic, located only about nine km from Monte Titano. The narrow-gauge electric railway that served the country until World War II has not been rebuilt.

In 1988 San Marino became a member of the European Council; in 1992 it became a full member of the United Nations. It presently has diplomatic relations with over 108 countries. And like the other microstates, it has agreed to bank procedures that lessen the perception of encouraging tax evasion. San Marino presently uses the euro—previously the Italian and Sammarinese *lira* were mutually exchangeable. The republic is not a member of the International Postal Union, so the stamps circulate only within the country or are sold to collectors.

San Marino is not a tax haven, and has VAT, corporate, and other taxes that are similar to Italy's. Over two million tourists visit the tiny state each year. San Marino has its own university. In 2008, the country was listed as a UNESCO World Heritage site.

San Marino now has a very high standard of living, with the annual per capital income being above $55,000. It has no national debt, and nearly 100 percent employment. These are characteristics of most of the other microstates of Europe as well, who have developed specialized service, industry, and trade niches in the larger economic community. There is an obvious correlation between continued existence and economic success. Being economically successful, it would seem, may be an enormous incentive to remain outside of larger, pluralistic states whose systemic problems of poverty, education, overpopulation, and medical care may seem impossible to solve.

Being founded as an early Christian community, San Marino existed as a refuge from a hostile, pagan Rome. It was a community before Constantine, before the seat of the Empire was moved to Byzantium, and long before the Papacy assumed dominance over Central Italy. This is the foundation of its national identity, and the reason it has insisted for seventeen hundred years that it is not now, nor ever has been, subject to the Bishop of Rome. That this ideal has prevailed through Sammarinese diplomacy rather than through violence is a testimony that nationalism and warfare are not inevitably paired. San Marino is also a strong example of the power of national identity to override many other considerations. Rather than joining the pan-Italy nationalist movement in the mid-nineteenth century, San Marino's ironic independence provided a refuge to Unificationists being trounced by Papal forces. And San Marino, despite appalling unemployment and poverty at the time, stayed out of the Italian union.

Notes

1. "San Marino history." http://www.sanmarinosite.com/eng/pcomunita.html (accessed 3/12/12).

2. "I leave you free from any other man."

3. "San Marino history."

4. *San Marino: Ancient Land of Liberty* (San Marino: Edition Souvenir SA International, n.d.), 73.

5. *San Marino: Ancient Land,* 4.

6. Peter De Rosa, *Vicars.* 108-110.

7. This duchy returned to France, where it was eventually recreated for the House of Grimaldi of Monaco. The title passed to Princess Charlotte, to her son Rainier III, and in 2005 to his son the current duke, Prince Albert II.

8. "History of San Marino. Napoleon." http:// www.Sanmarinosite.com (accessed 2/12/12).

9. "History of San Marino. From 1500 to beginning 1800." http:// www.Sanmarinosite.com (accessed 2/12/12).

10. "History of San Marino: 1800s to Garibaldi." www.Sanmarinosite.com (accessed 2/13/12).

11. *San Marino: Ancient Land,* 11.

12. "San Marino," *United States Diplomatic History.* U. S. Department of State. http://history.state.gov/countries/san-marino (accessed 4/25/12).

13. *San Marino: Ancient Land,* 14.

14. "Fascismo." http://www.storiaxxisecolo.it/fascismo/fascismo1c.html. (accessed 2/ 15/12).

15. Eccardt, *Secrets,* 65.

16. Charles Herbermann, ed. "Montefelto," *Catholic Encyclopedia* (New York: Robert Appleton Company, 1913).

Chapter Seven
State of Vatican City

At first glance, the State of Vatican City appears as a paradox. A central focus of twenty percent of the world's population is a mere 110 acres of gardens, churches, and palaces—an unlikely place for a country. It has no mountains, beaches, rivers, or lakes. More than many places described in this book, the Vatican expresses the central notion that the concept of nationhood is something more than "countryside," with cows, pastures, villages, and cities strewn over a certain landscape. The Egyptian obelisk, the great basilica with its dome, the colonnades, the walls and guards—the Vatican property is clearly set apart from Rome and the rest of Italy. The fact that the Vatican *appears* more of an imperial palace than a nation-state is telling, for it was designed exactly as the former. This apostolic palace and basilica of the Vicar of Christ on Earth represents, in timeless ideology, the heart of the Christian Roman Empire, the *axis mundi* of a universal and unified Christendom.

Well, that was the idea anyway. Through most of its sixteen hundred year history the state of the popes has been mired in controversy and warfare—hardly Christian values. And it very nearly disappeared in modern times: Initially after the unification of Italy in 1871 and the capitulation of Rome to King Victor Emmanuel II, the pope locked himself up in his palace, refusing to amalgamate the sanctuary of St. Peter into the new secular kingdom. After all, the central offices of the Papacy could not fall into the indignity of becoming a faceless department of the Italian State, a grim, functional bureau not unlike the local DMV. It was not until 1929, (a mere eye blink in the long history of the Papal States) that a compromise was signed, allowing the State of the Vatican City to pop to the surface of modern international relations.

This short essay is not a history of the Papacy—it is merely a snapshot of the state that grew around the Bishop of Rome, a state that became vitally necessary to Western European civilization when Emperor Constantine decided to move the imperial capital to Byzantium in 328. During the Early Middle Ages (fifth to tenth centuries), the Papacy provided some unity and focus after the fall of the Western Empire. The Papacy provided a conduit by which leaders of the German tribes could acquire legitimacy and triumph over their rivals, and continue now into the third millennium.

A Pagan Past

It all started on Vatican Hill, just outside the walls of the ancient Roman metropolis. The surrounding flat plains, the *ager*, were a fetid marsh that climbed away from the Tiber to the summit of the Mons Vaticanus. Like holy places throughout the world, this site had already long been considered sacred and thus out of bounds to ordinary settlement. During the Etruscan period, the hill was the home of soothsayers, the *Vates*, who worshiped the god of prophecy, Vaticanus. Located outside of the city, it was also a burial ground.

The prophecy of the Sybil of Cumae assured Roman victory in the Punic Wars if the Phygian goddess Cybele, the *magna mater* of Asia Minor, was adopted. She was installed by the state at the Mons Palatinus and in other locations. In later centuries, an altar to Cybele was established at Mon Vaticanus, a wild place for wild rites.

Envision twelve leagues of eunuchs in diaphanous gowns moving slowly up this hill, each with their flaming orange torches in one hand and grossly shocking silver bowls of ram testicles in the other. Here in the dead of night, as frogs croaked among the sulfurous fumes seeping from the marsh, the pious hierophants offered their grisly gifts symbolizing fertility at the altar of the great Phrygian earth goddess, Cybele. The priests represent her unfortunate consort Attis, who castrated himself for his lover. Two thousand years later, white and gold mitered priests, some in scarlet, others in purple, all of them celibate, move in stately procession to the Christian altar under clouds of burning myrrh and frankincense. The great organ of St. Peter's rumbles an explosive F# discordance, echoing across the marble and porphyry floors, splitting the calm. The sibyls of Cumae and Erythae, the oracles of Delphi and Libya, and the prophets of the Old Testament created by Michelangelo look down from the ceiling of the Sistine Chapel. Little has changed on the Hill of Prophecy.

With the great expansion of Roman Empire, peoples from throughout Europe, North Africa, and Asia Minor flowed into Rome, bringing their own religions. The imperial system was broadly tolerant of the introduced religions, such as that of Cybele and her fertility mysteries, as long as their adherents in turn respected the state cult of the Trojan-inspired *Aeneid* legend of Rome. Furthermore, the earth goddess Cybele easily merged with the Greek Gaia of Delphic fame. However, contrary to the Delphic myth, rather than being impaled by the powers of the great Apollo, Cybele took her own son, Attis as lover. He went mad and castrated himself, but was eventually restored to wholeness by Zeus. The self-castration of Cybele's priests, or a more convenient offering of animal testicles, was the chief ritual of this rather ironic fertility ritual of Cybele.[1] Numerous Cybele altars were found on Vatican Hill, some remarkably late. One dated 19 July A.D. 374 was found under present-day St. Peter's Square. The marble altar is decorated with the sacred pine tree of Attis, with bull and ram motifs.[2]

Agrippina the Elder (14 B.C.-A.D. 33) is credited with draining the marshes of the Vatican and planting gardens atop the hill. The demented Emperor Gaius Caesar ("Caligula"—A.D. 12-41) initiated construction of a circus at the foot of the hill in the year 40, which was completed by his successor Nero. The Circus Gai et Neronis was decorated with an obelisk taken from Heliopolis in Egypt and installed on the *spina* of the racetrack. Christianity was introduced to Rome about this time—its first converts were Greek-speaking Jews. Like the cult of Cybele, it was first seen as just another Oriental religion.[3]

After the great Roman fire of 64, Nero placed the blame on Christians, and had many of them executed in his circus, burning many alive on crosses to provide a grisly illumination. It was during this appalling time that an elderly Jewish leader named Simon Peter Bar-Jona was removed from his prison and crucified upside down at Nero's circus. His body was removed to the small cemetery up the hill from the stadium, on the immediate northern side of the Via Cornelia. This tomb of the Apostle Peter was marked by a simple cupola by A.D. 160, joining the other tombs, the Cybele shrine, and other pagan altars scattered along the hillside, in long association with the prophecy, sacrifice, martyrdom, and darkness of Mons Vaticanus.

Since the early Christians were considered outlaws of the Empire, the early church leaders could not own land nor transfer it. Fledgling churches therefore were temporary affairs, usually formed simply by congregations who met in the homes of well-to-do Roman citizens. These wealthy patrons, however, might hold title to properties in custody for the establishment of the first churches. This form of tenure was still followed when Constantine lifted the ban on Christians.[4]

Imperial Christianity

Constantine was greatly influenced by the Christian piety of his mother Helena and his own Christian-inspired victory during the battle of the Milvian Bridge against rival Maxentius in 312.[5] The Holy Cross with the motto, *In hoc signo,* was seen surrounding the sun by the emperor on that day. A doubly auspicious sign, the sun was a symbol of both the Roman emperor (as identified with the Graeco-Roman god Helios-Apollo Phoebus) and Christ. It was clearly a new direction for the imperial system. Rather than state-sponsored paganism, freedom of religion was decreed throughout the empire with Constantine's Edict of Milan. In the spirit of the new relationship with Christianity, the emperor donated the palace of the Lateran to the bishop of Rome, which was followed by the construction of the great basilica of St. John Lateran. This church remains the mother-church of the Catholic faith and has extra-territorial status as part of the Holy See.

Inspired by his mother Helena, Constantine began construction of another basilica at the sites of Calvary and the adjacent Holy Sepulchre in Jerusalem. Here he installed the True Cross, recently rediscovered by Empress Helena. In Rome, he replaced the simple cupola on Vatican Hill built over the tomb of St. Peter with a large basilica. He had partially leveled the hill, inevitably exposing other tombs and displacing some pagan altars. Often, the tops of tombs and other structures were merely clipped off and filled on the sides to level the site, thus setting up a treasure house of fourth century archaeological remains for future excavations. The building site was designed to have the extant tomb of St. Peter directly in the center. The flattened top of Vatican Hill was adjacent to the north. The A.D. 326 basilica of St. Peter's was built with a rag-tag assortment of columns and capitals scavenged from pagan temples around the city. The southern colonnades were placed directly on top of the extant northern stadium walls of the Circus, which caused instability problems in later years (see photographs).

In another part of town, the great basilica of St. Mary Major was built over another temple of Cybele. Under Constantine, the Christian Church began acquiring other properties in Rome and throughout Latium—this property was the nucleus of the Papal States. The first known palace in association with St. Peter's Basilica was built by Pope Symmachus (r. 498-514).

When the Christians were first tolerated by Constantine, the Bishop of Rome was but one among other religious heads in the imperial capital, all of whom were by law subordinate to the emperor. The pope assumed the office of *pontifex maximus*, at first only a high officer of state responsible for religion.[6] It was the emperor who was head of state and above the high priest of the state religion, regardless of who was in the pantheon. This religious aspect was a vestige of the sacred nature of the old Roman *rex*.

When Constantine left for Byzantium in 330, he created a tremendous power vacuum in Rome, one that would be increasingly filed by the Christian bishop, the pope. Constantine even allegedly took the venerable holy of holies, the Palladium. This was the ancient wooden statue (*xoanon*) of Pallas Athena that Odysseus and Diomedes stole from the citadel of Troy and had been taken to the future site of Rome by Aeneas.[7] The Palladium fell from heaven to safeguard the establishment of Troy, and was transferred to Rome. For centuries this most sacred object, which was necessary for the eternal safety of the empire, was kept at the Temple of Vesta. The emperor placed it in a sanctuary at the base of the Column of Constantine, symbolizing the transfer of imperial authority to Byzantium. Back in Rome, the Church adopted Roman law for the development of its own code, the Canon Law. The Roman Church is the last surviving institution from the ancient Roman Empire.

With the proliferation of cults and various points of interpretation even within the Christian Church, it was clear to Constantine that a systematic codification of the faith was needed. The great emperor called together three hundred Christian bishops to Nicaea in 325—this was the first great ecumenical council.

Pointedly, Pope Sylvester did not attend—the emperor presided, cloaked in purple and smothered with jewels. The emperor, rather than the pope, thus provided the leadership necessary to formulate Christianity as an instrument of state. More and more, Christianity became the route to power in the empire, the old gods being increasingly relegated to the superstitions of old women and ignorant peasants, the "pagans." On Vatican Hill, however, the eerie rites of Cybele and other pagan cults continued side by side with those of the Christian priests at St. Peter's for generations.

By A.D. 374, however, time was running out for the polytheistic cult of the state. Soon, Christianity would become the sole state religion of the Roman Empire, although to his dying day Constantine kept erecting pagan temples in Byzantium, his new capital on the Bosporus Straits. Much of this was a political expedient.

Finally in 380, the Emperor Valentinian was convinced by Bishop Ambrose of Milan to withdraw state support for pagan worship entirely. Christianity was declared the official religion of state. Valentinian's successor Theodosius continued the systematic process—the golden statue of Victory was removed from the Senate; the oracle at Delphi was silenced; and amid the tears of the elderly virgin priestesses, the eternal flame in the Temple of Vesta was finally extinguished, in 390. The beautiful gods, Apollo with his golden hair, lyre, and lover Hephaestus; Diana the moon-huntress; the voluptuous Venus, ancestress of Aeneas and the Julians—all were given their marching orders. These were the gods of the Indo-Europeans who trudged westward in their oxcarts from the plains of the Caspian Sea thousands of years before, the gods who defeated Troy, annihilated Carthage, and crushed the pharaohs. For the next sixteen centuries and counting, all remaining pagan worshipers would be branded as witches, wizards, and New Agers wearing patchouli and selling mugwort tea at flea markets.

Only two years after the abandonment of the Greco-Roman gods, Pope Damasus began to stake out his theological and spiritual primacy in the establishment of a Christian state by stressing a Petrine text for the first time. By now the Papacy had become a wealthy landowner in and around Rome, and the pope could state with alacrity that, Peter, the apostle that preached to the Romans in their capital, was the chief follower of Christ. In apostolic succession, the pope of Rome was declared the primate of the city, and by extension, the world, *urb et orbi*.

Ascendency of the German Tribes

After Constantine's departure, the Roman Empire was quickly divided into a western section at Rome and an eastern section at Byzantium, now named Constantinople—after Theodosius it became permanent. But the change in management structure did little to strengthen the western empire. It would not be an easy business to rule a crumbling, weakening Rome, now being covetously eyed by the Germanic barbarians to the north. In fact, the Teutonic tribes themselves were being displaced by the Huns and Tartars from Eurasia. The Germans, many tribes long allied with Rome, were moving into northern Italy.

In 410 Rome was sacked by the Visigoths under their king Alaric, the first foreign conquest of the city in eight hundred years. The western empire crumbled quickly—Britain was captured by the Angles and Saxons; Spain was invaded by Vandals and Sueves; Gaul was overrun by Franks, Burgundians, and Goths. Die-hard pagans suggested it was the wrath of the deposed, olds gods.

In the mid-fifth century, the Mongol hordes appeared in the West under the leadership of the "Scourge of God," Attila the Hun. Having raised havoc in the provinces and Constantinople, Attila turned his attention to Rome. Fortunately for all Christendom, St. Leo the Great was pope at the time. With superhuman courage, he rode directly into the encampment of Attila and convinced the Huns into sparing the city. Attila returned to Hungary, and died a short time thereafter. The great act of boldness immensely enhanced the prestige of the Papacy.

The Western Empire lingered on, ruled by a succession of weak emperors until in 476, when during the reign of Romulus Augustulus the Senate gave the empire to Zeno in Constantinople, and the rule of Italy itself to the local chieftain Odoacer. The Eastern Empire would labor on for a thousand more years, leaving the Papacy as heir to Roman law and other institutions in the West. The Papacy is the only surviving institution of the Roman *imperium*, and with it, its claim to universal rule.

The bishop of Rome, for all his humility, assumed the role of *pontifex maximus* in the absence of the emperor—indeed, argued the Church, the pope possessed the sole *plentitudo protestatis* (fullness of power) of the Empire. The increasing wealth of the church helped support this position, and the seating of the bishop as the de facto secular ruler of central Italy.

However, the seeds of a new Christian empire had been planted among some of the German tribes. Its doctrinal foundations were established with the rise of the great Frankish king Clovis (Chlodwig) (481-511) of the Merovech family.[8] After the Huns were defeated in Gaul by the Roman general Aëtius in 451 at Chalons-sur-Marne, Clovis' father Childeric entered Paris, then under the influence of a holy woman now known as St. Geneviève. Her influence, combined with the Merovech's success, prefigured the Frankish adoption of Roman Christianity. Clovis' tale largely mimes the conversion of Constantine: Clovis' wife, Clothilde of Burgundy, was a devoted Roman Catholic, and made slow inroads in converting her husband. Like Constantine, the decisive moment for Clovis came in war. Sensing imminent defeat in battle with the Alemanni near Cologne, the Frankish leader made a pact with Jesus that if he obtained victory, he would be baptized: "Christ, whom Clothilde calls the true God, I have called on my own gods, and they help me not! Send help, and I will own Thy name."[9] The king won the battle. Clovis, like Constantine, was predisposed to accepting and understanding a bit of Christianity, in this case through his wife. Many of the Franks themselves were already Christian, but of the Arian heresy. Clovis would bring them into the orthodox Roman fold and change the course of western Christendom.

While Pope Gregory was opposed to this new manifestation of Christian royalty, Clovis had established something entirely new to Western Europe. It was not a mere reproduction of the Constantinian miracle—rather his actions alluded to the divine appointment and anointing of Old Testament kings. The holy oil of Clovis' coronation replicated Samuel's anointing of David, as well as Solomon's unction at the hands of Zadok the priest. In fact, Clovis' elevation was an apotheosis and metaphorical of Christ Himself. According to the legend, when Clovis was baptized on Christmas day 506, the Holy Spirit itself descended as a dove from heaven bringing the holy chrism, in the manner that Jesus was baptized and initiated into His sacred ministry. The Holy Ghost also carried a lily, a sign of the Trinity. The heavenly blue banner of the French monarchy was thereafter strewn gold *fleurs de lis,* a sign of the Trinity.

Clovis and all his descendents were from that point empowered by Divine Right with a full panoply of mystical powers, including the healing touch for curing scrofula (a tuberculosis). Rather than being a Roman emperor who was divine in his own right, the new universal ruler served in Christ's stead on earth, and ruled by His right. The great historian Gregory of Tours (b. 539) called Clovis the New Constantine.[10]

The sacred chrism, another *acheiropoieton* not made by the hand of man, provided legitimacy to a forming nation-state of France, which France's neighbors, regardless of their political achievements, did not possess. The oil brought forth by the dove was the new Palladium, the source of all legitimacy. It was to serve as the model of absolute monarchy in Western Europe until the Enlightenment. A special relationship between the Most Christian King of the Franks and the Roman Church was established and served until the very end of the French monarchy, in fact to Napoleon III, whose defense of Papal rights probably cost him his throne in 1871.

The action of Clovis' baptism had profound significance in the transformation of the ghostly western empire from a Roman to a German one. While Constantine was consecrated by St. Sylvester, and later Charlemagne by Pope Leo, throughout the long history of the West, only Christ and Clovis are witnessed as being anointed by a literal epiphany of the Holy Spirit. The "Divine Right" of all European monarchs has its origin in the anointing of Clovis. More than any other action, the baptism symbolized the fusion of Greco-Roman, Germanic, and Judeo-Christian worlds in a new concept of universal empire. The Sacred Ampulla itself became among the most holy relics of the French monarchy, securing for the king the style "Most Christian" and "Eldest Son of the Church" until the very end of the *Ancien Régime.*[11] The French monarchy had become one of the great pillars of the Papacy.

Clovis' embracing of orthodox Roman Catholicism was a severe blow to the Arianism of Gaul. The Frankish king's profession helped establish the primacy of the Bishop of Rome in matters Christian. The miraculous materialization of the Holy Chrism at Clovis' investiture helped legitimate the West in opposition to the "error-ridden" Christian emperors of the East as well as the Arians. These events prefigure the Great Schism five hundred years later, which was to remove the Eastern Church from its pre-eminent position, one which theoretically had maintained a continuity of Roman Christian legitimacy from the times of Constantine.

Of course Clovis' conversion did not sit well with the *porphyrogénnētos* emperors at Constantinople, those "born in the purple." The Greek imperial government engaged in a war for the re-conquest of Italy throughout the sixth century, most forcefully by Emperor Zeno under the Gothic general Theodoric. The empire used Gothic tribes to fight one another. The Goths were successful against the Visigoths under Odoacer. Further energy and resources were poured in by Emperor Justinian, whose troops finally threw the Ostrogoths out of Italy at the decisive Battle of Mount Vesuvius in 553.

However, the war for reclaiming Italy for the Eastern Empire had worn down the people and the land, fostering the occupation of northern Italy by the Germanic Lombards ("Long Beards") from the Baltic coast within a few years after the Battle of Vesuvius. At the close of the sixth century, Byzantine authority was confined to a narrow strip of land extending from Ravenna on the east to Rome and Naples on the west, known as the Exarchate of Ravenna.

The Rise of the Papal States

As Greco-Roman imperial power weakened further, the Papacy rushed in to assume an ever-increasing role in defending Rome, its estates, and its spiritual authority against the Lombards. Fortunately, history's greatest pope, St. Gregory the Great (590-604) was at the helm of the Church. With the eastern empire's influence largely confined to the central portion of Italy's east coast, Gregory began to assume the ruling authority in what had been the Byzantine Duchy of Rome, which was essentially congruent with ancient Latium. It became the first papal state. The power of the popes, their popularity, and their wealth, enabled the bishops of Rome to increasingly defy Constantinople. They used the *plentitudo protestatis* in the absence of effective secular imperial rule. Quickly their powers increased. By the eight century, Pope Gregory II was even able to excommunicate the Byzantine Emperor Leo III.

In reality, the popes played a careful game of balance between the powers of Constantinople, Rome, and the Lombards. By 728 a boundary between Lombard and Papal claims was drawn up between Lombard king Liutprand and Pope Gregory II. It was known as the Donation of Sutri.[12] The Greek Exarchate of Ravenna, excommunicated and impotent, finally succumbed to the Lombards in 751, cutting Rome completely off from the Eastern Empire. The Papacy rightly decided that they could not defend their interests in Italy without the support of the more "reasonable" Germanic tribes. Building upon the lessons of *realpolitik* of his predecessors, Pope Stephen III began to court the current Frankish ruler, Pippin the Younger (Pepin III Carling), in 753. Pepin, the mayor of the palace under the weakening Merovech kings, had become the effective ruler of the Frankish kingdom. Stephen even traveled to Paris to beseech the new power to help him save the theocracy of Sts. Peter and Paul and the great city of Rome. He anointed and appointed Pepin and his sons, Carl and Carloman, as rulers of the Franks and patricians of Rome at the Abby of St. Denis outside of Paris.

At St. Denis, Pope Stephen showed King Pepin a seemingly ancient, secret document. Dated 30 March 315, and apparently signed by Constantine the Great himself, it granted to Pope St. Sylvester I and his successors rule over the entire Church, including the patriarchates of Antioch, Alexandria, Constantinople, and Jerusalem, and "all provinces and palaces and districts of the city of Rome and Italy and of the regions of the west."[13] In all matters, the pope was to be superior of the emperor, continued the document, as Christ, through the pope, had cured Constantine of leprosy. While this document, the "Donation of Constantine," was much later proved to be a notorious forgery,[14] it nevertheless had a profound effect at the time. Pepin marched his armies south in 754 and 756, defeated Lombard king Astolfo, and redeemed the promised lands for the pope. These were essentially the remains of the Exarchate of Ravenna. While the Donation of Constantine was disingenuous, it resulted in a real contribution by the king Pepin III—the pope became an independent, temporal ruler at the hand of the king of the Franks.

After the death of Pepin III and his son Carloman, Pepin's younger son Carl, known eventually as the Great, was enthroned as king of the Franks. He attacked the pagan chief Witikind of the Saxons, and in the subsequent victory of 785, forced Witikind to repudiate Odin and consent to be baptized. Charlemagne then made him duke of Saxony, one of the original core duchies of the precipitating eastern Germanic empire. The Frisian and Bavarian tribes followed suit. In 775 he had entered Italy and defeated the Lombard king Deiderio, assuming the Lombardic title for himself. With this victory, Charlemagne expanded the papal properties beyond the Duchy of Rome to include Ravenna, the Pentapolis, part of Benevento, Tuscany, Corsica, Lombardy, and several Italian cities by 781. Thus was established the several Papal States that were to endure for a millennium.

In gratitude for the gifts bestowed upon the Church, Pope Leo III provided the Frankish king with the supreme honor. On Christmas Day, 800, while Carl was kneeling at prayer upon the great circle of porphyry at St. Peter's basilica, the pope placed a crown upon his head, proclaiming the new "Augustus Romanorum." The pope had previous anointed two of Charlemagne's sons, Carl and Lodwig, to be kings of Lombardy and Aquitania, respectively.

In the next few generations, the Carlings suffered greatly under the invasions of the Vikings, the men of the North (Normans). The dynasty split and ultimately was replaced by other dynasties in both the German and French realms. The weakened Carlings settled in the third kingdom, Lotharingia or Lorraine, where they or their nobles continued to rule for the next eight hundred years. The Netherlands, Belgium, Luxembourg, Switzerland, Liechtenstein, the provinces of Burgundy, Lorraine, Lombardy, and Provence are all remnants of this ghostly central Germanic kingdom.

In hitching its fortunes to the rising star of the Germanic empire, the Papacy acquired a status that could not have been anticipated under Constantine. With the crowning of Charlemagne, Christianity was now bolstered by two swords, the secular and the ecclesiastic, in a mystical union under One God, One Rule for all of Europe, if not the world. The Holy Roman Empire illuminated the Middle Ages, the Renaissance, and the Enlightenment for a thousand years.

Unity was not to last. The split between the priestly and the secular powers developed slowly at first. The ghost of the ancient Roman Empire was still strong, and the Church was still seen as an organ of the state from the imperial point of view. Quite an opposite trend was being constructed by the Papacy in Rome. Having held the burden of protecting the Roman province for so long, the Papacy had developed a certain competency in dealing with affairs of state and had become a secular power in its own right. This would rather inevitably lead to conflict with other secular powers in Europe, especially at the top with the German emperor.

The pacts made with Pepin and Charlemagne and the popes were reconfirmed in the *Diploma Ottonianum* of 962 between Pope John XII and the Saxon king Otto I of the Germans. Otto was destined to become a great king, having routed the Huns decisively at the battle of Augsburg in 955 and united the powerful German dukes behind him. Now by far the greatest leader in all Europe, he yearned for the sacred anointing that had been performed for his ancestor in Rome—he wished to revive the Christian empire of Charlemagne, especially since the Carlings were out of the way.

Such was Otto's popularity that the very identity of the German nation could be said to have formed with him. Perhaps more importantly, the pope needed him. The young pope, all of twenty-five years old, had lost the war with Pandulf of Capua, and other lands had been occupied by Berengar of Ivrea, an old Lombard noble. John XII, who was elected pope at sweet sixteen, a youthful gambler and rambunctious libertine, summoned Otto to rescue him, as Charlemagne had with Leo III a century and a half before. The forces of Berengar were casually pushed aside by the advancing Otto.

On 2 February, 961, Otto entered Rome. He was barely tolerated by the Romans of long memory, this representative of the "barbarous" Germans. At St. Peter's Basilica Otto swore an oath to support the pope, issue no decrees without papal consent, and defend the patrimony of St. Peter. The next day the emperor issued the famous *Diploma Ottonianum* reconfirming the Donation of Pepin, codifying the relations between emperor and pope, and regularizing papal elections.[15] The emperor emerged with the privilege to confirm papal elections, a direct survival of the ancient Roman imperial rights. The two swords of Christ were to remain uneasily wedded for the next millennium.

When the peach fuzz-faced John placed the heavy crown upon Otto's head, the Holy Roman Empire of the German Nation was born. Yet it was different than the Frankish empire of Pepin and Charlemagne. Otto established the Kingdom of Germany as a hereditary state, in balance with the five core duchies of Franconia, Bavaria, Swabia, Saxony, and Thuringia. However, as portent for centuries of bickering to come, no sooner did Otto leave Rome that the Papal youth promised the imperial crown to Berengar.

This treachery led Otto back to Rome in 963, whereupon the emperor quickly convened a synod that deposed John. The erratic young man countered in poor Latin from his retreat in Tivoli, "if you do I excommunicate you by almighty God and you have no power to ordain no one or celebrate Mass."[16] The bishops responded that if John did not appear before them, it would be he who would be excommunicated. A few days later Otto secured the election of Pope Leo VIII. Otto marched back to Germany and John crawled back to Rome. Leo fled to Otto, who was occupied with battling Berengar's son Adalbert. But then hit the news that John had been killed in his lover's bed by a cuckold husband, and Leo's papal reign held. Thus, the great Christian empire was recreated.

Investiture Controversy

Perhaps the greatest unresolved issue that stemmed from the fall of Rome was the struggle of supremacy between civil and religious powers. The Bishop of Rome had since Constantine been an official of the Roman Empire, as *pontifex maximus*, head of the religious establishment. But as the empire departed Italy, it left the pope a secular leader as well. For centuries, the popes fought with kings and emperors for the right to consecrate bishops of their own choice, and thus to maintain local control and strengthen Christendom. Increased secularism after the eighteenth century finally began to separate church and state, but even contemporary social issues, like Right to Life, brings the issue to the forefront again. In a sense, the Investiture Controversy, as this struggle is called, is the basis upon which the popes have consistently demanded their own sovereignty, and thus the contemporary existence of the State of Vatican City.

Back in Germany around the turn of the second millennium, Saxon kings were succeeded by the Salian family of Hohenstauffen, whose power base had developed along the Rhine. The Hohenstauffen often treated the Papal States as an element of their domain. This did not set well in Rome, In 1075 Pope Gregory VII (a.k.a. Hildebrand) promulgated *Dictatus Papae*, which stated that the Roman church was established by God alone, that the sole power of empire was the pope, and that only he could appoint, depose, or assign clergy. This directly opposed the ancient theory of Divine Right from the Frankish monarchy of Clovis, which itself had been built on the position of the Roman emperor as head of state, the national cult, and on the Old Testament theology of the relationship between God, Christ, and the House of David. The Emperor Henry IV reacted strongly in a letter to Gregory: "I Henry, king by the grace of God, with all of my Bishops, say to you, come down, come down, and be damned throughout the ages."[17] Upon receipt, Gregory blithely had him excommunicated. Then, cutting a wide swath, the great pope deposed the emperor. The core dukes and other nobles, standing to benefit at the loss of central German administration and perhaps not wishing to burn in hell, supported the pope over the emperor.

The battle between pope and emperor faded with the extirpation of the Hohenstaufen dynasty, and left the Papacy in a strengthened position in Europe. By 1300, most of Italy, including the Papal realm, was essentially independent of German interference.

The rule of the popes increased as the influence of secular rulers decreased. In the eleventh century a reform movement within the Church ended most lay investiture of bishops. From now on, bishops owed their position to the pope, priests to bishops, in a diocesan hierarchy. Similarly, the pope would heretofore be chosen by a group of cardinals rather than by the Roman nobility. The Investiture Controversy was the most vociferous battle between pope and emperor in medieval Europe. It would result in a fifty-year civil war in Germany, lead in strong measure to the Protestant Reformation, which resulted in the atomization of the German nation until the reunification under Bismarck in the nineteenth century.

Between 1305 and 1378, the Roman popes ruled from Avignon in Provence. During this "Babylonian Captivity" they came under strong influence of the French kings. The Papal States in Italy remained under Papal control, however, and Avignon was annexed to this realm. It remained so even after the pope returned to Rome. It continued as an enclave of the Papal States within France until the French Revolution.

The Renaissance

The Renaissance saw a great expansion of papal territory and authority. Great wealth flowed into the coffers of the Church, allowing the pope to keep up with the Medici, Orsini, and other secular Italian dynasties in their patronage of the arts during the flowering of the Renaissance. Popes Julius II and Alexander VI Borgia notably added to the glory of the Papal edifice.

No more worldly pope could be dreamed of than Alexander VI. He lived openly with several of his many mistresses, who bore him sons and daughters who were recognized by their father, such as Cesare, who was appointed cardinal and the pope's captain general of the Papal armies, and Giovanni, who became Duke of Gandia, the family estate in Spain, and of Benevento, a microstate enclave surrounded by the Kingdom of Naples. Other family members received fiefs throughout the Papal States. Then there was the notorious daughter, Lucretia. Alexander is also remembered as the pope who divided the New World between Spain and Portugal, which he did in the Bull *Inter Caetera*. The Borgia papacy gained in power in direct proportion to a debasement of morals. Alexander, upon discovering that a certain cardinal had amassed a fortune, would concoct some reason to find offense, and subsequently confiscate the unfortunate cardinal's property. Rome was viewed throughout Europe as a cesspool of prostitutes, spies, thieves, and adventurers of all ilks. Niccolo Machiavelli's contemporary masterpiece *The Prince* found its inspiration from the corrupt reign of Alexander VI. Even the most loyal supporters of the Papacy, the Orsini and the Colonna, allied themselves against the Borgia debauchery. Despite the Papal highjinks, however, the world's newest Christian church would soon rise over Peter's ancient bones and the altars of Cybele.

A torturous decision was made by Alexander's successor, Julius II to dismantle the venerable Constantinian basilica of St. Peter and erect the largest church on earth on the site. During the long Avignon exile and the excesses of the Borgia family, the Vatican complex had fallen into great disrepair, especially the south side of the basilica that was built directly upon the walls of the Circus Gai et Neronis. If nothing else, the construction of a new basilica, the largest building ever conceived to that time, would be a bold statement of the power of the Holy See and the secular might of the Papal States.

Julius hired the finest artists of the day, including Bernini, Michelangelo Buonarote, and Raphael, and all would be on a most massive, even inhuman, scale. In 1513, Julius was succeeded by Leo X, of the great Medici family of Florence. Born Giovanni de Medici to Lorenzo the Magnificent and Clarice Orsini, the pope had been named a cardinal at the venerable age of thirteen. Rebuilding St. Peter's Basilica would severely strain even the abundant resources of Rome, the Papal States, and the Florentine Republic, to which Leo succeeded after the death of his father. And the capital campaign for the rebuilding of the basilica would have unanticipated results for all of Christianity.

The building of St. Peter's was the ignition point for centuries of smoldering resentment in other parts of Europe against the worldliness of the Papacy and the power of the popes. In calling for donations to the building fund throughout his flock, Leo was willing to grant an indulgence for those who contributed. This would remove some time spent in Purgatory for souls awaiting the move up to Heaven. Some thought this to be abusive of the line between spiritual and secular worlds, especially one German monk, Martin Luther. And so the Protestant Reformation and the Catholic Counter-Reformation were launched. In 1517 Luther published his *Ninety-five Theses*; in 1521 Leo published *Decet Romanum Pontificem* excommunicating Luther.

The Reformation, of course, severely divided the Universal Church. The Protestant movement was especially attractive to the northern tier of European states, including Germany, the Low Countries, Scandinavia, and England.

Many princes realized that with the Protestant faith, the king was again the head of church and state, as he had always been in the ancient Roman and Byzantine empires. The sacred chrism of Clovis overflowed. These lands won back the right of investiture once the pope had been dismissed. Here, the Reformation served a different kind of absolutism.

In Rome, as elsewhere in Europe, the Counter-reformation was also a feverish time of reform, artistic creativity, and rebirth—the Renaissance. Despite the loss of the northern realms, the Church was confident, so much so that an appreciation for Classical forms was embraced. Artists and sculptors dared to show the naked human body for the first time since Valerian closed the ancient Roman temples a thousand years before. The Renaissance became the springtime of the Modern Age.

The Papal States reached their greatest extent in the seventeenth century soon after the new St. Peter's Basilica was completed. At that time, in addition to the old Duchy of Rome and Latium, the Papal States included the Duchy of Benevento, Umbria, the Marche, and the *legations* of Ravenna, Ferrera, Bologna, and Pontecorvo. Enclaves in France included Comtat Venaissin and Avignon.

A primary symbol of the power of the Papacy was illustrated in the Papal tiara, which was used in some form for at least a thousand years, in fact down to the reign of Paul VI. Its symbolism is unclear: in its triple form it perhaps represents the Holy Trinity; it also may refer to the three dominions of heaven, earth, and hell. But the most logical explanation comes from the words of the Papal Coronation itself. As the senior cardinal-protodeacon places the beehive-shaped crown upon the pope's head, he intones a triple *magisterium*:

> *Accipe tiaram tribus coronis ornatam, et scias te esse patrem principum et regum, rectorem orbis in terra vicarium Salvatoris nostri Jesu Christi, cui est honor et gloria in saecula saeculorum* (Receive the tiara adorned with three crowns and know that thou art father of princes and kings, the ruler of the world on earth, the vicar of our Savior Jesus Christ, to whom is honor and glory through all ages).[18]

Aside from the coronation, the pope traditionally wore the tiara when giving his *Uri et Orbi* blessing and making the rare *ex cathedra* pronouncements, i.e. when speaking as universal sovereign.

End of the Papal States and Birth of Vatican City

The unification of Italy in the nineteenth century was a major turning point in the life of the Papacy, reducing the pope from ruler of the world to a mere sovereign of 110 acres (44 hectares). The Resurgence, *il Risorgimento*, was inspired by Enlightenment ideas, the French Revolution, and Napoleon, who proclaimed himself King of Italy and whose treatment of Pope Pius VI foreshadowed future

mistreatment of the Chruch. Among other things, the times set forth nationalistic goals that were notably anti-clerical. Many of the patchwork
Lombardic city-states of Italy were relegated to the Habsburg Empire after the
Congress of Vienna in 1815, which aggravated many Italians towards the
sentiments of unification. In general, the maintenance of microstates under
imperial and foreign domination was never popular. The Austro-Hungarian
Empire, under the leadership of Klemens von Metternich had been very harsh to
their Italian domains. Powerful nationalist leaders such as Giuseppe Mazzini and
Giuseppe Garibaldi, and monarchists like Count Cavour worked throughout the
early nineteenth century for the cause of unification. Furthermore, the Papal
States, existing as a belt across Italy's midriff, cut the prosperous north from the
populous south. Thoughts abounded at the time, ranging from creating a confederation of Italian states with the pope at its head to a secular republic. In almost every scenario, Rome, the historic center of the western world, would be
the capital of a unified state.

The state of the pope's realm (Figure 7.1) in the early nineteenth century
was that of a land dissatisfied during these times of the great Enlightenment.
Absolutism in the era of a perceived rebirth of liberty was not a popular stance
for any government, much less of the twin powers of the pope, both secular ruler
and absolute curator of souls. Much of the states' budget went to charitable activities of the Holy See, while infrastructure, such as road repair and other public
works often went neglected. There has been little evidence that the Papal States
would transform into a nation-state, for the entire emphasis of the Papacy was
the management of the universal church over the ethnogenesis of the people it
ruled locally.

The pan-European revolts of 1848 were significant in the Italian states, and
resulted in the regional leaders granting constitutions in four instances. Even in
the Papal States, adamantly opposed to unification, Pope Pius IX promulgated
the first constitution. He was in fact a remarkable reformer. The Papal States
began to take on many of the characteristics of a modern state, but without the
ethnic component. Pius created a cabinet of ministers from each of the states, a
representative council, and fostered the development of militia in each of the
Papal territories. But liberals were dissatisfied by the fact that laymen were excluded in this government, and that the College of Cardinals had veto power
over any decision of the representative councils. It was not enough. When Pius'
last prime minister was assassinated in 1848, the pope became markedly less
interested in the voice of the people.

A decisive event in the unification occurred when Austria first lost control
of Venice. At that time, unification hero Daniele Manin was declared president
of the Republic of San Marcos at Venice. Then the winds shifted when Sardi-
nian and Piedmont King Charles Albert was defeated, ceding Lombardy and
Venice to the Austrians. San Marino remained a haven for *risorgimentiste* despite being surrounded by the House of Savoy.

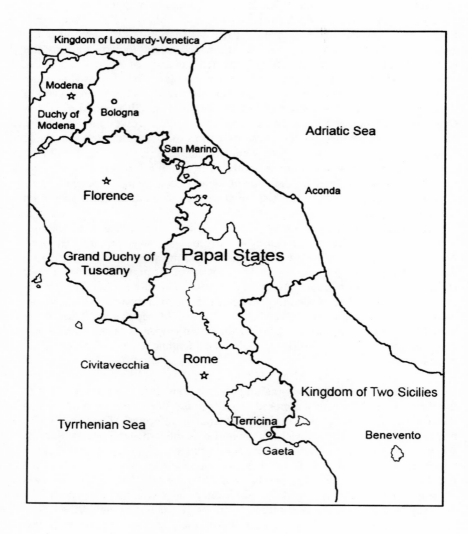

Kingdom of Lombardy-Venetica

Modena
Duchy of
Modena

Bologna

Adriatic Sea

San Marino

Aconda

Florence

Grand Duchy of
Tuscany

Papal States

Civitavecchia

Rome

Kingdom of Two Sicilies

Tyrrhenian Sea

Terricina

Benevento

Gaeta

Figure 7.1 Papal States in 1849

In 1849 Garibaldi managed to seize Rome and declare a republic. It was short-lived, as the French supported a restoration of the pope. Nevertheless, Pius IX abandoned the great Quirinal Palace for the Apostolic Palace at the Vatican. At the same time, the old King Charles Albert in Piedmont abdicated in favor of his son, Victor Emmanuel II. The new king's prime minister was the very able Count Camillo Benso Cavour. Through many battles, intrigues with Napoleon III, and other maneuvers, King Victor Emmanuel's kingdom grew and it was clear that the nucleus of the Unification lay with the House of Savoy. The southeastern Papal territories were gone by 1861, leaving just Rome and Latium the sole remaining possessions of the pope.

Not one to mince words, Garibaldi announced that the eventual capital of this new Kingdom of Italy would be Rome itself, the city of the popes. Pius IX reacted by dropping the nuclear bomb of universalist medieval weaponry: excommunication. Anyone who helped Garibaldi would be considered fallen from the Church, thus doomed to hell for all eternity. Catholics around the world rallied to the pope, sending him funds and volunteers to cobble together an army. The militia would be commanded by the French émigré, General Louis Lamoricière. Most of the Papal forces, in fact, were manned by foreign volunteers, as the papal nobility were largely disinclined to participate.

By 1861, almost all of Italy was united, save the truncated papal realm and Venetia in the northeast. Italy's first parliament met in Turin, its first acts to declare Victor Emmanuel II King of Italy and Rome the capital. The king, however, vacillated on any action—he was not willing to be seen as directly attacking the pope, which would of course be interpreted as an aggressive act against the Church. In August Garibaldi took actions in his own hands and attacked the volunteer papal forces. The battle was indecisive. The king, meanwhile, secretly negotiated with Napoleon III to remove the French emperor's troops from Rome, which he agreed to over the pope's vehement protest. Nevertheless, Pius had managed to build up his own troops during this time so the impact was minimal. A Palatine guard was established, again primarily with mercenaries. This is a clear sign the Papal States lacked a sense of national cohesion when the people and the nobles themselves would not defend the state.

During the Austro-Prussian war of 1866, Italy declared war on Austria. As a result of Prussia's superior forces and tactics, Austria was defeated and Italy won Venetia. Louis Napoleon reconsidered his support of the pope and sent a new French army to Rome. Napoleon III was very conscious that as the French sovereign, he remained the Most Christian of kings, successor of Charlemagne and Clovis, and had to defend the pope. The French Army remained effective in holding back Garibaldi until the onset of the Franco-Prussian War of 1870, when it had to be withdrawn. Victor Emmanuel waited until Napoleon III was completely defeated at Sedan and deposed soon afterward. The Italian king then sent a letter to Pius IX asking that Italian troops be allowed to peacefully enter Rome. The bombastic pope angrily denounced such a suggestion.

Events quickened. From April 1870 to October, the First Vatican Council was called to discuss the nature and constitution of the Church. Concerned primarily about maintaining the authority of the pope, the dogma of papal infallibility was passed by the Church's bishops and promulgated by Pius IX in *Pastor aeternus* in July. The concept had been used before, most notably in the proclamation of the Immaculate Conception of the Virgin Mary in 1854, *Ineffabilis Deus* by the Marianist Pius IX. In no uncertain language the document of 1870 defined the relationship of the pope to his Church:

> We teach and define that it is a dogma Divinely revealed that the Roman pontiff when he speaks *ex cathedra*, that is when in discharge of the office of pastor and doctor of all Christians, by virtue of his supreme Apostolic authority, he defines a doctrine regarding faith or morals to be held by the universal Church, by the Divine assistance promised to him in Blessed Peter, is possessed of that infallibility with which the Divine Redeemer willed that his Church should be endowed in defining doctrine regarding faith or morals, and that therefore such definitions of the Roman pontiff are of themselves and not from the consent of the Church irreformable.

> So then, should anyone, which God forbid, have the temerity to reject this definition of ours: let him be anathema.[19]

Soon afterward, the combined forces of the Kingdom of Italy set siege to the pope's capital.

On 20 September 1870, the Italian army breeched the Aurelian Walls at Porta Pia and entered Rome. Papal forces gave resistance, albeit token, until the very end. Rome and Latium were promptly annexed to the kingdom, an act which was ratified by a plebiscite three weeks later. The population of the Papal States and Rome had grown weary of papal rule and the absolutism it entailed, despite the reforms of Pius IX. Despite a thousand years of control by the apostolic successors of St. Peter, the people saw themselves as "Italians." Infallibility in the Age of Reason seemed to be too radical of an opposition to bridge for most Romans and the subjects of the Papal States.

Initially the king offered the deeply offended pope the Leonine City (the west bank of the Tiber flowing through Rome), the Lateran basilica and palace, and Castel Gandolfo, as his seat of sovereignty in the Law of the Guarantees. It also included a generous pension of over three million *lira*.[20] Pius again refused, considering such a move to show recognition of the agents that had destroyed the Church's ancient prerogatives in Rome and Central Italy. He then excommunicated King Victor Emmanuel and declared the kingdom illegitimate.

Now branded an apostate, Victor Emmanuel was still careful not to offend the pope further, a hopeless stand. He was reluctant to move into the traditional palace of the popes, the Quirinal, which had been unoccupied since the uprisings of 1848. Finally the government convinced the king to assume residence, and asked the pope for the keys. Pius reportedly said:

> Whom do these thieves think they are kidding asking for the keys to open the door? Let them knock it down if they like. Bonaparte's soldiers, when they wanted to seize Pius VI, came through the window, but even they did not have the effrontery to ask for the keys.[21]

The Italian government called a locksmith.

The pope's adamancy about his sovereignty stemmed from the fact that the Law of the Guarantees did not ensure that the popes' decisions would be clearly interpreted by the worldwide Christian community to be free from this or any other regional political influence. Furthermore the House of Savoy's Kingdom of Italy was a secular power. Total sovereignty was needed to assure that the spiritual dimension of life, i.e. Christianity, was forever free from domination by any civil authority. It was the same general argument as that between the Holy Roman emperors and the popes many centuries before. The "Roman Question" was really the old Investiture Controversy in a different place and time, a structural confrontation of the *longue durée*.

With the capitulation of Rome and the move of the pope to the Vatican, the massive gates of the Apostolic Palace and the great doors of St. Peter's Basilica were closed. The Papal nobility, whose titles originated from the pope as sovereign of the Papal States, boarded up their stately *palazzos* and villas, earning their nickname "Black" for their mourning of the pope's deposition. For fifty-nine years the popes went into self-imposed house exile, becoming "prisoners in the Vatican," and never leaving the holy hill. To do so would have acknowledged the legitimacy of the new Kingdom of Italy over Rome and its capture of the Papal States, considered the rightful property of the Church.

During this era, between the capture of Rome on 20 September 1870 to the signing of the Lateran Treaty on 11 February 1929, four popes would enter and die in the Vatican Palaces, having never officially left (Pius XI, the fifth "prisoner," died in 1939 in the new State of Vatican City).

During this period of righteous indignation, the lonely pope never appeared in St. Peter's Square, nor gave the *Urbi et Orbi* blessing to the city. He did appear occasionally from a balcony facing an inner courtyard or inside the Basilica. International diplomats continued relations with the Papacy, but through the Holy See, which was seen as an entity of international law and not dependent on the pope, who was now a subject of the Kingdom of Italy since he did not agree to the Law of Guarantees. This aspect of international relations has not changed—diplomats are still accredited to the Holy See rather than to Vatican City.

The Blessed Pius IX, the last monarch of the Papal States and the longest ruling pope save St. Peter himself, died of a heart attack induced by an epileptic seizure. He was succeeded by the wiry Leo XIII in 1878. Whereas Pius was the great statesman, Leo was the erudite theologian, an apt profession for the next prisoner in the Vatican. By all accounts his reign was successful, and brought many Marian practices to the center of the Church. Good-natured and curious about the modern world, he was the first pope to have his voice recorded and to appear in a moving picture. But he was as adamant as Pius IX about reclaiming his rightful sovereignty.

Pope St. Pius X succeeded Leo in 1904. His election was complicated by the archaic use of the imperial veto (*jus exclusivae*), during the second ballot. Emperor Franz-Joseph of Austria-Hungary had inherited the privilege from the Holy Roman Empire (an old Investiture Controversy concession) and unexpectedly used it—for the last time. The cardinals were appalled, but on the fifth ballot the new Pius X won.

The vexing "Roman Question" was not settled until the Vatican Pact of 1929, signed by Benito Mussolini for King Victor Emmanuel III, and Pietro Gasparri, Cardinal Secretary of State for Pius XI. Negotiations had labored on over three years. The primary lawyer for the pope was Francesco Pacelli, the elder brother of Eugenio, the future Pius XII. The Pacellis were among the most dedicated of the papal nobility. The Lateran Pact became actually less of a financial obligation for Italy as was offered in the Law of the Guarantees. The Lateran Treaty accepted the notion of complete independence for the Holy See, as seen in the establishment of the State of the Vatican City. The agreement also made Catholicism the state religion of Italy, and Mussolini had to agree to forbid divorce. The kingdom made a financial settlement with the pope for the loss of the Papal States. On the other side of the bargain, the new Vatican City also was sworn to perpetual neutrality. In gratitude for the long and difficult negotiations, Francesco was made a papal marquis; the king made him a prince; his brother Eugenio Pacelli was installed as the new Cardinal Secretary of State. The State of Vatican City remains essentially the same since the Lateran Pact.

The Holy See, in contrast to the modern State of Vatican City, is an international entity representing the 1.2 billion-strong worldwide Church. It represents the long-accepted sovereignty of the Papacy in regards to the operation of the Apostolic See of St. Peter, which had been granted by Constantine during Roman imperial days. Although both entities issue passports, the Holy See is not a state itself. The Holy See's Secretary of State is the foreign minister for the Vatican.

Mussolini was well pleased with the success of the Lateran accords, and commissioned the building of the Via della Conciliazione from St. Peter's Square to the Tiber, roughly along the ancient Via Cornelia. This opened up the approach to the Vatican to the City of Rome. The pope was now free to visit his cathedral, the Archibasillica of St. John Lateran, and his summer palace at Castel Gandolfo.

Remaining neutral during World War II, the Holy See allowed the Allies to be diplomatically represented in Rome. After Italy went to the Allied side in 1943, Germany was represented though papal auspices in Rome. As a result of Pius XII's skillful diplomacy, Rome was only bombed twice, by the Americans.

The pope continues to have absolute authority over all executive, legislative, and judicial functions of state. On an everyday basis, however, the executive is handled by the president of the Pontifical Commission for Vatican City State, a body of appointed cardinals that comprise the legislature. Giovanni Cardinal Lajolo presently serves as president. The office of the Cardinal Camerlengo (chamberlain) presides over the Apostolic Camera, which controls the property of the state and is especially important during an interregnum. It is the Camerlengo that taps a newly dead pope with a silver hammer to validate his passing, and removes and destroys the papal ring to prevent any illegal authorizations. The Camerlengo runs the government during a papal vacancy, and reports to the College of Cardinals. The current (2012) holder is Tarcisio Cardinal Bertone, who is also Secretary of State.

The tiny state has a trial judge, a tribunal, appellate court, and a supreme court. However, the pope at any time can assume any aspect of the judiciary, legislative, or executive bodies. The population demographics of the Vatican are of course much different than the Papal States. The states had regular households with women and children, whereas much of the Vatican's population could be said to derive from apostolic succession and appointment rather than biological reproduction. There are many Roman workers in the Vatican that return home to their families at night of course. The officers of the Swiss Guard are allowed to marry and have families, but their dependents remain Swiss citizens. These families may live in the Vatican, but the male children have to leave by age twenty-five, or upon marriage for girls. This helps assure that the Vatican will not develop a native population.[22]

Like SMOM, the Vatican has observer status at the UN. It has not asked for full membership. The Vatican is a member of the European Union and Eurozone, and uses the euro as currency. Previously it issued its own *lira*; during the Papal States, it used *scudi* (as did SMOM). While Latin remains the official language of the Holy See, Italian is the authorized language of the Vatican City State.

The stipulations of the Lateran Treaty were rolled over into the new Italian constitution when that country became a republic in 1947. In 1984 the agreement was amended, ending official state support of the Church. In 2008, the Vatican, in conflict over Pro-life issues, ended its automatic support of all Italian laws.

Following the reforms of the second Vatican Council, Pope Paul VI disbanded both the Palatine and Noble guards and removed many of the privileges of the Papal nobility (much to their dismay). This was a further deconstruction of the worldly Papal States. In a similar vein of humility, Paul set aside the tiara, another symbol of monarchy. The sole remaining militia, the Swiss Guards, assumed many of the ceremonial functions of the Palatine and Noble commands, assisted as needed by the Vatican and Italian forces. The Governorate of the

Vatican City State oversees the police force, the *Corpo della Gendarmeria dello Stato della Città del Vaticano*.

As a state, the Vatican has a population of around 800. Its citizens use regular passports, while the Holy See issues only diplomatic ones. The Vatican issues postage stamps, and is a member of the International Postal Union. The Vatican State is supported primarily by Peter's Pence and two thousand years of accumulation of treasure, augmented by the sale of these stamps and coins, by admissions to the immense Vatican Museums, by the sale of tourist souvenirs, by the manufacture of mosaics, and by the fabrication of uniforms. It has its own bank, *Istituto per le Opere di Religione*, notable for having the only ATM machine with instructions in Latin.

The Vatican operates its own railway station, which was built, ironically, long after the demise of the Papal States. The tiny country has a helipad, but the primary airports for the pope are the two international airports of Rome. Vatican Radio, the Vatican Television Center, and *L'Osservatore Romano* are organs of the Holy See, not the Vatican City State.

A look at the extraterritorial properties outside of Vatican City helps clarify the fact that it is the Holy See rather than Vatican City that is the locus of papal sovereignty. In fact, more papal acreage exists outside of the Vatican than within. All four papal basilicas are extra-territorial: St. John Lateran and the Lateran Palace, St. Mary Major, St. Paul outside the Walls and its monastery, and of course St. Peter's. Other Roman territories of the Holy See include the Palace of St. Callixtus, buildings of the Sacred College of Propaganda Fide on Gianicolo Hill, the Pontifical North American College, the Bambino Gesu Hospital, the Palace of the Holy Twelve Apostles, Palace of the Church of San Carlo ai Catinari, the Palace of the Dataria, the Palace of the Cancelleria, the Palace of the Congregation for the Propaganda Fide at the Spanish Steps, the Palace of the Congregation for the Doctrine of the Faith at the Piazza San Pietro a Porta Cavalleggeri, the Palace of the Congregation for the Oriental Churches, the Palace of the Vicariato, the College Bellarmino, the Pontifical Gregorian University, the Biblical Institute, the Archaeological Institute, Oriental Institute, Lombard College, Russian College, the two Palaces of Sant'Apollinare, the House of Retreat for the clergy of Saints John and Paul, the Nympheum of Nero, and the Campo Santo Teutonico. Sovereignty outside of Rome is extended to the Pontifical Palace, Villa Barberini, and Villa Cybo at Castel Gandolfo. Acreage at Santa Maria di Galeria, site of the antennae of Radio Vatican is also extraterritorial. The regions of Castel Gandolfo and Santa Maria de Galeria alone are both larger than Vatican City. But the properties outside of the Vatican are only extraterritorial to the Holy See, not necessarily sovereign, as the Holy See is not a state. They are not enclaves of the State of Vatican City.

The pattern of discontiguous state properties is not, of course, merely a model formed by the Lateran Treaties. The tiny enclaves of Holy See property scattered about the Roman countryside are the direct descendents of the old Germanic Lombard "fortress and field system" that fractured Italy and Germany into tiny principalities over the centuries. Liechtenstein, Monaco, and San Marino are additional examples that survive today. But these states have no discontiguous territory.

In international law, extraterritoriality is a type of sovereignty, in so far that any action committed in such territories is not subject to the laws of the host country; but extraterritorial possessions are not necessarily components of a sovereign state, either. Extraterritoriality lies precisely on the boundary between statehood and non-statehood, as we have seen in the Order of Malta. One wonders why the Holy See, being a sovereign legal persona under international law, needs territory at all, as represented by the State of Vatican City. The question is just as valid for the Sovereign Order of Malta, whose relationship with the Republic of Italy is exactly parallel to the Vatican's.

Notes

1. Mary Beard, "The Roman and the Foreign: The Cult of the 'Great Mother' in Imperial Rome," *Shamanism, History, and the State*. Edited by Nicholas Thomas and Caroline Humphrey, (Ann Arbor, University of Michigan, 1994), 164–90.
2. "Altar dedicated to Cybele and Attis." *Vatican Museums*. http://mv.vatican.va/3_EN/pages/x-Schede/MGEs/MGEs_Sala16_03_040.html.
3. Rodolfo Lanciani. *Pagan and Christian Rome* (Boston and New York: Houghton, Mifflin and Company) and New York, 1892.
4. As mentioned previously, the early Christian Church of St. Sabina, built on the Aventine, was the home of a Roman matron, Sabina. The Villa Malta was established next to it.
5. De Rosa, *Vicars*, 35.
6. "Chief bridge builder," or engineer, who figuratively constructed a "stairway to the gods." Before the Republic, the king had assumed this sacred function.
7. "Palladium," *Greece Myth Index*. http://www.mythindex.com/greek-mythology/P/Palladium.html (accessed 8/3/12).
8. Marie Tanner, *Last Descendent of Aeneas* (New Haven: Yale University Press, 1993), 36-9.
9. Gene Gurney, *Kingdoms of Europe* (New York: Crown Publishers, 1982), 55.
10. Gregory of Tours, *Historia Francorum* (Harmondsworth: Penguin, 1974), 31.
11. The sacred phial and chrism, the palladium of the Frankish empire, was intact until it was smashed by the mob in the public square at Rheims in 1793, during the French Revolution. Some of the holy oil was recovered, however, and was used for the coronation of Charles X in 1830, the last Bourbon king of the senior line. A new reliquary had been constructed to house it, which remains in the Treasury Museum of Tau at Rheims. (See photo section).
12. www.romeartlover.it/Civita3.html (accessioned 4/1/12).
13. De Rosa, *Vicars* 41.
14. For example, it was written in a vernacular Latin, not classical Latin.
15. "Pope John XII," *New Advent Catholic Encyclopdeia*. http://www.newadvent.org/cathen/08426b.htm (accessed 8/3/12).

16. Luidprand of Cremona. *The Complete Works of Liudprand of Cremona*. Edited and translated by Paolo Squatriti. Chapter 13, *Antapodosis*. (Washington: D.C.: Catholic University of America Press, 2007 [ca. 960]).

17. Letter from Henry IV to Gregory VII, 24 January 1076. http://www.fordham.edu/halsall/source/henry4-to-g7a.html (accessed 2/12/12).

18. Francis Patrick Henrick, *The Primacy of the Apostolic See Vindicated* (Baltimore, London and Pittsburgh: John Murphy, 1857), 252. Also, according to the *Encyclopaedia Americana*, article "Tiara," the words are "*... scias te esse patrem, principem, et regem* (know that you are father, prince, and king).

19. "On the Infallible Teaching Authority of the Roman Pontiff. Decrees of the First Vatican Council." Session 4, 18 July 1870. Chapter 4 (9). *Papal Encyclicals Online.* http://www.papalencyclicals.net/Councils/ecum20.htm#Chapter%204.%20On%20the%20infallible%20teaching%20authority%20of%20the%20Roman%20pontiff (accessed 8/3/12).

20. David Kertzer, *Prisoner of the Vatican* (Boston, Houghton Mifflin, 2006), 45.

21. Kertzer, *Prisoner*,79-83.

22. Eccardt, *Secrets,* 63.

Chapter Eight
Principality of Monaco

Monaco is another vertical country where the residents spend more time riding elevators than their Ferraris. Perched on the cliffs where the Maritime Alps meet the sea, the tiny principality is the jewel of the Côte d'Azur. Its spectacular setting is reason enough for its natives to have fought hard to maintain its independence. For most of the twentieth century, Monaco, with its elite casino, its megaweathy residents, and its colorful ruling family, was known primarily through a tabloid lens. Cheap journalism has tainted the international image of this most intriguing sovereignty, a country certainly more demi-monde than all other microstates in Europe. At thirty-one thousand people (2011)[1] Monaco has nearly the same population as San Marino. However, the tiny principality is only two sq. km (0.76 sq. miles).

Of Ancient Times

Monaco is an ancient place, a small natural harbor along a rocky coast. Above the waters rises a flattened mesa, defendable on all sides and studded with caves and grottoes. This is Monaco-Ville, the old chateau. The caves of Balzi Rossi on the Italian border, now known as the Grimaldi Grotto, yielded Pleistocene mammals such as rhinoceros, elephant, reindeer, bear, as well as human remains, including a pre-Cro-Magnon group and a Cro-Magnon one, complete with associated artifacts. These were later supplemented by Holocene finds in the gardens of Saint Martin and in the grotto of the Observatory. From prehistoric times through the Phoenician era, Monaco was utilized as a shelter from the storms, "where neither the strength of the Eurus and the Zephyr does not reach."[2] Sometime in the sixth century B.C. the Phocaeans of Massalia (Marseilles), originally from Greek Anatolia, founded the colony of *Monikos*. The historian Diodorus Siculus and the geographer Strabon described the rock of Monaco and the hardy Ligurians who toiled there. The ancient trail between Italy and Spain ran along the coast, its construction and fortifications attributed to the hero Heracles (Hercules). Altars were thus dedicated to the Hero at great crossroads along the highway, but at the Rock of Monaco a Temple of Hercules was established, and the name Port Hercules was used throughout antiquity. The term Single One (*Monoeci*) or *Monoikos*, the Single House, refers to the uniqueness of Hercules, his temple, or the community living isolated around the Rock.

Monaco is located where the Maritime Alps meet the sea. The port was a useful one for the Oratelli people of Peille, who lived inland. In 43 B.C. Julius Caesar held up at Monaco awaiting Pompey before sailing to Greece. The entire Ligurian Coast was plunged into barbarian warfare and piracy after the fall of the Roman Empire in the fifth century. In A.D. 973 a certain Gibelin aided William, comte de Provence, to drive the Saracens out of the area. He was rewarded with the land that had been named for a dog: he became Gibelin de Grimaldi.

The legend of the servant Torpes, the dog Grimaud, and a rooster recalls a Christian martyr who died after refusing to renounce his religion at the insistence of his master, Emperor Nero. The emperor decapitated his Christian attendant and his head was tossed into the Arno. His body was placed in an old boat with a rooster and a dog, which had been placed there in order to nourish themselves on the saint's body. The boat floated towards Liguria and landed southwest of modern Nice. The body was founded to be miraculously untouched by both the rooster and the dog. Upon landing, the cock flew away towards the village later named Cogoline after it; the dog headed towards another village later named in its honor, Grimaud. The local people named their village in honor of the martyr Torpes, i.e. Saint-Tropez.[3]

Under Gibelin de Grimaldi, local inhabitants began to return to the coast and to Monaco. With the formation of the Holy Roman Empire, the unsure days of the Dark Ages were drawing to an end. Monaco soon struck out with its first taste of independence. Frederick Barbarossa's successor, Emperor Henry VI, gave Genoa the sovereignty of the entire Ligurian coast up to Monaco. In 1215 Genoese Ghibellines led by Fulco del Cassello laid the foundation stones for a fortress upon the rock of Monaco, marking the birth of the principality. The foundations serve as the base of today's Princely Palace. Ramparts were built around the fortress, completely encircling the rock. Land concessions and tax exemptions encouraged people to settle here.

During this time, however, the Grimaldis of Genoa were becoming a rival business and political family. They were descended from Otto Canella, a Consul in Genoa in 1133. Moreover, they were Guelphs, supporters of the pope against the Imperial Ghibellines. By 1270, Genoa was in a state of civil war between the Ghibellines and the Guelfs. In 1295, the Ghibellines took control of Genoa, forcing the Grimaldis into exile westward into Provence. Rainier Grimaldi became an admiral of France and died try to rid the coast of Genoese ships. With the rousing of a small army, his relation François Grimaldi succeeded in capturing the fortress of Monaco in 1297 by disguising himself as a Franciscan monk and passing around the guards. This action is memorialized in Monaco's coat of arms. Unfortunately, the family lost Monaco in 1301.[4] It was not until generation later that the Guelphs returned to power. In 1331, Charles Grimaldi occupied Monaco. In 1341, Charles received the possessions of the Spinola family at

Monaco, and purchased the adjacent lordships of Menton and Roquebrune (Figure 8.1).[5]

The family continued building a strong relationship with France, serving in the courts of Paris and of Provence. Rainier I was an admiral of France under Philip the Fair, King of France. Charles I was an officer at the Battle of Crecy of 1346. The Monégasques were continuing to develop an identity away from the Genovese and the other Ligurian Coast peoples. They continued to speak, however, a dialect of Ligurian from Genoa strongly influenced by the Occitan of Nice. Today, Monaco is the only country in the world that uses Monégasque as its national language.

John I, son of Rainer II, worked his entire life for the independence of Monaco, which was still considered a part of the Genoan realm. The succession passed through his granddaughter Claudine, who married Lambert of the Antibes branch of the Grimaldi family. Lambert was successful in achieving the recognition of independence of Monaco by Charles VIII of France and the Duke of Savoy around 1490.[6]

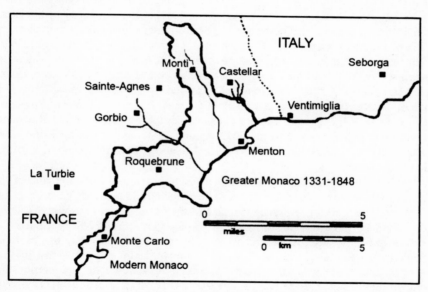

Figure 8.1 Greater Monaco

By 1506, the Grimaldi family, under Luciano, son of Claudine and Lambert, were well entrenched in the fortress, withstanding a four-month siege by a huge Genoan army. Subjected nevertheless to French sovereignty in 1509, they succeeded in wresting letters patent from Louis XII awarding the independence of Monaco with a perpetual treaty of alliance between the two states. Luciano was assassinated in 1523 by his cousin Bartholomew Doria. His successor, Honoré I, and the Regent Bishop Augustin, succeeded in alienating the French court. But these are defining moments for the European microstates: Bishop Augustin merely approached the Spanish Holy Roman Emperor Charles V, in a manner not unknown to the Andorrans, Knights of Malta, and the House of Liechtenstein in their nation-building efforts. Clearly, the Gueph/Ghibelline wars had ended, as the former Papal Grimaldi family made friendly overtures to the Imperial Court. This diplomacy resulted in the Treaties of Burgos and Tordesillas in 1524, which recognized the autonomy of the tiny state under the Empire. The Bishop of Grasse, Augustin Grimaldi, was ensconced as the head of government, in fief directly under the Emperor Charles V, in a manner not unlike that held by the Prince of Liechtenstein. Monaco thus became an imperial immediacy. The great emperor himself visited the chateau in 1529. A large Spanish garrison took up residence at the Rock.[7]

With the passing of Bishop Augustin, the regency of the state passed to Stephen Grimaldi for life. Eventually, Honoré I took up the reigns of rule. He was succeeded by his sons Charles II and Hercules. Their reigns were also filled with conflicts and intrigues, and Hercules was assassinated in 1604.[8]

Hercules' son Honoré II assumed the throne under the regency of his uncle, the Prince of Valdetare. The Prince Regent convinced his nephew to assume the title of Prince of Monaco in 1612, which was recognized by the Imperial Court. But fortunes were slowly beginning to change for the Empire, which was being eclipsed by the rise of the nation-states of France and England. Monaco wasted no time changing alliances: Honoré II, assisted by his cousin John Henry Grimaldi, Marquis of Courbons and Lord of Cagnes, and the governor of Provence, Marshal de Vitry, signed a treaty (1641) with the French Cardinal Richelieu, representing King Louis XIII in 1641.[9] Again, the sovereignty of the Principality was recognized. This reestablished cordial relations with the French Court that have remained to the present day.

The new relationship ushered in a French garrison at the command of the prince. It was soon standing face-to-face with the old Spanish garrison at the fortress of Monaco. The French troops and the Monégasques threw the Spanish out. Monaco gave up the lordships in Naples that were given by Charles V. France replaced these by the Duchy of Valentinois, the Viscounty of Charlat in Auvergne, the Marquisate of Baux, and the lordship of Sant-Rémy in Provence—known today as the French Lands. (The scourge of San Marino and many others lands, Cesare Borgia was the first Duke of Valentinois). Honoré II was received many times at the French Court. He was entertained by Cardinal Mazarin. Louis XIV became the godfather of his grandson, Prince Louis I.[10]

Prince Honoré II launched a building project that resulted in the construction of the South Wing of the Princely Palace, which houses the Grand Apartments. The prince amassed a collection of seven hundred paintings, great objects of furniture, silver, and tapestry.

When Honoré II died in 1662, he left a grandson, Louis, to succeed him. His son Hercules had died previously. Louis I married Catherine-Charlotte de Gramont. She founded the Convent of the Visitation in Monaco. The couple spent a considerable amount of time in the French Court. Catherine-Charlotte became Lady in Waiting to the Princess Palatine, while Prince Louis fought in the War of the United Provinces against England in battles in Flanders. When he returned to Monaco, King Louis XIV made him ambassador to the Holy See. The struggle over the Spanish Succession was beginning, and the king wished the support of the pope to ensure the appointment of the Dauphin to the throne on the passing of Charles II of Spain. Unfortunately, Prince Louis spent most of his House's fortune on maintaining his court in Rome.

Louis died in 1701 and was succeeded by his son Antoine, who by the life-style of his parents had spent much of his life in Paris. He was close to the Duc d'Orleans, future Regent of France. Antoine also served in the army as Colonel of the Soissor de Infantry, where he obtained the nickname "Goliath." Antoine married Marie de Lorraine, a noblewoman in the French Court. While she stayed in Paris and Versailles, Antoine returned more or less permanently to Monaco. When the Duke of Savoy invaded Provence in 1707, Antoine set about fortifying the fortress of Monaco. His buildings are seen today in the Oreillon, a tower that commands the ramp leading to the Princely Palace. Fortunately, Monaco was not invaded.

Antoine and Marie left only daughters. The eldest, Louise-Hippolyte, was married to Jacques-François-Léonor Matignon, a Normandy nobleman. By arrangement, he gave up his Normandy estates and adopted the name and arms of the Grimaldi. He was created Duke of Valentinois by Louis XIV. When Louise died ten months later, Jacques became Prince of Monaco, which was followed by the regency for their son Honoré III. Jacques I abdicated in favor of his son in 1733. He spent the remainder of his life collecting paintings at his mansion in Paris, the Hotel Matignon, which is currently the residence of the French premier.

Honoré III was to reign longer than any other sovereign of Monaco. Following tradition, he served in the French army, and took part in campaigns in Flanders, the Rhineland, and the Low Countries. He became a field marshal. The years 1746-47 saw the War of the Austrian Succession over the inheritance of Maria Theresia in the Holy Roman Empire. Due to the Salic Law, she could not claim the crown of the Holy Roman Empire, but she held the Habsburg inheritances including Austria, Hungary, and Bohemia. She wished her husband, Franz of Lorraine, to be elected emperor. Despite the Pragmatic Sanction, which was supposed to have worked out this matter among the European princes, France disputed the candidacy, and supported the Elector of Bavaria. Meanwhile, Frederick of Prussian seized her Silesian provinces. At her Hungarian coronation, Maria Theresia appealed to the nobles, and raised at that moment six regiments. The Bavarian army was driven out of Habsburg lands, and Franz became Holy Roman Emperor.[11] Monaco was thrown under a blockade by Austrian forces. This was eventually broken with the aid of Marshal de Belle-Isle.

Honoré III married Marie-Catherine de Brignole-Sale, one of the wealthiest heiresses in Italy. They had two sons, Honoré and Joseph. The prince, like other Monegasque rulers of the time, spent most of his time on his French estates, in this case the Normandy lands. Honoré the younger also married a great heiress, Louise d'Aumont Mazarin, who inherited the Duchy of Rethel and the Principality of Château-Porcien.

On the eve of the French Revolution, Monaco's territories and scattered fiefdoms were at its greatest extent. Its subjects were well-governed and prosperous—Monaco exacted taxes from shipping traffic headed to Italy, and its estates in Provence, Alsace, and Normandy provided great revenue. In August 1789, the French Constituent Assembly abolished feudal privileges and these sources of revenue disappeared. Despite the invocation of the Treaty of Péronne, Honoré III was ineffective in restoring his rights and revenues in the French lands.

Revolutionary fervor swept into Monaco itself—many Monégasques supported the people and their representatives over the princely monarchy and its sovereignty. French troops were sent to Nice. On 15 February, the French Convention annexed Monaco. It was made a canton. The Palace was looted, paintings sold at auction. The building itself first housed soldiers, then became a hospital and a poor house.

Most of the princely dynasty survived the ordeal. The Grimaldi family was imprisoned for awhile, and then freed. Only poor Princess Marie-Thérèse de Choiseul-Stainville met a fate on the scaffold. By 1795, while most kept their heads, the Grimaldis were left nearly destitute. Two young princes, Honoré-Gabriel and Florestan, served in the French army.

With the abdication of Napoleon in May 1814, the matter quickly reversed itself. The Treaty of Paris restored most deposed monarchs to their thrones, *status quo ante bellum*. Suddenly Monaco was a sovereign state again. In poor health, Honoré IV, son of Honoré III, was unable to rule. After a family squabble, he passed the crown to his son Honoré-Gabriel. The father returned to Monaco in 1815, where he was arrested by General Cambronne. He was taken to Napoleon, who had just escaped from his first exile on Elba.

The principality survived, but the prior cordial relationship between the restored Bourbon monarchy and Monaco was not resumed. This was to become a disadvantage for post-Napoleonic Monaco. The Second Treaty of Paris in 1815 placed the principality under the Kingdom of Sardinia, which was recognized on 8 November 1817 by King Victor Emmanuel I at Stupiniggi. The tiny state still had not recovered from the privations of the French Revolution, which put a great stress upon the reign of Honoré-Gabriel, who ruled as Prince Honoré V. The population, especially in the town of Menton, rose up in rebellion in 1833.

In 1841, Honoré V died and was succeeded by his brother Florestan. He had married Caroline Gilbert, a bourgeois from Lametz. Her great business sense helped Florestan restore some measure of prosperity in the principality. But revolution was again brewing. When Charles Albert, King of Sardinia, gave his subjects a liberal constitution, the Monégasques were upset that Florestan did not give them one. Two constitutions that were prepared were rejected by the citizens of Menton. The great 1848 revolutions sweeping Europe exacerbated the problem. Florestan abdicated in favor of their son Charles (III). But it could not stop the dissatisfaction—on 20 March 1848 Menton and Roquebrune seceded from the principality and declared their own independence. Furthermore, they resisted annexation by the Kingdom of Sardinia. They formed an unusual no-man's land for twelve years. It was not until the Treaty of Turin in 1860 that the counties of Nice and Savoy were ceded to France and with them the rebellious towns of Menton and Roquebrune. Although the House of Savoy lost its home-land as a result of a war with Austria, the Kingdom of Piedmont-Sardina was proclaimed the Kingdom of Italy under Victor Emmanuel II in 1861. That year Prince Charles III gave up his claims to the two townships in exchange for an indemnity of four million *francs* and the guaranteed independence of Monaco. After nearly three hundred years, Monaco reestablished its sovereignty freed of any feudal relationships. But now, the tiny state had to become viable as an economic entity, or run the risk of absorption again.

The loss of Roquebrune and Menton reduced Monaco by a further eighty percent. Prior to this, the state was roughly the size of Liechtenstein, and functioned very similarly to an "immediate" principality of the Holy Roman Empire. In older times, it also had great revenues from its estates in France. Monaco, now very much a microstate, was reduced to the Rock and the immediate coastal areas. The loss of the productive estates of Roquebrune and Menton was a great blow to the economic viability of the Principality. It could not simply raise taxes on the remaining impoverished population with no agrarian base, and attempts to increase commercial activity failed.

The Casino at Monte Carlo

Desperate times engender genius. Reigning Prince Charles III and his parents Princess Caroline and Prince Florestan, great patrons of the performing arts and possessing great taste in the art of living, fell upon the brilliant idea of establishing a gaming house in tiny Monaco. After the revolutions of 1848, with the Industrial Revolution in full swing, a new class of wealth was established in Europe based in commerce, banking, and manufacturing. With the development of steamships and railroads, holiday travel became available for the wealthy industrialist. Europe, especially in the mountains and along the southern coastline, sprouted with spas and casinos, watering holes for the nouveau riche tourist. The successes of Baden Baden and Marienbad attested to the arrival of a new leisured class. What a more lovely setting for such a resort as sunny Monaco on the Côte d'Azur?

Resorts were already being built at Cannes and Nice, with its "Promenade des Anglais." Caroline and Charles launched the Société des Bains de Mer, the concession of which was awarded to François and Louis Blanc, directors of a gaming establishment at Homburg. The Bains de Mer built hotels, a theater, and the casino to attract tourists on a small promontory east of the fortress of Monaco known as the *Spélugues* (Cave [of Thieves]) Plateau. In 1856, the owner of the land sold the beach-slum property for a mere twenty-two *centimes* per square meter.[12] In honor of Charles III, it was renamed Monte-Carlo. The Bains de Mer concessionaire had the obligation of establishing hotels, cafes, and theatres in addition to the casino. The elegant Hôtel de Paris was built by Dutrou in 1864. It remains one of the most prestigious inns in the world. Similarly, the Café de Paris was established at Monte-Carlo in 1865.

From nearly the beginning the operation of the Bains de Mer was a resounding success— François Blanc was called the "Magician of Monte-Carlo" despite the fact that Monaco was still isolated. In 1868, the rail line between Nice and Ventimiglia added a stop at Monaco. Suddenly the principality was accessible overland from France and Italy and the number of visitors radically increased. The chic aphorism for Monaco during the Belle Époque that was enveloping the Second Empire was "whether it's red or black, it's always Blanc that wins."[13] In 1869, the casino was such a success for the country that it stopped collecting income tax. This drew wealthy residents from throughout Europe.

Monaco became a world of flowers and perfume, of sunshine and sensuality, with the added cachet of mystery and intrigue generated by the possession of hard-won sovereignty. Monaco remained a meeting place for high society and the glitterati of Europe. In 1890, the grand resorts already established in Monaco were joined by the Belle Époque Hôtel Hermitage, built by Jean Marquet. It was designed after the Grand Trianon of Louis XIV. The immense wealth, languorous lifestyle, and brilliant Technicolor settings are the reasons that exposés of modern life in the principality are more often found in *People* and *Point de Vue/Images du Monde* glamour magazines.

Monaco, its economic base established, began to exercise its sovereignty. Not wishing to become a haven for pirates and other renegades, the country signed extradition treaties with Italy, Belgium, France, Netherlands, Russia, Switzerland, Austria-Hungary, Great Britain, and Denmark. It was a signatory of the Paris Convention (1883), Berne Convention (1886), and the Madrid Arrangement of 1891.[14] The principality exchanged ministers and chargés d'affaires with Paris, the Vatican, Madrid, Rome, and Brussels. In 1865, Charles III issued the first Monégasque postage stamp. Ironically, while building the sovereign character of the Principality, Charles III spent most of his time at his chateau Marchais in Champagne and relied on the advice of his lawyer, Eynaud, to rule his distant country. In 1889, Charles III passed away and was succeeded by his son, Albert I. Prince Albert married an English noblewoman, Marie Victoria Douglas-Hamilton.

The Bains de Mer, as required by the terms of their princely commission, formed the Salle Garnier Theatre in 1879. Europe's finest performers found a home here. Moreover, it was soon to lead the world of dance. While wealthy industrialists and their mistresses drank their Lillets amid the fuchsias on mid-afternoon terraces, and Great Britain's Edward VII gobbled down plates of crêpes Suzette at the Café de Paris, Serge Diaghilev moved the Ballet Russe from the Théâtre Mogador in Paris and ensconced his tempestuous lover Vaslav Nijinski as lead dancer in Monaco. When Nijinski stormed off after an argument, Diaghilev replaced him with the Ukrainian marvel Serge Lifar. Nijinski and Lifar were easily the greatest male ballet dancers of their time, if not in history. Anna Pavlova, Mathilde Kschessinska, and Ida Rubinstein were some of the ballerinas—all originally from the Imperial Ballet in St. Petersburg under Marius Petipa. Having found a glamorous home in Monaco, the Ballet Russe attracted composers such as Prokofiev, Debussy, and Stravinsky. Its set designers included Braque and Picasso. After Diaghilev's death in 1929, ballet was reorganized as the Ballet Russe de Monte-Carlo in 1932 under Colonel Basil and René Blum—George Balanchine and Tamara Toumanova were principals. Reorganized again in 1985 as the Ballet Monaco by Princess Stephanie, it has never lost its leadership within the world of dance.[15]

Sovereignty, culture, and the arts—with Albert I, Monaco added a third indelible characteristic. It acclaimed a monarch who was a scientist—an oceanographer and paleontologist. In 1901 he founded the Anthropological Museum to exhibit the fossils and skeletons he had excavated from the grottos of the Balzi Rossi on the Italian border. In 1910, Albert established the Human Paleontology Institute in Paris.

Prince Albert I established the institutions and environment from which Jacques Cousteau emerged. Perhaps from the site of the ancient temple of Hercules on the cliff of La Roche rose the great Oceanography Museum, among the finest in the world. Where walruses and scallops reign, the Beaux Arts edifice grows out of the Rock. It dominates even the Princely Palace in grandeur.

Much of Monaco's current notoriety stems from the hijinks of its princely family in the twentieth century. As Cesare Borgia rose to great power as the illegitimate son of Pope Alexander VI, the Grimaldi line was not hindered by the taint of out-of-wedlock children. Among the ancient dynasties of Europe, however, running a casino seemed a bit demi-monde, despite Napoleon IIIs enthusiastic support. When matchmakers conspired to marry off future Prince Albert I to Princess Mary Adelaide of Cambridge, the emperor wisely argued that Queen Victoria's family would never agree to such a marriage, and suggested Mary, sister of the twelfth Duke of Hamilton. They were wed in 1869. Unfortunately the terribly Teutonic Mary took one look at Monaco and left permanently for Baden, where she gave birth to Albert's only son, Louis. Divorce followed—little Louis kept his legitimacy by a special bull issued by the pope.

In 1889 Albert succeeded to the throne and married an American widow, the Dowager Duchess Marie de Richelieu. She had a fine sense of culture and business, and helped Prince Albert further transform Monaco into the gem of the Riviera.[16] In 1910, however, the population, banned from working in the casino, without agricultural land or industries, rose up in revolt against the prince. They demanded a constitution, and the end to French political manipulation in the affairs of the country. The prince gave in to their demands.

Albert tried desperately to prevent World War I, appealing directly to Kaiser Wilhelm II. When war was inevitably declared, Monaco remained neutral. However, they supported the Allied effort through hospitals and by Prince Louis, who served in the French Foreign Legion. While stationed in Algeria in

1897, Louis had a romance with a cabaret singer, Marie Juliette Louvet. Their daughter, Charlotte Louise Julliette, was born the following year. Louis returned to France in 1908, and had a distinguished military career, attaining the rank of brigadier general in the French Army.

In that year of revolt, 1911, Louis had his father legitimate his daughter, as the throne would otherwise pass to a collateral branch of the family in Germany. There were irregularities in the law, however. A solution was found in 1918-19, with Louis legally adopting Charlotte, with rights of succession. To prevent future intrigue with Germany, France and Monaco subsequently passed a treaty that required French approval on many dynastic matters, including the forfeiture of the throne to France on the demise of a legal heir. Fortunately, Monaco does not practice the Salic Law, and allows for the succession of women, effectively doubling the chances that the forfeiture stipulation would never be invoked. In 1922, Louis II succeeded his father Albert I.

Louis brought the Monaco Grand Prix auto race to the tiny country in 1929, again fuelling the tourist industry. The Grand Prix is now one of the most prestigious auto races in the world, with its harrowingly steep courses and hairpin turns through the main drag of downtown Monaco.

Princess Charlotte became the Hereditary Princess. In 1919, she received the title Duchess of Valentinois, which may have raised an eyebrow or two, considering the first Duke of Valentinois was no less than Cesare Borgia. She married Comte Pierre de Polignac, from one of the oldest and most prestigious French noble families. Upon marriage, he changed his name to the dynastic Grimaldi and was made a prince.

Pierre was known as one of the most exquisitely well-mannered gentlemen of his time, descended as he was from the courtiers of the *Ancien Régime* where the affections of studied manners were serious competition among noble families. Pierre's refinements, apparently, could have made Madame de Pompadour herself appear like a borborygmus fish monger in comparison. Versatile in his charms, Pierre was also bisexual, which strained the marriage to Charlotte. Nevertheless, they had a daughter Antoinette, followed soon after by a son, Rainier. Pierre and Charlotte separated in the mid 1920s, and a divorce followed. Deeply disappointed, Louis II vowed he "would call out the Monégasque army if the prince ever set foot in the principality again."[17] The tabloids loved it.

Princess Charlotte took up a new romance, with Del Mass of Italy. Louis II rescinded Pierre's banishment in 1933. On the eve of Prince Rainier's twenty-first birthday in 1944, Charlotte gave up succession rights in favor of her son.

Monaco was officially neutral during World War II, although at times it was overrun by Fascists of Italy, Germans, and the French Resistance. Rainier himself was a strong supporter of the Allied Powers, which put him in a strong position with the subsequent victory.

With the death of Louis II in 1949 and the waiver of Hereditary Princess Charlotte, Rainier III became the monarch of the Principality. Charlotte moved to the family's estate near Paris, Le Marchais, with her new lover, René Girier, a jewel thief. She opened her house as a rehabilitation center for ex-convicts. In her later years she attended college, receiving a degree in social work.

Princess Antoinette did not become the legal hereditary princess when her younger brother Rainier became sovereign because her mother stipulated that if Rainier predeceased her, Princess Charlotte would assume the throne. Antoinette was quite intrigued with the idea, however, of the succession eventually coming to her and the children she had with her lover, Alexandre-Athenase Noghès. When she married Alexandre-Athenase in 1951, it was her now-legitimate son Louis Christian who was next in line after her aging mother and her. It is said she tried to poison the ten-year relationship Rainier was having with Gisèle Pascal, to remove potential competition, by spreading rumors she was infertile.

By now Antoinette had left Alexandre for a new beau, Jean-Charles Rey. Rey was not just a Riviera beach boy, but president of the Monégasque parliament, the Conseil National. This may have emboldened Antoinette, for apparently she continued planting rumors. The gossips had it that Antoinette was even considering having Rainier deposed and usurping the throne for herself and her son.[18] Mme. Pascal did indeed depart, but then Rainier thumped his sister and promptly married the American actress Grace Kelley, in 1956. Rainier and his bride wasted no time in having children: Caroline was born in 1957; Albert arrived the following year. Rainier's throne was secured.

Grace Kelley brought her own prim luster to a court decadently glamorous. And she provided a much appreciated domestic touch of social housekeeping. One of Princess Grace's first acts after securing the throne for her family was to banish Antoinette from the country. Antoinette moved down the road and became a *grande dame aux chats*, adopting stray felines from around the neighborhood. Like Pierre and Charlotte, she was eventually reconciled with the family, and died in 2011 at the stout age of ninety.[19]

When Rainier ascended the throne in 1949, ninety-five percent of the country's revenue was based in gambling. But what had served as the golden hen of the country was in jeopardy. The central bank, the Societé Monégasque de Banques et de Métaux Précieux, which held fifty-five percent of the country's reserves, was bankrupt. The casino company, the Société des Bains de Mer, was held by Aristotle Onassis, who felt that Monaco should only promote the resort. Rainier, on the other hand, was determined to wean the country off of the casino. The old clientele base of the casino, the European aristocracy, had found themselves in reduced circumstances after the War. Rainier's reign was characterized as diversifying the country's economy, through real estate development, banking, and promoting the principality as a tax haven. He regained control of the Société des Bains de Mer in 1964. By the end of his rule in 2005, only three percent of the country's revenue was based in gambling.

In 1958, Princess Grace and Prince Rainier inaugurated the new railroad tunnel that burrows under the city rather than taking up valuable real estate on the surface.[20]

Prince Rainier promulgated a new constitution in 1962, which put limits on his own powers. The elected National Council, on the other hand, increased its authority. It now has twenty-four members elected for five-year terms. The Tribunal Supreme is composed of judges nominated by the sovereign at the advice of the National Council. Monaco has several political parties including Monaco Together, Rally and Issues for Monaco or REM, Union for Monaco or UPM (including National Union for the Future of Monaco or UNAM).[21]

In 1965 Princess Grace gave birth to the ruling couple's last child, Stéphanie. The princess would experience the horror of losing her mother in an automobile accident. In 1982, the car driven by Princess Grace went off the road on a steep mountain grade above Monaco. Stéphanie, who was with her, was slightly injured but Grace died the next day.

Badly shaken, Rainier continued the transformation of his little kingdom. In several areas along the tiny coastline, such as Fontvieille, reclamation projects added extremely valuable land to the country. A heliport was built, which whisks air travelers to the Côte d'Azur International Airport at Nice.

Rainier spent much of his efforts grooming his son Albert for the responsibilities he would eventually handle. Albert has maintained a deep interest in the Olympic movement, as an athlete and a promoter. But as the decades went by, and Albert remained unmarried, the tabloid wags began to speculate that Albert was homosexual, despite his widely reported dating of female fashion models. The magazines also saw the widower Rainier finding solace with his distant cousin, Princess Ira von Fürstenberg. And the romances of his two glamorous daughters were additional fodder, especially in the years before there was a Diana of Wales.

In 1992, Tamara Rotolo from California filed a paternity suit against Prince Albert, claiming that her daughter, Jasmin Grace Grimaldi was fathered by him. A DNA test eventually proved this, and Albert finally acknowledged his daughter in 2006. In 2005, a Togo flight attendant, Nicole Coste, claimed that her son Alexandre was fathered by Albert. Again a positive DNA test was secured. On the eve of his inauguration in 2006, Albert confirmed his second illegitimate child. They are ineligible for the throne.[22]

The 2002 treaty between France and Monaco finally revised the Grimaldi succession provision, that lacking an heir, the country would revert to France. That stipulation was abolished—Monaco will continue its independent status regardless. In this treaty Monaco also won the right to name its own head of government, or Minister of State. Prior to this agreement, the minister was French. Also, a change in the law of succession stipulated that the legitimate siblings of a succeeding ruler could inherit the throne. Princess Antoinette and her family thus were removed from the succession with the passing of Rainier and the accession of Albert, since she was not a sibling of the succeeding ruler. Caroline became the Hereditary Princess.

Caroline is now styled a Royal Highness due to her marriage with the heir of the Kingdom of Hannover. She was first married to Philippe Junot (1978-1980), then to Italian industrial heir Stefano Casiraghi. He died in a tragic speed boat accident in 1990. In 1999 she married Ernest von Hannover. Her eldest son, Andrea Casiraghi, is second in line to the throne of Monaco. All other Grimaldi dynasts are Serene Highnesses, including the reigning prince. In July 2011, Albert II married Charlene Wittsock, a South African swimmer.

A Singular House

In many ways, Monaco is a unique land. What Monaco possesses as diminutives are matched by various superlatives: Monaco, like Andorra, has the longest life expectancy in the world, at about ninety years. Monaco's employment is one hundred percent; the principality has the highest per capita income, at $185,000, and the most expensive real estate, at $56,000 per square meter. It is also the most densely populated of countries. Its thirty thousand residents have had to build upwards. Not surprisingly, it has the lowest poverty rate in the world, and the highest number of millionaires and billionaires per capita. It has recently fallen behind Liechtenstein as the first ranking GDP per capita state, however. It appears that much of Monaco's wealth derives from outside sources.

Monaco is not a member of the European Union, but does use the euro and has the right to issue its own versions of the coins. It is a member of the International Postal Union, so issues its own postage stamps. The principality is linked to France by a customs union. Monaco has been a member of the United Nations since 1993, with full rights since 2002.

Although the defense of the country is primarily maintained by France, the principality mans the Corps des Sapeurs-Pompiers de Monaco and the Compagnie des Carabiniers du Prince, with their red, white, and blue uniforms ornamented with pith helmets and feathers.

With such wealth, it is not surprising that Monaco has a substantial number of day workers commuting in from France and Italy. Like the tides, the principality uptakes 160 percent of its daytime population at morning rush hour, and similarly disgorges 48,000 workers at sunset, or when the casino and the clubs wind down in the wee hours.

Like all of the European microstates, Monaco is primarily Catholic, complete with its own archbishop. It does have a small Jewish population, mostly European retirees. Monégasque identity is strengthening, and the language, which was almost extinct in the 1970s, has made a strong comeback. Since the new succession laws and the new treaties with France, the threat of French incorporation have retreated and the microstate, under Grimaldi leadership, can confidently continue weaving its course through history as a place something other than France or Italy.

Notes

1. "CIA Country Index, Monaco" https://www.cia.gov/library/publications/the-world-fact-book/geos/mn.html (accessed 2/14/12).

2. Attributed to Virgil. See also Virgil, *Aeneid,* Book 6, Line 830. John Dryden, trans. The Internet Classics. http://classics.mit.edu/Virgil/aeneid.htm (accessed 4/25/12).

3. "Saint Tropez." http://www.nrj-saint-tropez.com/saint-tropez/st-tropez-135.html (accessed 3/10/12).

4."Monaco."http://www3.monaco.mc/monaco/info/history3.html(accessed3/12/12).

5. "Monaco"/history3.

6. "Monaco"/history3.

7. "Monaco"/history3.

8. "Monaco"/history3.

9. "Monaco/history3.

10. "Monaco"/history3.

11. Gies McGuigan. *The Habsburgs* (New York: Doubleday, 1966), 229.

12. Editions Molipor-Editorial Escudo de Oro, S.A. *All the Principality of Monaco* (Barcelona: Editorial Escudo), 54.

13. Editions, 56.

14. "Monaco." http://www3.monaco.mc/monaco/info/history5.html (accessed 1/15/12).

15. Lynn Garafola, *The Ballet Russe and its World* (New haven: Yale University Press, 1999).

16. Anne. Edwards. *The Grimaldis of Monaco: Centuries of Scandal/Years of Grace* (New York: William Morrow, 1992).

17. Charles J. V. Murphy, "The New Riviera," *Life,* 10 November 1947, 152.

18. "Princess Antoinette of Monaco," *Telegraph.* 27 March 2011.

19. "Princess Antoinette."

20. *Annales Monegasques* (Monaco: Des Archives du Palais Princier, 1999), 86.

21. "CIA Country Index, Monaco."

22. "Monaco prince admits love child," *BBC News*, 6 July 2005. http://news.bbc.co.uk/2/hi/europe/4656797.stm (accessed 8/3/12).

Chapter Nine
Flotsam, Jetsam, and Survey Errors

The true microstates of Europe can be better appreciated by examining several claims for sovereignty that are simply not accepted by the "club," and others that have rarely appeared in either history books or travel guides. There are dozens of these anomalies scattered throughout the planet—hidden corners of the world that for some reason were never registered on any map. We will examine a few in Europe (Figure 9.1). Their inclusion here is useful to show the evolution of sovereignty and the development of recognized territoriality under international law. To be a nation-state is to be a member of a most exclusive club. So powerfully attractive is the concept of nationhood—nothing stands between the founder of a country and his deity. It is the ultimate worldly conceit.

Sealand (1967 to present)

The gulf between the smallest true microstate, the Sovereign Military Order of Malta and the "Principality" of Sealand is immense. While the former is recognized by 104 countries, Sealand has but a shaky stake in the family of nations, begrudgingly acknowledged by perhaps only two powers—and those are based on coercion.

Sealand is located six miles (ten km) off the coast of Suffolk, England—a man-made platform built by the British as H.M. Fort Roughs during World War II. It is similar to an off-shore oil rig, but was designed as a watching post to guard the nearby port of Harwich from German incursion. Along with other platforms, it was designed by Guy Maunsell. They were known as the Maunsell Sea Forts. Fort Roughs was constructed in the U.K., towed to 51°53'40"N and 1°28'57"E and scuttled on Roughs Sandbar in the North Sea near Ipswich.

Abandoned after the war, the Maunsell Sea Forts were occupied by a succession of pirate broadcasters during the 1960s. Reminiscent of the ancient Viking raids of the Middle Ages, these no-man lands became prized targets for modern day privateers. The pirate radio stations could gain large audiences and sell lucrative advertising. They were established primarily to avoid paying high

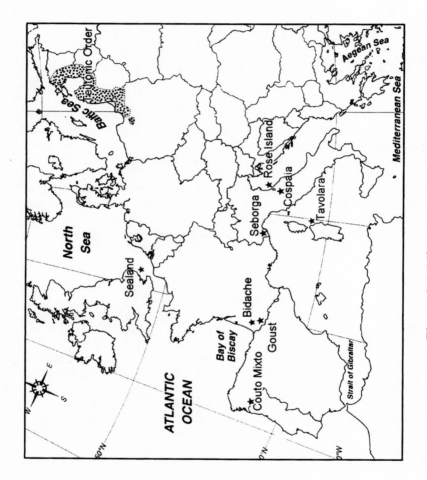

Figure 9.1 Microstate Also-rans

licensing fees in the U.K. H.M. Fort Knock John was used by offshore station. Radio City, until its occupancy was physically overthrown by the Englishman Paddy Roy Bates. Bates had previously operated the pirate Radio Essex. Because Fort Knock John was within the three-mile territorial waters, Bates was found guilty in the U.K. courts for illegally broadcasting. H.M. Fort Roughs was similarly being used for broadcasting by Ronan O'Rahilly, part of the Radio Caroline network of pirate broadcasting ships. Bates and O'Rahilly had plans to operate Roughs as a health club for entertainers, but soon had a falling out. Bates mounted a siege to take over Roughs, with the fighting lasting until September 1967. Bates "conquered" the platform, and moved his own radio equipment there.

All of this did not sit well with the British government. Soon after Bates' occupation of Roughs, the Royal Navy attempted to remove him. In defiance, Roy declared the platform's independence (2 September 1967). As the British ships grew closer, Bates' son Michael fired warning rounds from the big gun left after World War II. Consequently, father and son were summoned to court on weapons charges. It ultimately ruled, however, that because Fort Roughs was outside of the three-mile territorial limit, it was beyond British jurisdiction. It was learned much later, under an expiry of confidentiality, that the U.K. had plans to lay siege to the tower, but wished to avoid loss of life and subsequent embarrassment to the government.

After the ruling, Bates moved his family to the platform and declared the establishment of the Principality of Sealand with himself as monarch, Prince Roy I. According to the monarch, the principality was founded on the "principle that any group of people dissatisfied with the oppressive laws and restrictions of exiting nation states may declare independence in any place not claimed to be under the jurisdiction of another sovereign entity."[1] Sealand issued its first postage stamps in 1969. A helicopter service was established between the tower and Brussels, Belgium. Remarkably, a considerable amount of post was carried through the Belgian system and passed on to the international mails without surcharge. Sealand cancellations are also seen passing through the British system, although it's against official policy. Incoming mail is addressed to U.K. box numbers near Ipswich.

Prince Roy introduced a constitution, flag, national anthem, currency, and passports in 1974-75. Roy's consort is Princess Joan and together they have a son, Michael, as Crown Prince. The latter is currently Prince Regent and head of government due to Roy's advancing years and poor health. The Sealand dollar is the official currency, and several dozen coin styles of various denominations have been struck, mostly of precious metals. Most carry the profile of Princess Joan.

Bates' 1974 constitution consists of a preamble and seven articles, the latter of which deals with the appointment of governmental bureaus, the role of the appointed senators, tribunal responsibilities, the sovereign's exclusive right to formulate foreign policy, and the succession through the male line. Current bureaus include External Affairs, Internal Affairs, and Post, Telecom, and Technology. The legal system follows British Common Law, and laws are issued as decrees from the sovereign.

The watery principality even saw its own attempted coup d'état in 1978 when Professor Alexander Achenbach, then the prime minister, seized control of Roughs Tower while Roy was away. The professor, originally from Netherlands and Germany, arrested Michael. However, Prince Roy's mercenary "army" soon overpowered Achenbach and his men. Achenbach, a citizen of Sealand, was tried by Bates for treason. He was held as prisoner of war. The Netherlands and German governments pleaded with their British counterparts to intervene, but Britain conveniently acknowledged that Sealand was "outside of their jurisdiction." This of course was seized upon by Bates as de facto acknowledgement of Sealand's independence. Germany sent an official to negotiate with Bates for the release of Achenbach, which was granted. The deposed prime minister then established a Sealand "government-in-exile." His Website is www.principality-of-sealand.de. Achenbach's group has, predictably, issued its own coins in the early 1990s, with the likeness of new Prime Minister Seiger.

Sealand's Claims under International Law

What separates Sealand and Roy Bates from the daydreams of Walter Mitty is that circumstances have caused the case of Sealand to be placed before several courts of law. Sealand had to claim independence or Bates would have been liable for the violation of strict British licensing laws. Bates' claim states that when the tower was first reoccupied in 1967, it was located in international waters and outside of the jurisdiction of the U.K. and all other states. Bates used the old "law of the high seas," to form the basis of Sealand's alleged *de jure* status. Furthermore, court action and official negotiations in Germany and U.K. over Sealand, according to Bates, constituted a type of *de facto* recognition.

Bates was getting at the heart of the definitions of statehood and provided pause for other microstates and would-be sovereignties.

Although no country in the world has exchanged diplomatic representatives with Sealand, Bates argued that his negotiations with Germany formulated a type of recognition of existence under the constitutive model of nation-building. Furthermore, the qualifications of territory, population (under ten), and governance uphold Sealand's independence under declarative principles of sovereignty. In 1978, the Administrative Court of Cologne ruled that Sealand was not an acceptable nation, "A man-made artificial platform, such as the so-called Duchy of Sealand, cannot be called either "part of the earth's surface" or "land territory" and only structures which make use of a specific piece of the earth's surface can be recognized as State territory within the meaning of international law."[2] A state needs land; it cannot be a sunken platform, a vessel, or a website.[3]

In 1936-1937, Christian Holmes, an heir to the Fleischmann Yeast Company, added sixteen acres to a pre-existing twelve-acre island, Coconut Island, in

Kane'ohe Bay, O'ahu, in the U.S. Territory of Hawaii. In December 1955, the Territorial Tax Office raised the issue of the filled lands of Coconut Island. Although Holmes had clear title to the original island, the 16.3 acres of land created by his dredging and filling was apparently never assessed and taxed. The reclaimed land did not appear on tax maps. Federal law requires that any accretion of land to an ocean shoreline becomes federal property unless overridden by an act of Congress. The attorney general of Hawai'i stated that the territory would be interested in collecting back taxes should the artificial section of the property be deemed to belong to Holmes and his successors. Although not an issue of sovereignty, Holmes' improvements created a potential tax liability and clouded the title on an otherwise attractive property. Many years later the problem was solved by the current owners simply giving the land to the state for the state university's marine biology institute.[4] Based in ancient British Common Law, land accreting to a shoreline belongs to the state, not to the individual who may have created it, or to any local government. Similarly, in 1971, the 2.94 acre Fontvielle was added to the territory of Monaco from reclaimed seashore. It formed a foundation for the nation's heliport, providing land for the construction of a stadium, condominiums, and a garden. It is considered sovereign to Monaco. Back in Hawai'i, land is constantly accreting to the Big Island of Hawai'i through active lava deposition. It technically belongs to the United States.

In 1982 the United Nations Convention on the Law of the Sea concluded that artificial islands may no longer be constructed and then claimed as sovereign states, or as state territories, for the purposes of extension of an exclusive economic zone, territorial waters, etc. No doubt this decision was influenced by the technicalities encountered by the Sealand example.

In 1987 Britain passed an Act of Parliament that extended its territorial sea to twelve nautical miles. This helped alleviate certain ambiguities about other artificial islands built offshore. Sealand, however, followed suit by extending its territorial waters twelve miles, which brought its "jurisdiction" to the very suburbs of Ipswich. In any case, Sealand would claim that its sovereignty was established prior to the change in the British law, and thus enforcement of the new law by U.K. forces would be considered a violation of Sealand territory and an act of war.

In 1990 the United States got into the act by also ruling that Sealand was not a valid sovereign nation from evidence from the Federal Communications Commission (FCC). Sealand had tried to register a broadcast ship, Radio New York International, off the coast of Jones Beach, NY. The FCC court judgment was upheld on appeal to U.S. Federal Court, that the state of Sealand has never existed!

In 2004, the British Crown Estate, which owns the sand bar underneath Roughs Tower, decided not to claim back rent from Bates due to their opinion that the Ministry of Defense is the lawful owner of the fort. The Crown Estate is an institution dating back to the Act of Settlement of 1688 that granted certain privileges to the monarchy for its giving up of political power to the government. The sand bank became a Crown land under the Territorial Sea Act of

1987. According to British law, Bates has maintained an unlawful adverse possession of the property, further exacerbated by failing to file a squatter's rights petition in a U.K. court of law.

Niche market appears to be a common aspect of microstate sustainability. Certainly Andorra, SMOM, the Holy See, and Monaco continue to enjoy great prosperity due to their unique economic enterprises rather than their natural resources. This is no less a challenge for Sealand, which essentially has no resources other than that which can be generated by sovereignty itself. From its initial position as a pirate radio station, ideas for economic development have also included a fun house and recuperation center. The sale of stamps and coins provided some income, as it does for other microstates, but the Bates subsidies were not infinite. By the late 1990s, family wealth was wearing thin and things were getting desperate. Enter HavenCo, a dot com start-up that proposed to Prince Michael to use Sealand as a Web hosting facility. Unregulated informational broadcasting was Sealand's original raison d'être anyway. Sealand would become a high-security "collocation," a kind of Swiss bank for data. Launched in 2000, the domain was popular for gambling sites, and even the Tibetan government-in-exile used Sealand for their website, due to the fact that the Dalai Lama was proscribed from engaging in political activity in his exile in Dharamsala, India.

Gaming might just have been the salvation for Sealand in the twenty-first century as it had been for Monaco in the nineteenth and twentieth, and as it has for hundreds of American Indian tribes operating casinos in newly constituted states of sovereignty under federal law. HavenCo founder Ryan Lackey had Prince Michael appointed CEO. Almost immediately, Michael's authoritarian ways came into conflict with HavenCo libertarian outlook. Michael wanted to use HavenCo to work with other governments on cyberterrorism, thus boosting Sealand's claims to sovereignty. This grated against HavenCo's anti-establishment philosophies. High costs and unfulfilled promises further clouded the operations. According to Lackey, Bates did not inform him about the U.S. Court decisions of 1990-1991 that declared Sealand a nonentity. In 2002, visas to Sealand were curtailed, most likely due to the decline of HavenCo.

Still Sealand marched on. In 2003 Darren Blackburn of Ontario, Canada represented Sealand at several competitive marathons and other races. He was appointed "Athleta Prinicpalitas" by Prince Michael. The Danish football team Vestbjerg represented Sealand in 2003-2004, scheduling matches against such entities as the Åland Islands, Northern Cyprus, and Tibet-in-Exile.

On 23 June 2006, the Sealand platform caught fire, and one person was injured. An RAF helicopter was dispatched to the platform to transfer the individual to the hospital at Ipswich. A local tug boat managed to extinguish the fire, which destroyed Sealand's offices and main power generator. Soon thereafter the official Sealand Website announced that it had contracted with Church and East Limited to renovate the platform. Solicitations were made on-line to help pay for the rebuilding:

Knowing the loyalty shown by those across the globe who have supported the Principality, we have added a 'donation' option for persons who might wish to contribute to the reconstruction required.
Preliminary estimates put the figure at approximately a million dol-
lars.[5]

By 2007, it appeared that all the damages had been repaired. The platform was
then offered up for "transfer," as apparently a principality cannot be sold (it
seems that Michael Bates is unaware of the creation of Liechtenstein from purchased estates). The Bates family has retained the Spanish estate company Inmo
Naranja to broker a transfer. The price is set between £65,000,000 and
£504,000,000 (U.S. $1 billion).

Republic of Rose Island (1968)

The swinging '60s was a time of social experimentation. It was inevitable that
copy-cat Sealands would be in the making. A most notable experiment was the
Republic of Rose Island, another nation-building project focused on a man-made
platform in the Adriatic Sea a few miles off the coast of Italy at Rimini. The
400-meter platform was constructed by Giorgio Rosa on nine pylons sunk into
the sea. Rosa plastered a restaurant, bar, nightclub, gift shop, post office, and
radio station on the artificial island. On 24 June 1968 Rosa declared his island's
independence. He adopted Esperanto as its official language, and issued the
perfunctory flag, stamps, currency, and allegedly coins. The style of these in-
struments of sovereignty clearly resembled those of the genuine Republic of San
Marino located a few dozen miles west of Rimini.

Rose Island was short-lived, however, as the Italian government's reaction
was succinct and swift. Soon after independence, a group of revenue agents and
police landed on the platform and took control. The platform's Council of Government sent a futile telegram to the Italian government protesting the violation
of sovereignty and the loss of tourism. The Italian Navy evacuated the platform,
strapped explosives to the pylons, and consigned the Serene Republic to Nep-
tune's realm. The Rose Island government-in-exile subsequently issued postage
stamps commemorating the complete destruction of their country.[6]

Several other artificial island-building exercises in nation building were similarly foiled, ultimately culminating in the 1982 UN Convention of the Sea,
prohibiting the recognition of man-made platforms and artificial islands as sovereign entities.

Principality of Seborga (954—present)

What Rose Island was to San Marino, Seborga is to Monaco, with the exception
that Seborga is made of real earth and may indeed still have an ancient but legal

claim to sovereignty. Located northeast of Monaco on the Ligurian coast of Italy, Seborga was early on a fiefdom of the Counts of Ventimiglia, when it was known as "Castrum Sepulcri." The name morphed to "Sepulcri Burum," then to "Serporca," finally to "Seborga." In A.D. 954, Count Guido gave the castle, St. Michael's Church, and some land to monks of Lerins, and the following year it minted its first coins (the Lerins were islands off the coast of Cannes).[7]

The four sq. km territory became an immediate imperial principality of the Holy Roman Empire in 1079 with the abbot becoming the ruling prince. It was the first and only Cistercian state in history. St. Bernard of Clairvaux arrived at Seborga in 1117, joining abbots Gondemar and Rossal. In 1118 the Prince-Abbot Edward invested nine knights in the new Order of the Temple of Solomon, who went off to the Crusades as the "poor militia of Christ."[8] The knights were named Gondemar, Rossla, Andre de Montbar, Count Hugues I de Champagne, Hugues de Payens, Payen de Mont Didier, Geoffroy de Saint Omer, Archambaud de Saint Amand, and Geoffroy Bisol. They arrived in Jerusalem in May 1119. The Knights Templar returned to Seborga on the first day of Advent in 1127, to further support the ecclesiastic state. Their leader, Hugues de Payens, was ordained grand master of the Order of the Temple by St. Bernard himself at Seborga. He was accompanied on this occasion by the Blessed Frà Gerard, the founder of the Hospitallers of Jerusalem. As part of the Templar investiture, Saint Bernard, the Bishop of the Cathars, and the knights swore to uphold the "Great Secret."

After the power of the Templars was destroyed in the fourteenth century, however, there was still a flicker of the candle left in Seborga. Many of the Templar knights had also been princes of Seborga. In 1611, the last vow of silence was taken in the presence of Father Cesario da San Paolo, the Grand Master of the Order of St. Bernard. To mark the event, every roof in the principality was decorated with thirteen tiles incised with the number thirteen, the date 1611, the letters C.S., and the Templar cross. Seborga remained a Cistercian state until 1729 when it was sold to Vittorio Amedeo II of Savoy, Prince of Piedmont and King of Sardinia. Somehow, however, the king failed to register the transaction in either Savoy House records or through the auspices of the Kingdom of Sardinia, an inaction that forms the basis of the modern claim to independence. When this section of Liguria was integrated into the Republic of Genoa under the Treat of Aquisgrana of 1748, Seborga was not mentioned. When the Congress of Vienna of 1815 met to re-establish old Europe, Seborga was not explicitly included in the Kingdom of Sardinia.[9] Neither was the principality mentioned in the Unification of Italy in 1861. Seborga belonged to no one, it would seem, but the Seborgians.

The legalists claim that upon the failure of King Vittorio to register his claim, Seborga, at the expiration of the ecclesiastic state, would have simply returned to Ventimiglia. That territory had been a fiefdom of Genoa since 1139, much as Monaco had been. When the Republic of Genoa became a part of the Kingdom of Piedmont-Sardinia and the subsequent Kingdom of Italy, Seborga would have automatically been integrated into the Italian state. But we have also seen a tendency for the borderlands between France and Italy to act independently of either larger state. Menton and Roquebrune, adjacent to Ventimiglia, we have seen, separated from Monaco for a time and Monaco itself coveted its own sovereignty. It should not be too surprising that nearby Seborga would share in some of that collective memory.

In the early 1960s, the late Giorgio Carbone (1936-2009), head of the Seborga flower-growing cooperative, championed the idea of independence as a natural expression of Seborga's historical anomaly. So convincing and popular were Carbone's arguments that in 1963 they elected him head of state, becoming "Sua Tremendita" Prince Giorgio I of Seborga.[10] The inevitable stamps and coins, the *luigino*, were issued. The blue and white flag of Seborga, looking very much like that of San Marino, was flown over the little town. In 1995, the electorate of 308 persons voted 304 to 4 to reassert Seborgan independence and establish a new constitution. Capturing the whimsy of the tourist market, Seborgia began to exploit its image as a "postage stamp principality." It rapidly revitalized the modest economy of the traditional horticulture-based economy. Prince Giorgio established several orders of knighthood to support his state, and issued national identity cards, passports, and automobile license plates. Seborgan stamps are accepted for mail within the village, and the principality's currency and coins are legal tender within the country and are accepted at the local bank. The central piazza of Seborga was charmingly restored through the affluence created by marketing its uniqueness. The great irony is that despite the official sanction of nationhood from the international community, the state has succeeded financially in a manner wholly without the design or control of Italy. As such, it could be favorably compared with the success of the grand resort of neighbor Monaco, whose historical roots are not so dissimilar with Seborga's.

It could be argued, under the rules of the declarative model of statehood under the Montevideo Convention that the state really does exist. It has territory, a population, a system of governance, and evidence that it has engaged directly with other states in the past. Furthermore, under the U.N. charter, the Seborgans would have the fundamental right to self-determination.

In 2010 Michael Menegatto, a former sailor and heir to a to a hosiery company succeeded to the Seborgan throne at the passing of Giorgio I through an election by the people.[11] He claims to have opened consulates in various countries. His wife serves as Minister of Exterior. Prince Michael was recently featured in the United Airlines in-flight magazine, *Hemispheres.* Stores in town now accept the local currency. While Prince Michael did not initially take things seriously, the local Seborgans do. The tourism that has built up from its microstate status is very valuable to shopkeepers, hoteliers, and restaurateurs throughout the principality. Evidently, even the travel giant United Airlines has caught on.

The path that Seborga is on is the usual way that many states have formed: an idea, shared by the people, emboldens self-determination, which may lead to declarations of independence and recognition by other states.

To a limited extent, Seborga was initially for the Templars what Rhodes and Malta were for the Hospitallers and what Prussia became for the Teutonic knights. They were states based not upon territorial gain as much as bases from which lateral, religio-political ideologies could be supported. The same holds true with Vatican City, which the Holy See consciously argued during Lateran Treaty negotiations that it needed a temporal base from which it could exercise unimpeded divine authority.

The Teutonic Order State (1224-1525)

No discussion of motile sovereignty would be complete without an acknowledgement of the Teutonic Order, which still survives today, albeit shorn of national sovereignty. Like SMOM, the Vatican, and Seborga, it was an ecclesiastic state. It was of great importance, seeding the development of the Kingdom of Prussia and modern Germany. Although not technically a microstate, the territories of the Teutonic Order, like SMOM, were wherever the knights happened to settle. Thus, they serve as another example of a "lateral" sovereignty not dependent upon a land base.

The little brother of the great military orders of the Latin Kingdom of Jerusalem, in terms of numbers and power was the Order of St. Mary of the Teutons. Like the two other great military hospitaller orders, the Teutonic knights moved throughout time. Their first great center was at Acre in Palestine (1190-1309); then they became lords of Prussia at Marienburg (1309-1525); with the loss of Prussia when their Grand Master converted to Protestantism, they became rulers of Mergentheim in Franconia (1526-1805); after the Napoleonic wars, they settled in Vienna under the patronage of the Habsburgs, where they remain to this day. A Protestant branch exists in the Netherlands.

A hospital for German pilgrims was established early during the Latin kingdom known as St. Mary's of the Teutons. It was originally operated under the auspices of the Order of St. John under the rule of St. Augustine. It was wrenched away from St. John by Saladin in 1187. Their mission was reassumed in 1190 by Hanseatic knight hospitallers from Bremen and Lübeck, under the leadership of the Duke of Holstein, arriving in the Holy Land during the Third Crusade. They established a hospital in a makeshift tent made from their ships' sails under the besieged walls of Acre, inspired by the original hospital in Jerusalem. With the victory at Acre, and with the sponsorship of Frederick II of Swabia (son of Frederick Barbarossa), leader of the German crusade, a permanent hospital was established. The knights adopted the hospital rule of St. John and the military organization of the Templars. In 1199, again following the examples of the Temple and St. John, it was transformed into a knightly order and granted exemption from diocesan control by the Bull of Pope Innocent III, *Sacrosancta romana*. The ceremony was attended by the Patriarch of Jerusalem, the King of Jerusalem, the general of the Crusaders, and the masters of the Templars and St. John. Forevermore it would be beholden to the pope alone, who granted the privilege of wearing a white habit with black cross. The knights, whose membership was nearly exclusively German nobility, were professed to the vows of poverty, chastity, and obedience, with a mission to administer to the sick and fight the Infidel.[12]

Rapid growth followed the victories of the Latin empire. The Order built the castle of Montfort, a rival of the Krak des Chevaliers of the Order of St. John, in the Holy Land. In Germany it had estates from Styria to Saxony, Bavaria, and the Tyrol; other lands were in the Byzantine Empire, Netherlands, Switzerland, and even Spain. The thirteenth century saw the establishment of several Commanderies or *kommenden*, exceeding some three hundred by the year 1300, organized under provinces or bailiwicks. National commanders were the *Landmeisteren*. By this time, two other orders, the Dobriner and the Brothers of the Sword, had merged into the Teutonic Order. The provincial master for Germany became the *Deutschmeister*, a title that was eventually merged with that of grand master or *hochmeister*. The older *kommenden* were endowed with cash and property by pious crusaders, and popes, emperors, bishops, nobles, and burghers were numbered among their benefactors. Other high officers included the grand commander, marshal, quartermaster, hospitaller, and treasurer elected by the chapter general. The Order was divided into various classes, including knights, priests, lay brothers, sisters, and "familiars." A large body of people supported the professed knights, from auxiliary knights down to slaves. Secular knights had a place in the Order, as did the old local crusader mercenaries, the Turcopoles. There were squires (*knechte*), sergeants-at-arms, and foot soldiers drawn from the local peasantry.

The imperial House of Hohenstaufen heaped favors upon the Teutonic Order, to whom they remained loyal. When Frederick II broke with the papacy and stood in opposition to the orders of St. John and the Temple, the Teutonic Knights were at his side. The original title of the grand master, conferred on Hermann von Salza in 1209, was *Magister Hospitalis Sanctae Mariae Alemannorum Jerusolimitani* (Master of the Hospital of Saint Mary of the Teutons in Jerusalem), and with the substitution of *Theutonicorum* for *Alemannorum*, has remained the title of the master ever since. From 1226-27, the masters enjoyed the rank of Imperial Prince at court and were seated in the Diet as immediate vassals of the emperor.[13] This was centuries before the Knights of St. John were so privileged.

During the Fourth Crusade, the Teutonic Knights reclaimed their original house, St. Mary of the Germans, under the banner of Emperor Frederick II. In 1291 the remaining knights left the Latin Empire that had now fallen to Islam. Since 1230, however, the knights had begun a new military career in the pagan Baltic lands of the Prussians. Grand Master Hermann of Salza was asked by Duke Conrad of Massovia to come to his aid in a region of the

Baltic lands that was encountering resistance by the indigenous, Odin-wor-shipping Prussians. The Order was promised the sovereignty of Courland and Livonia as a reward of victory. The emperor and pope agreed, sending an army of crusaders under Hermann Balk and twenty-eight knights. The battle lasted a full twenty-five years, the conclusion of which led to the establishment of a military principality and Germanic colonization of this largely uninhabited, Letto-Slavic wilderness. The Grand Master had stayed at Venice until 1309, when he transferred his residence to the Fortress of Marienburg in Prussia following the decisive battle of Rudau.[14]

The ancient Prussians (linguistically and culturally similar to Lithu-anians) were among the last of the Indo-Europeans in Europe to be converted to Christianity. Within their old religion were ancient gods, like Potrympus, Pecols, and Pocols,[15] who would be recognized among Classicists as within the Zeus-Jupiter-Odin pantheon, ironically the same gods the ancient Germans worshipped. The modern Catholic German knights, however, brought their own culture and settlers, cultivating the land and established towns and cities, including Danzig (Gdansk), Thorn, Kulm, and Königsberg. Only about a thousand knights held the country together, a country spanning parts of modern Estonia, Latvia, Lithuania, Poland, and Russia. They became a Hanseatic power, and dominated trade in the eastern Baltic.

The Order, in its process of occupation and conversion, set about with a forced "Germanification" of the region. The knights frequently had to defend their territory from insurrection. However, when the native Grand Duke Jagellon embraced Christianity with his marriage to Hedwig, heiress of the Kingdom of Poland in 1386, much of the religious motivation for the occupation of Prussian ended. The Order's enemy now became the kings of Poland. The decisive battle of Tannenberg (1410) went to Grand Duke Jagellon. Over six hundred knights were killed and their fortunes ruined. Struggling to overcome the defeat of the Thirteen Years War, the Order lost the western half of its territory to Poland outright and the remaining lands remained under the suzerainty of Poland under the terms of the Treaty of Thorm in 1466. The knights lost Marienburg and transferred the Hochmeister's residence to Königsberg in East Prussia (Rus. Kalingrad, now an enclave of Russia on the Baltic), which remained the symbolic capital of Prussia until modern times.[16]

Hochmeister Albert, Duke of Brandenburg took advantage of his position to secularize Prussia. In 1525 he became a Lutheran, and made the Teutonic Order's East Prussia a hereditary fief of his House of Hohenzollern under the suzerainty of the Crown of Poland.[17] It was the first Protestant state. Albert became the first Duke of Prussia and renounced his Grand Mastership. In 1640, his descendent Frederick Wilhelm became an Imperial Elector—in1701 his successor became the first King of Prussia, being crowned in Königsberg; the last king was the colorful and bombastic Kaiser Wilhelm II of WWI fame.

Despite the tremendous setback caused by Albrecht, the Order carefully picked up the pieces, and chose a new Grand Master. Walter von Cronenberg moved his residence to Mergentheim in Franconia in 1526. The Order still had twelve bailiwicks in Germany for a time. The Reformation had greatly affected the Order—Saxony, Messe, and Thuringia became Protestant bailiwicks. Emperor Charles V provided the Order with certain rights and privileges under imperial law; additional benefits were offered under Canon Law in 1530. The bailiwick of Utrecht was lost in 1580, and Louis XIV, following the example of his predecessor Philip the Fair with the Templars, secularized the Teutonic Order's possessions in France.[18]

Thus, the Order became a national one under the Imperial Crown. The position of Hochmeister became reserved for an archduke of the House of Habsburg. Archduke Eugen was the last holder of the title in the family. During this era, there were about twenty professed knights bound to celibacy, and thirty non-celibate knights of honor who were required to pay a reception fee of fifteen hundred *florins* and an annual donation of one hundred *florins*. The knights also represented one of the most exclusive of all European aristocracy, and had to prove a nobility of sixteen-quarterings, down from an astonishing thirty-two at the height of the feudal period.[19] The revenues of the Order are devoted to religious works, being in charge of fifty parishes, seventeen schools, nine hospitals, six congregations of religious. The Order traditionally performs ambulance service during wartime. The ancient bailiwick was re-established under King Willem I of the Netherlands as an order for Calvinist nobles.

Gradually the military activity of the Order diminished. An army was raised to support the Austrian defense against the Turks, but little is heard about military action from the eighteenth century beyond.

The Treaty of Lunéville in 1801 removed the Order's lands on the west bank of the Rhine; in 1809 Napoleon gave the east Rhine's possessions to his allies in the Confederation of the Rhine. This left the Order with only the bailiwick of Tyrol and that of Austria. In 1839 Emperor Ferdinand I reconstituted the Order as the Deutscher Ritterorden with a sole mission as hospitallers. In 1866 an "Honorable Knights of the Teutonic Order" was inaugurated, followed in 1871 by the Marianer des Deutschen Ordens for women. The knights provided hospital care for about three thousand wounded soldiers in World War I.

Burleigh's remarks in his article on the Teutonic Order have been used in various episodes of German history in the making of modern myth—especially during World Wars I and II. Symbols referring to the Order "have been used to provide historical legitimisation for a variety of political objectives."[20] Despite the positive ideals that were often conveyed, historians such as Herder in the eighteenth century compared the forcible conversion of pagan Prussians to the genocide inflicted by the Spanish upon the Indians of South and Mesoamerica. Yet with the ascendancy of Prussia among German states in the nineteenth century, some writers looked upon the Order's activity as "the northward and eastward rush of the German spirit and the formidable activities of our people as conqueror, teacher, discipliner of its neighbours."[21] This jingoistic, social Darwinism supported a fabricated continuity between the *Ordensstaat* and the Hohenzollern ascendancy among German states, and the Order was seen as being the font of Prussian militarism. The Iron Cross was modeled on the badge of the Order. So popular was this revision of history that Wilhelm II threw a grand fête to celebrate the restoration of the Order's capital in Marienburg.

The post-World War I Austrian Republic was wary of the Order, with its Habsburg grand master, even more so because like SMOM, it was independent under Canon Law. War hero and field marshal Archduke Eugen (1863-1954)[22] was the last secular grand master—he resigned in 1923 to allow a priest to take his place and resume relations with the anti-Habsburg Austrian government. Like the Knights of Justice in the Order of St. John, Eugen was a professed knight sworn to the evangelical counsels of poverty, obedience, and chastity. By putting the Order directly under the Church, Archduke Eugen possibly saved it from extinction.

Hitler also juggled the symbols and stories of the Order to justify the re-expansion of the German occupiers to the East at the expense of the Slavs. And to seal his cryptohistory from inconvenient contamination by historical fact, he had the real Order disbanded in 1938-39, persecuting both its priests and the Prussian nobility.

After WWII the Order rebounded and its Austrian possessions were returned. The Order's headquarters, treasury, and archives are located in Vienna, ironically close to the embassy of the Sovereign Military Hospitaller Order of Malta, their brother institution of over nine hundred years. The present head of the Order is Grand Master Abbot Dr. Bruno Platter, who was elected sixty-fifth *Hoch und Deutschmeister* in August 2000 and who uniquely is the male head of a religious order composed mostly of nuns. It is headquartered in the Deutschordenskirche in Vienna near St. Stephansdom. It operates one hospital in Carinthia and a nursing home in Cologne, and is represented in other hospitals in Germany. It still has about 350 Marian knights in the German Bailiwick, and a handful elsewhere, including ten in the United States, but alas, no sovereign territory.

Cospaia (1440-1826)

Remarkably, Seborgia, a territory overlooked by sloppy bookkeeping, is not alone in Europe. An even more absent-minded error resulted in a space of free territory that existed for nearly four hundred years. The fact of Cospaia says something about people's powerful interest in sovereign liberty. It seems that just as soon as these survey errors are noticed, the local inhabitants act almost immediately to establish their independence.

Cospaia, in the Italian Apennines is another example. Not too far away from San Marino on the Italian peninsula, the Republic of Cospaia was an accidental country.[23] Poor Pope Eugene IV, in debt to the Grand Duke of Florence for twenty-five thousand *ducats*, pledged the town of Borgo San Sepolcro and its district along the northern border of the Papal States to the grand duke for relief. San Sepolcro was to be transferred from Papal Umbria to Tuscany. The treaty established the new boundary line between the states at a creek noted as "Rio." Rio, however, is just a generic term for any river. One could image that a local stream might not have a proper name, especially on a large-scale map. Fortunately for the residents of San Sepolcro, there are two streams that run down from Mt. Gurzole about five hundred meters apart. The grand duke claimed the land up to Rio #1 near San Sepolcro, while the pope claimed the land up to Rio #2 (now called the Riascone, between Sangiustino and Cospaia). The "mesopotamia" was a roughly triangular strip of land that included the village of Cospaia. It did not register on either claim, thus Cospaia disappeared from any outside jurisdiction.

Bureaucrats soon noted the error, but the time and effort needed to get the emissaries of the pope and the grand duke together was not worth the effort. Neither party made a subsequent claim for the no-man's land. The area was only 330 hectares (825 acres or about one square mile). But for the residents of Cospaia, it was their world. They promptly declared independence. No popes, grand dukes, taxes, couvée labor, or burdensome laws to worry about. They established for their motto, *Perpetua et firma libertas*, "constant and strong liberty."

Remarkably, Cospaia was largely ignored by its neighbors. One of the defining points for sustainable sovereignty among the microstates is the creation of a "national niche" that its bigger neighbors cannot provide. Casinos, VAT free shopping, religious privilege—all the European microstates seem to have their economic *shtick*. The economic strength does not necessarily create national aspirations, but the resources serve to maintain and defend them. For tiny Cospaia, it was tobacco. Having managed to exist for over 125 years without doing anything special, Cospaia developed this niche market in 1574. Nicolò Cardinal Tornabuoni, returning from Spain, brought seeds of the New World plant, tobacco, to his nephew, local Bishop Alfonso. The highly addictive and popular plant was sweeping Europe. Like coffee, tea, and liquor, it could be highly taxed and the production regulated as a substantial source of state revenue. In fact, it was indeed heavily taxed in Tuscany, and outright banned in the Papal States under the threat of excommunication. Since the residents of Cospaia were not vexed by either proscription, tobacco soon became the sole crop of the Republic. Originally called "Tornabuoni's plant, tobacco kept the minuscule republic in business for hundreds of years.[24]

Slowly things changed for Cospaia, however. In 1724 Pope Benedict XIII revoked the ban on the devil weed, and Cospaia lost all semblance of orderly propriety, becoming a haven for thieves, pirates, and outlaws of all descriptions. Finally on 25 May 1826, Grand Duke Leopold II of Tuscany and Pope Leo XII moved into Dodge. They cleaned out the riff-raff, and divided the tiny parcel between the two states, the pope getting the lion's share. Most of Cospaia became attached to San Giustino. However, the Papacy allowed the Cospaiesi to continue to grow tobacco, with a quota of a half million plants. To this day "Bright Cospaia" is a well-known cultivar of tobacco in the industry, and tobacco production is widespread throughout Umbria.

Kingdom of Tavolara (1836-1934)

A mighty rock, Tavolara Island off the northeastern coast of Sardinia was ruled by the Bertoleoni family as the Kingdom of Tavolara—at two square miles, one of the smallest countries on the planet. Never formally annexed, is it now a *de facto* part of Italy.

   In 1836, Charles Albert of Savoy, King of Piedmont-Sardinia visited the large limestone island of Tavolara and befriended the shepherd Giuseppe Bertoleoni, who lived by himself on the rock. Finding him intelligent and capable, King Charles, with a certain tongue-in-cheek verve, invested humble Giuseppe as an independent sovereign monarch of the island. Giuseppe promptly moved his two families over to the island, giving the title "prince" to his heir and "lords" or "ladies of the Sea" for his other children. In 1839, his son Paolo even obtained a royal patent for the claim from King Charles Albert. In 1845, Giuseppe passed the kingdom to Paolo, dying in 1849, the same year as Charles Albert.

   King Paolo was successful in obtaining recognition of Tavolara from the new king of Italy, Victor Emanuel II, son of Charles Albert—Tavolara, like San Marino, was not included in the Italian unification. In 1861 the Italian government paid twelve thousand *lire* for land at the northeast end of the island to build a lighthouse, which began operating in 1868. When Paolo fell ill in 1882, his wife Queen Pasqua Favale became regent. Paolo stipulated that a republic be established at his death, in 1886. A president and a council of six were elected every six years by universal suffrage of the people. Tavolara had its third president by 1896. He too was recognized by the Italian Kingdom.[25]

   However, the republican form of government was not popular, and Paolo's son, Carlo I, assumed the throne in 1899. A year later the British ship HMS *Vulcan* visited the island, and photographed the royal family for Queen Victoria's collection. Carlo was a humble man, however, who was more interested in his lobster pots than being king. Nevertheless, he soldiered on until late 1927 or '28, depending on the source, passing away at Ventimiglia on the Italian Riviera. He was succeeded by his sister Mariangelia, at the request of Carlo's son Paolo who was not resident on the island. Paolo, son of Carlo I and Queen Maddalena Favale, did ascend the throne in 1929. In 1930 Paolo II married Italia Murra.

Old Queen Mariangelia died in 1934, and had stipulated in her will that the kingdom be given to Italy.[26] Mariangelia's nephew Paolo II still claimed the kingdom, however, and ruled it until his death in 1962. That year marked the installation of a NATO station on the island and the effective end of Tavolaran sovereignty. The throne in pretence passed to Carlo II, son of Paolo II, and he lived until 1993. During this time the crown had been contested by his cousin, Maria Molinas Bertoleoni.

There is still a king of Tavolara, Tonino I, another son of Paolo Bertoleoni II and Queen Italia Murru. He is an Italian citizen who runs "Da Tonino," a restaurant on the island. Politically, the interests of the island are represented internationally by Prince Ernesto Geremia di Tavolara, of La Spezia, Italy, who has written a history of the island.[27] The king's children by Pompea Romano are Princess Loredana, Princess Paola, and Crown Prince Giuseppe.[28]The royal tomb of King Paolo I is in the graveyard on the island, surmounted by a crown.

One wonders if Giuseppe I and Charles Albert of Savoy took the Kingdom of Tavolara seriously, or if they were merely playing pirate. There is little evidence that the tiny island kingdom sought broader international recognition in over a hundred years of existence, and it is doubtful that King Charles had the authority to make anyone a king in the first place. Still, the recognition by the House of Savoy seems to be the key. When Crown Prince Vittorio Emmanuelle was permitted to leave his exile and return to Italy in 2003, King Tonino vowed to contact the pretender of the Italian throne for renewal of Savoy's recognition of Tavolara's sovereignty. However, since Vittorio has been arrested several times for general hooliganism, and is at bitter odds with his rival for the throne, Amadeo, Duke of Aosta, it is hard to say which Savoyard pretender is to be sought out to recognize the pretender of Tavolara.

Goust (1648 to present)

Remarkably, Andorra is not alone as an isolated sovereignty among the Pyrenees. As discussed previously, a suite of border states between France and Spain were created by Charlemagne to secure the empire against the Moors of Iberia (see Chapter Two). Of these, the Basque lands of Navarre are perhaps best known. At some unknown time, Goust, to the west of Andorra, either split from Navarre or perhaps never was included in surveys of neighboring kingdoms and counties. The tiny Goust perhaps generates the most questions about the general viability of microstates: One wonders if Goust is still technically independent. The former (?) Republic of Goust is an enclave within the territory of the French commune of Laruns. It occupies a hefty two and a half square km (one square mile)[29] on a plateau at the southern end of the Gave d'Ossau valley in the Western Pyrenees, across the river from the town of Eaux-Chaudes. At an elevation of 995 m (3,264 feet), it is accessible only by a narrow mountain footpath across the Pont d'Enfer. The nearest town is Laruns in the valley below.

The community is made up of a dozen households, with a population fluctuating between 59 (1865 estimate) and 150 residents (1900 estimate). The traditional economy was based on animal husbandry, wool, and silk production, augmented more recently by tourism. All church baptisms, weddings, and burials are performed in Laruns. Due to its isolated situation, the inhabitants of Goust have evolved a curious funeral custom: the deceased is placed in a coffin and sent down the mountainside via a specially-constructed chute, to be collected at the bottom for burial in the Laruns cemetery. Thus, no one is buried in the country.

Neither the founding nor the termination of Goust has been determined. However, in 1648 it was recognized by both France and Spain as independent. The government consisted of a Council of Ancients composed of between three and twelve citizens, who elected a president for a term of five years. In 1896 the president of Goust proclaimed a ban on publication of any newspaper without executive authorization, which led to an uprising of the citizens, or neighbors as it were.[30] Although never formally annexed, Goust has not recently asserted its claim to independence. Like the Kingdom of Tavolara, Goust may well be an example of a *de jure* state that is, in practice, not one at all!

Bidache (1570-1789)

The little principality of Bidache, another territory arising from the Spanish March, separated from the French kingdom of Lower Navarre in 1570, when the local ruler of the Gramont family proclaimed himself Prince Antonio I. Bidache is 30.43 sq. kilometers, or 11.75 sq. miles. The commune currently has a population of 1,189 and is located in the Pyrenees-Atlantiques department. Bidache as a sovereign entity survived until the French Revolution, when France became a unitarian republic.[31]

Couto Mixto (Tenth Century-1868)

Couto Mixto (Mixed Territory in Galician) is a scrap of land with three villages (Santiago and Rubiás now in the municipality of Calvos de Randín, and Meaus in the municipality of Baltar), located in Ourense, Galicia, on the border between modern Spain and Portugal. This land was neither

Portuguese nor Spanish for centuries, until the Treaty of Lisbon (1864) partitioned the land between the two kingdoms. It gave the inhabited land to Spain, which it annexed in 1868.[32] The fact of their independence is noted by their sovereign privileges, such as exemption from conscription to either Portugal or Spain, freedom from having licenses to carry firearms, and the issuance of stamps. A revitalization movement is in progress now, as residents attempt to memorialize past achievements.

Wheel of Fortune

There were hundreds of state-like entities existing through the long history of Europe. As we have seen, there were quite a few along the Ligurian coast and in the Spanish March until modern times. Most memorable, perhaps, were the former states that participated, willingly or not, in the unification of Italy and the formation of the Second German Empire in the nineteenth century. Places like the principalities of Waldeck-Pyrmount, Saxe-Coburg-Gotha, the discontiguous Reuss states, and Anhalt-Zerbst were sovereign states that minted their own coins, had their own little capitals, armies, flags, and ruling houses. But most were not ministates. Many of the extinct states of Germany and Italy included, in fact, large polities such as the Grand Duchy of Bourbon-Parma, Lombardy, and the kingdoms of Hanover, Saxony, and Bavaria. Why these much larger entities have been subsumed into even larger units underscores the irony of the continued existence of the extant microstates. Sometimes the incorporation into larger entities is voluntary, sometimes it is coerced. But on other occasions, given the opportunity, groups opt out. We have seen with Cospaia, Goust, and Seborga that even the slightest legal irregularity can propel people to detach and create their own international boundaries. These decisions are often made on the basis of affective affiliation, without concern for economic consequences. This indicates that the emotional dimension to ethnogenesis and nationalism should not be overlooked, that the "irrationally" seen by a determinist and purblind social science is perhaps nothing more than the illogic of affect.

The scattering of territories presented here are just a small sample of serious and not-so-serious attempts at nation-building. Lonely Planet's volume on Micronations presents a worldwide sample of counties, homesteads, and apartment flats, *ad ridiculum*, whose owners have proclaimed their independence. As predicted, the requisite carriers of national sentiment are produced by these entities: stamps, passports, coins, maps, and national anthems. Most are monarchies; some, like Sealand sell patents of nobility on the Internet. Under the principles of self-determination, are they candidates for sovereignty? Under the Montevideo model, a unilateral declaration of sovereignty may indeed be legal, provided these areas have population, government, and the ability to make agreements with other sovereign states. Is paying off your parking tickets an agreement with another sovereign state? It is possible that the difference is merely a matter of scale rather than kind.

Notes

1. "Sealand." http://www.sealandgov.org (accessed 7/15/07).
2. "In the Duchy of Sealand" (1978) 80 ILR 683, 685. http://www.uniset.ca/ naty/80 ILR683.htm (accessed 7/10/07).
3.There is no limit to the extent of this required land. Thus, under this interpretation, the 1.6 acres in Rome extraterritorial to SMOM supports the criteria of statehood there.
4. "Millard Purdy, Tax Office Raises Problem of Coconut Isle Ownership," *Honolulu Star-Bulletin*, 16 December 1955, cited in P. Christiaan Klieger *Moku o Lo`e: A History of Coconut Island,* (Honolulu: Bishop Museum Press 2007).
5. "Sealand."
6. "History of the Principality of Seborga." http://seborga.net/ history/index. html (accessed 8/2/07).
7. "History Seborga." The secrecy of the Templars, and the suspicion it caused, was one of the agents of its downfall. In 1312 French King Phillipe II broke up the order, executed Grand Master de Molay. He confiscated the Order's lands, and gave the bulk of their wealth to the Knights Hospitaller.
8. "History Seborga."
9. "History Seborga."
10. Douglas Martin. "Giorgio Carbone, Elected Prince of Seborga, Dies at 73," *New York Times,* 12 December 2009. http://www.nytimes.com/2009/ 12/13/world/europe/ 13carbone.html?_r=3 (accessed 8/2/2012).
11. Jennifer Miller. "A Land Apart," *Hemispheres Inflight,* January 2012. http://www. hemispheresmagazine.com/2012/01/01/a-land-apart (accessed 4/26/12).
12. "Teutonic Order," *The Catholic Encyclopedia.* http:www.knight. org/advent/ cathen/14541b.htm (accessed 4/28/98).
13. Guy Stair Sainty. "The Teutonic Order of Holy Mary in Jerusalem." http://www. chivalricorders.org/Vatican/teutonic.htm (accessed 10/13/98).
14. "Teutonic Order."
15. Endre Bojtá. *Foreword to the Past: A Cultural History of the Baltic People.* (Budpest: Central European Press, 1999). 315.
16. "Teutonic Order." Like the Habsburgs, the Hohenzollerns were originally a Swiss family.
17. "Teutonic Order."
18. "Teutonic Order."
19. The Bavarian Order of St. George still requires 32 quarters of nobility for investiture.
20. Michael Burleigh. "The German Knights: Making of a Modern Myth." *History Today* 35, no. 6 (June 1985), 21-34.
21. Heinrich von Treitschke, *The Origins of Prussianism*, trans. E. and C. Paul, (Sidney: Allen & Unwin 1942).

22. A public relations boon for the Habsburgs, manly Archduke Eugen stood a striking two meters high without his beplumed helmet. He was considered by some in the insecure Austrian government to be ideal for appointment as regent/ head of state after World War I.

23. Angelo Ascani. *Cospaia: storia inedita della singolare Repubblica.* (Tuscany: Città di Castello, 1963).

24. Ascani. *Cospaia*

25. "Tiny Republic Signs Treaty," *Atlanta Constitution*, 22 November 1903, 10. 26. "Italy Gets Queen's Island of Tavolara," *Hartford Courant*, July 9, 1934, 15.

27. "Nation of 55 People: Republic of Tavolara in Its Third Presidential Campaign," *Boston Globe*, 10 January 1897, 34.

28. "Tavolara's King Dies; Ruled Tiniest Realm; Charles Bartoleoni Was Monarch of Small Island Off Sardinia's Coast," *New York Times*, 1 February 1928, 27.

29. Louis F. Post (ed.) "Little Nations Little Known," *The Public: A journal of democracy,* 2 (96), 3 February 1900. 15–6.

30. Post. "Little Nations."

31. Raymond Ritte. *Bidache Principauté souveraine*, (Lyon: Éditions Audin,1958).

32. Luis Manuel García Mañá. *Couto Mixto. Unha república esquecida* (Vigo, Spain: Universidade de Vigo, 2000). 36–7.

Chapter Ten
The Limits of Globalism

We have examined some aspects of perceived pernicious and illogical nationalism, created as all nationalisms have been at the intersection of human affinity, family, and the sentiment of place. This work is motivated on the observation that the explanation of a phenomenon, in this case the modern nation-state, is clearer through the exceptions rather than the norm. Far from being marginal, the existence of the microstates says much about cultural change and persistence everywhere.

In the process, we have excavated concepts of the tribe and ethnic identity in the formation of nation-states, and have acknowledged the power of structural history to help account for the extremely long persistence of most of the extant European microstates. We have looked at a few functional aspects of the modern state to suggest than many of the microstates might be actually post-modern, occupying boutique economic niches in a relatively unified European Community. We have even tried to deconstruct the perception of improbability that many of these tiny nations maintain in popular culture. It leaves us with the question that has always been overarching in the social sciences: are there patterns in the data, or are all of these examples *sui generis*, in our case, to their unique historical trajectories? I am hoping for the former.

In Europe, the conflicting tides of fission and fusion, the battles between pope and emperor, the great schisms of the Universal Church, have pitted national, or tribal agenda against a philosophy of universalism since the Roman Empire. It has left us with the microstates and two institutions of the Church that are themselves microstates. Improbable to some at the point of whimsy for many, these tiny scraps of sovereign territory have survived Attila the Hun, the development of the centrist kingdom of France, the fractionalized Holy Roman Empire, the War of the Austrian Succession, the Thirty Years War, Napoleon, the Congress of Vienna, Bismarck, Garibaldi, World War I, Hitler, the European Union, and the Internet. Why do the tiny principalities of Liechtenstein and San Marino still exist when the great duchies of Burgundy, Parma, and Hesse-Darmstadt do not? If not merely serendipitous, there may be many lessons to learn on the survivals of peoples and identities through time. In an era of rampant transnationalism and the McDonaldization of cultural difference, the sublime sovereignty of sun baked Monaco and spa-encrusted Andorra gives one pause if not pleasure.

Despite great advances in the development of a global community, with the foundation of the United Nations, the European Union, NATO, OPEC, and the development of the Internet and social media, the most exclusive club remains the sovereign state. As Smith points out, "a growing cosmopolitanism does not in itself entail the decline of nationalism; the rise of regional culture areas does not diminish the hold of national identities."[1] It appears as if the tendency for the "flattening" of cultural idiosyncrasies through globalism is counterbalanced by the expressions of the individual, and the "individualisms" of the collective. This dialectic has been steadily articulated in the Western World since the emancipation of the individual from the universal collective, which is high-lighted by events such as the Reformation and the Enlightenment.

More obscure than even SMOM are numerous wannabee realms whose de-mands for recognition by the sovereign states have largely gone unnoticed. Sea-land, an old radio platform in the English Channel, Rose Island in the Adriatic, Seborga in Italy, and other not-so-serious contenders have all petitioned the powers to be recognized as sovereign entities in the last few decades. Through-out Europe and the world are dozens of other scraps of earth whose "people" covet the ultimate prize of sovereignty.

Andorra, Liechtenstein, Malta, Monaco, and San Marino are remote, small territories located at the edges of empires. Their physical or political marginali-ty, in this sense, have directly contributed to the development of cultural solidar-ity apart from the assimilative agencies generated through the competition of greater regional powers. These five are also affective nation-states whose citi-zens practice shows of "tribal" solidarity through national symbols such as flags, anthems, national festivals, sporting events, cuisine, and the utilization of "di-alects" as national languages.

The other two microstates, the modern Vatican City and SMOM, on the other hand, are polities derived from universalistic ideologies, i.e. the Catholic Church and the Christian Crusades, respectively. They have always been trans-national, but maintain their sovereignty functionally, to operate in the world without subordination to any secular power. Vatican City and SMOM, as non-localized, lateral organizations, tend not to emphasize the state as the zenith of their existence. Their populations are usually citizens of other states, in fact. Rarely is seen the type of patriotic performance noted in the other microstates, as energies are directed towards their global operations instead. Similarly, the pope is accorded universal acclaim because he is the pope, not because he is the sovereign of the Vatican City state. But in the Vatican and at the SMOM, the sovereignty of the state is considered necessary for the free operation of the ac-tivities of these two religious organizations.

What is the mystique of the sovereign state, a status that seems to be the gold standard of collective identity? It resides precariously in the balance be-tween a high-level collective and the individual, and is presented in a myriad of styles in response to unique historical trajectories. It is an articulation of differ-ence that simultaneously builds in-group solidarity as well as invites comparison between groups. The seven microstates discussed in this study are merely a successful, European sample of the scores of small ethnic, niche, or mission-based communities throughout the world who clamor for an unfettered expression of the collective self. Their continued existence may say something about the affective importance of sovereignty. Membership in the club of sovereign nations is highly coveted, even if they are areas hardly bigger than some backyards.

National identity is not mutually exclusive of other sorts of identities. One remains a father, sister, "best friend forever," and co-worker, in addition to being a subject or citizen of a country. The same can be said of global identity references. Identities are often nested, but can also exist in parallel, compartmentalized relationships to one another. But nationality seems to be one of the most affective of identity markers, encouraging people to leave their jobs and families in times of war to defend the greater collective, sometimes to the point of death.

Several of the European microstates, i.e. San Marino, Liechtenstein, Vatican City, and SMOM, have been maintained in their independence by their powerful neighbors partially as a reward for service to humanity, the Church, or to other states.. For many, however, the continuation of nationalism foretells a world perpetually mired in strife, as new countries tear themselves away from irredentist motherlands. Smith states: "the conflicts between nation-states, and between states and their constituent *ethnies*, are likely to continue and perhaps proliferate, mobilizing tomorrow ethnic communities and categories that are dormant today."[2]

Considering the wealth and influence of most of the microstates of Europe, one wonders if fragmentation will continue in preference to universalism, or that both trends will continue in an uneasy balance.

Having your own microstate is perhaps a billionaire's dream—with your own sovereignty one would be beyond the long arm of eminent domain, taxation, conscription and other duties. But even most billionaires would not have the prophetic knowledge to be in the precise time and place to hatch a successful microstate—the Liechtenstein family and the stonemason St. Marino did. All of the microstates represented here fought long and hard to achieve and maintain their sovereignty when the most unusual vicissitudes of history permitted it.

Like Llobera, I have focused this discussion of nationalism on Europe, as Europe is where nationalism first developed. Understanding it here allows us the possibility of examining the phenomenon on a worldwide basis. Llobera has also presented us with outcomes and assignments from which an analysis of European nationalism might provide:

1. An understanding of the subjective feelings or sentiments of ethnic and national identity, along with the concomitant elements of consciousness. This is the task of an anthropological theory *sensu stricto*.
2. An account of the genesis and evolution of the idea of the nation and of national identity and consciousness in the Middle Ages and in early modern Western Europe. This is the task of a history of mentalities.
3. A spatio-temporal explanation of the varying structures (ideologies and movements) of nationalism in the modern period. This is the task of a structural history.[3]

To the third point, I suggest that through the telling of the various historical narratives presented here, one may at least glimpse structures of long-duration from which the national collectives are built and rebuilt. The seven extant microstates have had success in transforming themselves throughout the vicissitudes of the centuries and remain viable, having successfully maintained their boundaries. They now exist at the level of independent states, no different in this sense from the USA or the People's Republic of China.

We have come a long way in the social sciences from the pretense that the observer could discern certain "social laws" that would everywhere apply. On the other hand, while historical trajectories are everywhere different, and the events that pepper these trajectories unique, the narratives that are produced in process are not chaotic. There is always a certain structure or predisposition, based on a collective knowledge of the past that interacts with event. Although as Sahlins might say, the outcomes of these interactions may have unintended consequences for the actors, the intent is usually to reproduce cultural patterns and maintain the status quo.

The seven states presented here have at least one thing in common—they have successfully articulated a concept of nation or sovereignty for centuries and have no intention of doing away with it. They have successfully reproduced a sense of collective memory that is presently articulated as states. Accordingly, they are identical to other states and size may have had nothing to do with it. What does appear to be unusual is the modernist prejudice that tiny entities are doomed to be absorbed into larger, more powerful entities. This logic has been applied not only to states, but to indie book stores and music producers, restaurants, indigenous peoples everywhere, and many small corporate business institutions. While increasing globalism is most likely inevitable due to the great advances in communication, the homogenization of difference is not. The two trends will most likely operate in tandem.

The odds have always seemed, at least, to be stacked against the microstates, with little fishes being eaten by larger fishes. But even the greatest empires fall. Statecraft does not conform to natural laws—nation-building and maintenance is completely dependent upon human agency. And as such, it is conditioned upon human subjectivities—people's greed, fear, loyalties, and tribal pride of affiliation. Who knows, a thousand years from now, how many more unique clusterings of souls, with colorful names and invented traditions linking them to a perceived past, will be minted? As cultures and languages disappear, new ones take their place. Such is the nature of humanity.

Notes

1. Smith, *National Identities*, 175.
2. Smith, *National Identities*, 170.
3. Llobera, *Foundations*, 188.

Bibliography

"Addresses of the Andorran diplomatic missions." *Government of Andorra—Ministry of External Affairs.* http://www.exteriors.ad/index.php?lang=en (accessed 8/3/12).

"Altar Dedicated to Cybele and Attis." *Vatican Museums.* www.mv. vatican.va/ 3_ EN/ pages/x-Schedel/ MGES/MG (accessed 7/4/2012).

"Ancient and Illustrious Order Knights of Malta." *The Royal Black Institution.* 1880s. www2. prestel.co.uk/church/sjcross/ancient.htm (accessed 2/19/08).

Anderson, Benedict. *Imagined Communities: Reflections on the Origins and Spread of Nationalism.* London, Verso, 1991.

"Andorra history." www.andorramania.com (accessed 3/3/2012).

Angier, Natalie. "Cooperate or Die," book review of E.O. Wilson, *The Social Conquest of the Earth.* (New York: Liveright, 2012), *Smithsonian,* April 2012.

Annales Monegasques. Monaco: Des Archives du Palais Princier, 1999.

Ascani, Angelo. *Cospaia: storia inedita della singolare Repubblica.* Tuscany: Città di Castello, 1963.

Attard, Joseph. *The Knights of Malta,* San Gwann, Malta: Publishers Enterprises Group, 1992.

Beard, Mary, "The Roman and the Foreign: The Cult of the 'Great Mother' in Imperial Rome." *Shamanism, History, and the State.* Edited by Nicholas Thomas and Caroline Humphrey. Ann Arbor: University of Michigan, 1994.

Bojtár, Endre. *Foreword to the Past: A Cultural History of the Baltic People.* Budapest: Central European Press, 1999.

Buchmaier, Lix. *Fürstliche Desserts.* Vaduz: Fürst von Liechtenstein-Stiftung, n.d.

Burleigh, Michael. "The German Knights: Making of a Modern Myth." *History Today* 35, no.6 (June 1985), 21-34.

Cachia, Francis. Interview of Russian Ambassador Dr Sergey S. Zotov. *The Times,* Malta. http://smom-za.org/smom/saints/philerme.htm (accessed 4/ 30/2007).

"CIA Country Index—Monaco." https://www.cia.gov/library/publications/the-world-fact-book/ geos/mn.html (accessed 2/14/12).

"CIA World Facts—Liechtenstein. Economy." 2008. https://www.cia.gov/library/publications/the-world-factbook/geos/ls.html (accessed 4/24/12).

"CIA World Facts—Malta." https://www.cia.gov/library/publications/the-world-factbook/geos/ mt.html (accessed 3/15/12).

Comaroff, Jean. *Body of Power, Spirit of Resistenace*. Chicago: University of Chicago Press, 1985.

Cooper, Robert. "Conflict Resolution and Sustainable Peace Building." www.world-governance.org/spip.php?article86 (accessed 7/4/2012).

Danspeckgruber,W., editor, *Self-determination and Self-Administration: A Sourcebook*. New York: Lynne Rienner Press, 1997.

De Rosa, Peter. *Vicars of Christ* . New York: Crown, 1988.

Dharmananda, Subhuti. *Cynomorium: Parasitic Plant Widely Used in Traditional Medicine*. Portland, OR: Institute for Traditional Medicine, 2004.

Dunant, Henry. Wikipedia entry. http://en.wikipedia.org/wiki/Henry_Dunant (accessed 4/22/12).

Duursma, Jorri. *Fragmentation and the International Relations of Micro-states: Self-determination and Statehood*. Cambridge: Cambridge University Press, 1996.

Eccardt, Thomas. *Secrets of the Seven Smallest States of Europe* (New York: Hippocrene Books, 2005.

Editions Molipor-Editorial Escudo de Oro, S.A. *All the Principality of Monaco*. Barcelona: Editorial Escudo, n.d.

Edwards, Anne. *The Grimaldis of Monaco:Centuries of Scandal/Years of Grace*. New York: William Morrow, 1992.

Elias, Norbert. *Power and Civility*, Volume 2, The Civilizing Process. New York: Pantheon Books, 1982.

"Fascismo." http://www.storiaxxisecolo.it/fascismo/fascismo1c.html (accessed 2/ 15/12).

Forsythe. David P. *The Humanitarians. The International Committee of the Red Cross*. Cambridge: Cambridge University Press, 2005.

Foster, Michael. "The Patronage of the Order of St. John, Knights Hospitaller (OSJ) by the Karageorgevitch House and the Claims Concerning the Sacred Relics" 5. www.homeusers.prestel.co.uk/church/kposj/relics.htm (accessed 4/17/00).

"France's Sarkozy to Andorra: Behave or I quit as co-prince." *Today's Zaman*. 29 March 2007. http://www.todayszaman.com/news-170741-frances-sarkozy-to-andorra-behave-or-i-quit-as-co-prince.html (accessed 4/25/12).

Fried, Morton H. *The Notion of Tribe*. New York: Cummings, 1975.

Garafola, Lynn. *The Ballet Russe and its World*. New Haven: Yale University Press, 1999.

García Mañá, Luis Manuel. *Couto Mixto. Unha república esquecida*. Vigo, Spain: Universidade de Vigo, 2000. 36–7.

Gellner, Ernest. *Nations and Nationalism*. Ithaca, NY: Cornell University Press, 1983.

Gregory of Tours, *Historia Francorum*. Harmondsworth, UK: Penguin, 1974.

Gurney, Gene. *Kingdoms of Europe*. New York: Crown Publishers, 1982.

Halm, Heiz. "Al-Andalus und Gothica Sors," *Der Islam,* 66, 1989.

Handler, Richard and Jocelyn Linnekin. "Tradition, Genuine or Spurious," *Journal of American Folklore*. 97, no. 385, 1984.

Harris, Ruth. *Lourdes: Body and Spirit in the Secular Age*. London: Penguin, 1999.

Henrick, Francis Patrick. *The Primacy of the Apostolic See Vindicated*. Baltimore, London, and Pittsburgh: John Murphy, 1857.

Henry IV, Letter to Gregory VII, 24 January 1076. http://www.fordham.edu/halsall/source/henry4-to-g7a.html (accessed 2/12/12).

Herbermann, Charles, ed. "Montefelto," *The Catholic Encyclopedia*, New York: Robert Appleton Company, 1913.

"History of the Principality of Seborga." http://seborga.net/history/index.html (accessed 8/2/07)

"History of San Marino. From 1500 to beginning 1800." http://www.Sanmarinosite.com. (accessed 3/1/12).

"History of San Marino. Napoleon." http:// www.Sanmarinosite.com (accessed 2/12/12)

"History of San Marino. 1800s to Garibaldi." www.Sanmarinosite.com (accessed 2/13/12).

"In the Duchy of Sealand" (1978). 80 ILR 683, 685. http://www.uniset.ca/naty/80 ILR683.htm (accessed 7/10/07).

"Italy Gets Queen's Island of Tavolara," *Hartford Courant*, 9 July 1934.

Kahoun, Ladislav. "Liechtenstein Prince Hans-Adam II: I want my property back." http://www.blisty.cz/art/17123.html (accessed 3/15/2012).

Kant, Immanuel. "Thesis from the Third Antimony," *A Critique of Pure Reason*. Cambridge: Cambridge University Press, 1999 (1781). http://praxeology.net/kant.htm (accessed 7/4/2012).

King, Edwin J. (revised by Harry Luke). *The Knights of St. John in the British Realm: Being the Official History of the Most Venerable Order of the Hospital of St. John of Jerusalem. Order of St. John*. London: St. John's Gate, 1967.

Klieger, P. Christiaan. *Moku'ula: Maui's Sacred Island*. Honolulu: Bishop Museum Press, 1997.

———. *Moku o Lo`e: A History of Coconut Island,* Honolulu: Bishop Museum Press, 2007.

———. "Envisioning a Tibet outside Tibet." Paper presented for the panel, *Who's Afraid of China's Tibet?* Association of Asian Studies, Atlanta, Georgia. April, 2008.

Klimczuk, Stephen and Gerald Warner, *Secret Places, Hidden Sanctuaries*. New York: Sterling, 2009.

"La Constitució del Principat d'Andorra, 1993." http://www.andorramania.ad/constitucio-principat-andorra.php (accessed 4/24/12).

Lala's Kitchen blog. "Fenkata." http://oliveoilandheart.blogspot. com/ 2010/07/fenkata.html (accessed 3/29/12).

Le Goff, Jacques. *History and Memory*. Translated by Steven Rendall and Eliza-
    beth Claman. New York: Columbia University Press, 1992.
"LGT History." http://www.lgt.com/en/lgt-group/history/index.html (accessed
    8/3/12).
Llobera, Josep R. *Foundations of National Identity*, New York: Berghahn
    Books, 2004.
Luidprand of Cremona. *The Complete Works of Liudprand of Cremona*. Edited
    and translated by Paolo Squatriti. Chapter 13, *Antapodosis*. Washington:
    D.C.: Catholic University of America Press, 2007 (ca. 960).
"Malta in World War I." http://www.killifish.f9.co.uk/Malta%20WWII/ WW1/
    Malta_WWI.htm (accessed 2/15/12).
"Malta in World War II." http://www.visitmalta.com (accessed 2/19/12).
Martin, Douglas. "Giorgio Carbone, Elected Prince of Seborga, Dies at 73,"
    New York Times, 12 December 2009.   http://www.nytimes.com/2009/
    12/13/world/europe/ 13carbone.html?_r=3 (accessed 8/2/2012).
Marx, Karl and Friedrich Engels. *The Communist Manifesto*. New York: Pen-
    guin Group, 1998 (1848).
McGuigan, Dorothy Gies. *The Habsburgs*. New York: Doubleday, 1966.
Miller, Jennfier. "A Land Apart," *Hemispheres Inflight*. 1 January 2012. http://
    www.hemispheresmagazine.com/2012/01/01/a-land-apart   (accessed   4/26/
    12).
"Monaco." http://www3.monaco.mc/monaco/info/history3.html (accessed 3/12/
    12).
"Monaco prince admits love child," *BBC News*, 6 July 2005. http://news.
    bbc.co.uk/2/hi/europe/4656797.stm (accessed 8/3/12).
"Montevideo Convention on the Rights and Duties of States (1933)." Council
    on Foreign Relations. http://www.cfr.org/sovereignty/montevideo-conven-
    tion-rights-duties-states/p15897 (accessed 8/2/12).
Morell, Antoni. *Boris I, Rei D'andorra*. Barcelona: La Magrana, 1984.
Morello, Giovanni. "The Origins of the Knights of Malta," *Rivista*, 31, 1999.
Murphy, Charles J. V. "The New Riviera," *Life,* 10 November 1947.
"Nation of 55 People: Republic of Tavolara in Its Third Presidential Campaign,"
    Boston Globe, 10 January 1897.
"Navarre." www.heraldica.org/topics/france/navarre.htm (accessed 3/3/2012).
Nicholson, Helen. *The Knights Hospitaller*. Woodbridge, Boydell Press, 2001.
Norbeck, Edward. "Anthropological Views of Play," *American Zoologist*, 14(1),
    1971.
"On the Infallible Teaching Authority of the Roman Pontiff. Decrees of the First
    Vatican Council." Session 4, 18 July 1870. Chapter 4 (9). *Papal Encyclicals
    Online.*   http://www.papalencyclicals.net/Councils/ecum20.htm#Chapter
    %204.%20On%20the%20infallible%20teaching%20authority%20of%20the
    %20Roman%20pontiff (accessed 8/3/ 12).
Order of Malta. *Constitutional Charter*, Title I, Article 3. Rome: SMOM, 1961.
    http://www.orderofmalta.int/wp-content/uploads/2010/06/order-of-malta-
    constitution.pdf (accessed 4/25/12).

——. "News Archives, 2002." www.orderofmalta.int (accessed 3/12/12).

"Our Lady of Philermo," *Sunday Times of Malta*, 26 April 1998, 42.

"Our Lady of Philermo," 2. http://www.smom-za.org/ smom/ saints/ philerme. htm (accessed 2/3/06).

"Palladium," *Greece Myth Index.* http://www.mythindex.com/greek-mythology /P/Palladium.html (accessed 8/3/12).

"Pan Am 103—Lockerbie Appeal Judgment." www.Terrorismcentral.com (accessed 3/2/12)

Peter of Yugoslavia, *A King's Heritage.* London: Putnam, 1955.

Pfeiffer, Eric "The Sideshow." *Yahoo News*, 23 March 2012. http// news.yahoo. com/blogs/sideshow/borat-anthem-played-during-actual-kazakh-gold-metal. htm (accessed 7 April 2012).

"Pope John XII," *New Advent Catholic Encyclopdeia.* http://www.newadvent. org/cathen/08426b.htm (accessed 8/3/12).

Post, Louis F. (ed.) "Little Nations Little Known," *The Public: A Journal of Democracy,* 2 (96), 3 February 1900.

Press and Information Office, *Liechtenstein—Principality in the Heart of Europe.* Vaduz: Press and Information Office, 1996.

"Princess Antoinette of Monaco," *Telegraph*, 27 March 2011.

Relics of the House of Karageorgevitch. http://www2.prestel.co.uk/church/ kposj/relics.htm (accessed 7/31/05).

"Representación de los Copríncipes," *Govern d'Andorra.* http://www.exteriors. ad/index.php?option=com_content&view=article&id=223&Itemid=59&lan g=es (accessed 7/22/12).

Ritter, Raymond. *Bidache Principauté souveraine*, Lyon: Éditions Audin, Lyon, 1958.

Roelker, Nancy Lyman. *Queen of Navarre: Jeanne d'Albret.* Cambridge: Harvard University Press, 1968.

Ryan, John, George Dunford, and Simon Sellars. *Micronations.* Oakland, CA: Lonely Planet, 2006.

Sack, John. *Report from Practically Nowhere.* New York: Harper & Brothers, 1955.

"Saint Tropez." http://www.nrj-saint-tropez.com/saint-tropez/st-tropez-135.html (accessed 3/10/12).

Sainty, Guy Stair. "The Teutonic Order of Holy Mary in Jerusalem." http:// www.chivalricorders.org/Vatican/teutonic.htm (accessed 10/13/98).

——."The Order of Malta, Sovereignty, and International Law." *SMOM.* 1998. www.chivalricorders.org/chivalric/smom/maltasov.htm (accessed 7/15/02).

San Marino: Ancient Land of Liberty. San Marino: Edition Souvenir SA International, n.d.

"San Marino history." http://www.sanmarinosite.com/eng/pcomunita.html (accessed 3/12/12).

Savona-Ventura, C. and A. Mifsud "Paleolithic Man and his Environment in the Maltese Islands," 2009. http://pmhem.org/old/palaeol.html (accessed 4/22/ 12).

"Schoss Liechtenstein." http://www.liechtenstein-schloss-wilfersdorf.at/eng/eng
_02.html (accessed 2/20/12).

"Sealand." http://www.sealandgov.org (accessed 7/15/07).

Seger, Otto. *A Survey of Liechtenstein History.* Vaduz: Press and Information
Office, Government of the Principality of Liechtenstein, 1984.

"Self-styled Orders which illegitimately claim to be an offspring of the genuine," *Order of St. John/Order of Malta.* www.smom-za.org/smom/ self-
styled.htm (accessed 3/15/09).

Seymour, Joseph. "The National Question in the Marxist Movement, 1848-
1914." *Workers Vanguard,* 123, 125, 3 and 17 September, 1976. www.icl-
fi.org/english/wv/931/national-question.html, 27 Feb. 2009 (accessed 6/
21/2012).

"Siege of Malta in World War II." http://www.bbc.co.uk/history/worldwars/
wwtwo/siege_malta_01.shtml (accessed 2/20/12).

Sire, H.J.A. *The Knights of Malta.* New Haven: Yale University Press, 1994.

"Sixth Language-Scottish Branch." Chapter 3. http://members.tripod.com/
~Blessed_Gerard/PA-3.htm (accessed 4/23/08).

Smith, Anthony D. *National Identity.* Reno: University of Nevada Press, 1991.

———."Gastronomy or Geology? The Role of Nationalism in the Reconstruction
of Nations," *Nations and Nationalism,* 1, no. 1, March 1995.

Smith, Whitney. *Flags.* New York: McGraw-Hill, 1976.

Strage, Mark. *Women of Power.* San Diego: Harcourt Brace Jovanovich, 1976.

Szantova, Olga. "Liechtenstein sues Germany over Czech property." *Radio
Praha News.* http://www.radio.cz/en/article/10871 (accessed 3/10/2012).

Tanner, Marie. *Last Descendent of Aeneas.* New Haven: Yale University Press,
1993.

"Tavolara's King Dies; Ruled Tiniest Realm; Charles Bartoleoni Was Monarch
of Small Island Off Sardinia's Coast," *New York Times,* 1 February1928.

"Teutonic Order," *The Catholic Encyclopedia.* http:www.knight.org/advent/
cathen/14541b.htm (accessed 4/28/98).

Times of Malta, 28 May 1997, 60.

"Tiny Republic Signs Treaty," *Atlanta Constitution,* 22 November 1903.

Turner, Victor. *The Ritual Process: Structure and Anti-Structure.* Piscataway,
NJ: Transaction Publishers, 1995 (1969).

van Gennap, Arnold. *The Rites of Passage.* Chicago: University of Chicago
Press, 1960 (1909).

Virgil. *The Aeneid.*6. John Dryden, translator. *The Internet Classics.* http://clas-
sics. mit.edu/Virgil/aeneid.htm (accessed 4/25/12).

von Treitschke, Heinrich. *The Origins of Prussianism,* trans. E. and C. Paul,
Sidney: Allen & Unwin, 1942.

U.S. Department of State, "Background Note—Andorra." http://www.state.gov/r
/pa/ei/bgn/3164.htm (accessed 3/19/2012).

U.S. Department of State. "San Marino," *United States Diplomatic History.*
http://history.state.gov/countries/san-marino (accessed 4/25/12).

Vorres, Ian. *The Last Grand Duchess*. New York: Charles Scribner's Sons, 1964.

"Waldensese." *The New Advent Catholic Encyclopedia*. http://www.newadvent.org/ cathen/ 15527b. htm (accessed 8/2/12).

Wallace, A.F.C. *Rochdale: The Growth of an American Village in the Early Industrial Revolution*. New York: Alfred A. Knopt, 1978.

Wilson, E.O. *The Social Conquest of the Earth*. New York: Liveright, 2012.

"World at War—Andorra 1866-1957." www.schudak.de/timelines/andorra1976 (accessed 3/1/2012).

"World Heritage Sites in Malta." http://www.visitmalta.com (accessed 2/20/ 12).

Index

Index

About the Author

P. Christiaan Klieger was born in Montana but lived most of his life in Hawai'i. He received his doctorate in anthropology from the University of Hawai'i in 1989 on the process of national identity formation. He is a leading expert on the principle of self-determination among the peoples of Tibet. He has also worked extensively with Native Hawaiians and Native North Americans on self-determination and the application of Native voice in museums. He is the author of several books on the history of Tibet and the Hawaiian kingdom and dozens of articles. *Microstates of Europe* is a unique study of how peoples create and maintain notions of allegiance to state and statehood. He currently lives in the San Francisco Bay Area, and is a knight of the Order of Malta and the Equestrian Order of the Holy Sepulchre, and is a Fellow of the Royal Anthropological Institute of Great Britain and Northern Ireland.